Brush Up Your Bible!

Other Books by Michael Macrone

❧

Brush Up Your Shakespeare!

It's Greek to Me! : Brush Up Your Classics

By Jove! : Brush Up Your Mythology

Brush Up
Your Bible!

MICHAEL MACRONE

Illustrations by Tom Lulevitch

Cader Books

HarperCollins*Publis*

Created by Cader Books, 151 East 29th Street, New York, NY 10016.

FIRST EDITION

Designers: Michael Macrone and Michael Cader

Library of Congress Cataloging-in-Publication Data

Macrone, Michael.

           / Michael Macrone : illustrations by
            ed.

         . 2. Bible—Language, style.   I. Title.

                                             93-4350

---

97   DT/HC   10 9 8 7 6 5 4 3 2 1

Contents

Introduction

And further ... my son, be admonished: of making many books
there is no end; and much study is a weariness of the flesh.

Ecclesiastes 12: 12

People disagree about many passages in the Bible, but few will
dissent from this one. The rewards of Bible study are great, but
life is increasingly distracting and time-consuming, leaving
precious little time for weariness of the flesh.

This is a shame, not just because the Bible—which includes
the holy writings of Judaism and Christianity—is a sovereign
source of spiritual and ethical teaching and a treasure of dramatic stories and intriguing questions. It is also the most important single influence on our language, literary and spoken.
The Bible has lent us phrases from "in the beginning" to "the
Alpha and the Omega"; inspired ideas such as "feet of clay,"
"a city on a hill," and "a labor of love"; and introduced characters who have become figures of speech, including Methuselah,
Jezebel, and Doubting Thomas. Yet we often forget—or never
learn—the original sense of their scriptural source.

Brush Up Your Bible! is a guide to the most memorable words
and phrases found in various English versions of Scripture.
Many reference works list biblical quotations, but this book,
like others in my "Brush Up" series, sets famous lines in their
original context, untangling the often archaic phrasing of the
original. In the process, I introduce the historical background,
famous figures, and larger stories of the Bible, with a smatter-
ing of scholarship on the side.

The result, I hope, is an informative and entertaining companion to the Bible for both those who have and those who have not read it. Readers new to the Bible's language, teachings, stories, and ideas may use *Brush Up Your Bible!* as a primer, and perhaps as an inspiration to explore the original text. Those better acquainted with Scripture will find both familiar and unfamiliar passages set in a new light and will learn how the Bible has influenced English over the centuries.

As this book is aimed at everyone interested in the Bible and its language, I have tried to stay neutral where people differ, especially on matters of faith. The varieties of belief (and of skepticism) are many, but virtually all agree that the Bible is a great literary work in which fallible human beings had a hand. Thus I approach the Good Book principally as literature, secondarily as history, and only implicitly as theology. The truth of Scripture and its degree of truth are largely matters of faith. While faith is based on the literal claims of the text, it also transcends them. Even the most orthodox theologians acknowledge the inconsistencies and implausibilities of certain scriptural passages, some of which I note in my commentary. I intend no disrespect to anyone's beliefs; I wish only to enrich the reader's understanding and enjoyment of the Bible as a literary work that is of central importance in our culture.

HOW TO USE THIS BOOK

Brush Up Your Bible! is a series of brief entries on the most famous words, phrases, and stories of the Bible. Each entry is headed by the relevant quotation or phrase, which is followed by an excerpt from the Bible book in which it is found (or on which it is based).

This book is divided into two main sections: "The Hebrew Bible" and "The New Testament." (Christians call Judaism's sacred books the "Old Testament," which they see as the precursor to those books collected in the New Testament.) Within these sections, entries follow the arrangement of books in the King James Bible and all other Protestant Bibles in English. This order differs from that of Hebrew and Catholic Bibles, but as excerpts are cited from the King James text, I observe its arrangement of books for the sake of consistency.

This arrangement should make it easy to locate particular passages, at least if you are familiar with the books of the English Bible. If you are not, I supply a list of them beginning on page xiii. This sequence also enables me to tell longer stories (covering a series of entries) in narrative order; reading entries one after the other, though not necessary, will give the best overview of the larger biblical story. Cross-references are supplied in case you're skipping around in the text and would like to consult other entries that enrich the context. If you would simply like to find a particular phrase, there is a special index designed for that purpose on page 355.

GENESIS OF THE ENGLISH BIBLE

I cite Scripture from the King James Bible (or "Authorized Version"), first published in 1611, because it is that text more than any other that English-speakers (not only Anglicans) think sounds like Scripture—like the language of God. And because the King James translation remains popular to this day, it has had the greatest impact on the language: most people quote from the Bible in this Renaissance rendition.

The committee appointed by King James I for the task of supplying a standard English Bible did not, however, work from scratch; many of its phrasings are borrowed from older editions. I will often cite these editions and their translators, so a brief overview is in order. I begin with English translations rather than with the original texts, which will be discussed in the preludes to the two main portions of this book, "The Hebrew Bible" (p. 1) and "The New Testament" (p. 161).

Before any English translation was attempted, the standard Bible was a Latin text called the "Vulgate" (because when it was produced Latin was the most "vulgar"—that is, common—tongue in Europe). This text was largely produced by or under the supervision of St. Jerome, an influential cleric of the fourth and fifth centuries. Jerome's Vulgate was the basis for the first printed book in Europe: the Gutenberg Bible (1456).

No complete English translation of the Bible survives from before the fourteenth century, although it is believed that the Venerable Bede attempted one six hundred years earlier, and fragments of an Old English version by Ælfric survive from the tenth century. What Bede accomplished is unknown, but we do know that slightly before his death in 1384 John Wyclif published an English version of the standard Latin Bible. Though some of Wyclif's views were unorthodox in his day, his translation is reasonably faithful to the Latin, and he was the first to put certain biblical expressions (such as "graven image") in their familiar form. Wyclif's text became popular among the people, who were generally ignorant of Latin, but Church authorities in England were not so enamored. Wyclif was posthumously denounced as a heretic, copies of his Bible were destroyed in 1415, and in 1482 his body was exhumed and burned.

Things were little better for William Tyndale, who in 1520 was forced into exile after the English Church accused him of heresy. While in Germany he fell under Martin Luther's influence and, as Luther had, determined to publish a vernacular Bible, from texts in Hebrew and Greek, that would speak plainly to the common man. Tyndale did not live to realize his vision—he was arrested and executed in 1536—but he did manage to publish an English rendition of the entire New Testament, along with the Pentateuch (or Torah, the first five books of the Hebrew Bible) and Jonah. He also left behind manuscript translations of nine other Hebrew texts.

When copies of Tyndale's New Testament—complete with anti-Catholic notes—were imported into England in 1525, the bishop of London seized and burned them. But only ten years later the government of Henry VIII (who had subsequently split from the Church) commissioned the Coverdale Bible (1535), which relied heavily on Tyndale's work. Where the translator, Miles Coverdale, could not borrow from Tyndale, he used other translations, principally in German and Latin. (His knowledge of Greek and especially of Hebrew was slight.) Subsequently (1537) an old associate of Tyndale's issued the so-called "Matthew Bible" (from his pseudonym "Thomas Matthew"), which used both Tyndale's published and unpublished translations, supplemented by Coverdale's Old Testament. Coverdale himself revised this work; his new edition, published between 1539 and 1541, was called the "Great Bible" after its unusual dimensions. The Great Bible became the first translation officially sanctioned by the English Church.

Challenging the Great Bible, however, was a revision of Tyndale produced in Geneva by conservative Protestant exiles during the reign of the Catholic Queen Mary. The resulting "Geneva Bible" (1560) had a Puritan slant, despite or because of which it became wildly popular among the English people (it was read, for example, by Shakespeare). Its success may have had mostly to do with its directness, simplicity, and accuracy— it was, to date, the translation most faithful to the original text. But the immoderate and tendentious tone of some passages and notes made this edition unacceptable to the English Church; so the Protestant Queen Elizabeth ordered a panel of bishops to conduct a toned-down revision of the Geneva Bible. The resulting "Bishops' Bible" (1568) became the second official English Bible of the Church.

Its stylistic and doctrinal inconsistencies, though, were manifest, so soon after King James came to power in 1603 he authorized yet another revision. The best biblical scholars in the land came together in 1607 to begin work, and within four years they had produced what we now call the King James Bible. It is based largely on the Bishops' Bible, and therefore on Tyndale's original work, but the editors also consulted all other English editions save Wyclif's, including the Catholic New Testament that had been published in 1582.

Surprisingly, though later generations would consider this Authorized Version the very model of English prose, it was at first attacked as barbaric, and the more ornate and familiar Geneva Bible held the hearts of the people for another forty years. After that, though, the King James Bible monopolized the field; another revision wasn't even attempted until the 1870s. The Revised Version of 1881–1885, the Revised Standard Version of 1946–1957, and the New Revised Standard Version of 1989, though all based on the King James text and all recognized by the English Church, have never managed to break the grip of the original Authorized Version on English quotation. The vast influence of the King James text, as well as its longevity, are the reasons I will cite from it here.

BIBLICAL BOOKS AND THEIR ABBREVIATIONS

The King James Bible published today is shorter than the one published in 1611, because it excludes Old Testament books (called the "Apocrypha") that Protestants have never accepted as divinely inspired, but which were still included in vernacular Renaissance Bibles, in a separate section, for reference. The order of canonical books is the same today as it was then, and I will follow this order in the text. I list these books here in the abbreviated form by which I will cite them hereafter, along with the full titles [in brackets] as given by the King James headings, where they differ.

The Hebrew Bible (Old Testament)

Genesis [The First Book of Moses, called Genesis]
Exodus [The Second Book of Moses, called Exodus]
Leviticus [The Third Book of Moses, called Leviticus]
Numbers [The Fourth Book of Moses, called Numbers]
Deuteronomy [The Fifth Book of Moses, called Deuteronomy]
Joshua [The Book of Joshua]
Judges [The Book of Judges]
Ruth [The Book of Ruth]
I Samuel [The First Book of Samuel, otherwise called,
The First Book of the Kings]
II Samuel [The Second Book of Samuel, otherwise called,
The Second Book of the Kings]
I Kings [The First Book of the Kings, commonly called,
The Third Book of the Kings]

II Kings [The Second Book of the Kings, commonly called,
The Fourth Book of the Kings]
I Chronicles [The First Book of the Chronicles]
II Chronicles [The Second Book of the Chronicles]
Ezra
Nehemiah [The Book of Nehemiah]
Esther [The Book of Esther]
Job [The Book of Job]
Psalms [The Book of Psalms]
Proverbs [The Proverbs]
Ecclesiastes [Ecclesiastes; or, The Preacher]
The Song of Solomon
Isaiah [The Book of the Prophet Isaiah]
Jeremiah [The Book of the Prophet Jeremiah]
Lamentations [The Lamentations of Jeremiah]
Ezekiel [The Book of the Prophet Ezekiel]
Daniel [The Book of Daniel]
Hosea
Joel
Amos
Obadiah
Jonah
Micah
Nahum
Habakkuk
Zephaniah
Haggai
Zechariah
Malachi

The New Testament

Matthew [The Gospel according to St. Matthew]
Mark [The Gospel according to St. Mark]
Luke [The Gospel according to St. Luke]
John [The Gospel according to St. John]
Acts [The Acts of the Apostles]
Romans [The Epistle of Paul the Apostle to the Romans]

Introduction

I Corinthians [The First Epistle of Paul the Apostle to the Corinthians]
II Corinthians [The Second Epistle of Paul the Apostle to the Corinthians]
Galatians [The Epistle of Paul the Apostle to the Galatians]
Ephesians [The Epistle of Paul the Apostle to the Ephesians]
Philippians [The Epistle of Paul the Apostle to the Philippians]
Colossians [The Epistle of Paul the Apostle to the Colossians]
I Thessalonians [The First Epistle of Paul the Apostle
to the Thessalonians]
II Thessalonians [The Second Epistle of Paul the Apostle to the Thessalonians]
I Timothy [The First Epistle of Paul the Apostle to Timothy]
II Timothy [The Second Epistle of Paul the Apostle to Timothy]
Titus [The Epistle of Paul to Titus]
Philemon [The Epistle of Paul to Philemon]
Hebrews [The Epistle of Paul the Apostle to the Hebrews]
James [The General Epistle of James]
I Peter [The First Epistle General of Peter]
II Peter [The Second Epistle General of Peter]
I John [The First Epistle General of John]
II John [The Second Epistle of John]
III John [The Third Epistle of John]
Jude [The General Epistle of Jude]
Revelation [The Revelation of St. John the Divine]

The Apocryphal books not included in this list are Tobit, Judith, The Wisdom of Solomon, Ecclesiasticus, Baruch, I–II Maccabees, I–II Esdras, the Prayer of Manasseh, and additions to the books of Esther and Daniel. All of these except I–II Esdras and Manasseh are accepted by Catholics as Scripture, though of secondary ("deuterocanonical") status. None have contributed phrases to English that are very familiar, though some lines from Ecclesiasticus may be found in "Purgatory" (p. 325), where I collect less familiar, less important, or erroneous citations.

I will cite biblical books by chapter and verse in abbreviated form. "Matthew 13" indicates chapter thirteen of the Gospel according to St. Matthew; "Matthew 13: 9" indicates verse nine of that chapter. (Chapters were first divided into verses in the Geneva Bible.) Consecutive verses are divided in epigraphs and other citations by a vertical slash (|).

SOURCES AND ACKNOWLEDGMENTS

I made use of numerous reference works in preparing this book, the most important of which are *Harper's Bible Dictionary,* Paul J. Achtemeier, general editor (HarperSanFrancisco, 1971); *Harper's Bible Commentary,* James L. Mays, general editor (Harper & Row, 1988); and *The Jerome Biblical Commentary,* first edition, edited by Raymond E. Brown et al. (Prentice-Hall, 1968). For illustrative quotations I often referred, beyond my own reading, to the *Oxford English Dictionary,* second edition (Oxford, 1991; abbreviated "OED"), and to *The Kenkyusha Dictionary of English Quotations,* edited by Sanki Ichikawa et al. (Kenkyusha, 1952).

My principal text is the Authorized Version of the Bible; I follow the spelling and punctuation of the undated sextodecimo Cambridge University Press edition. I also made use of the Revised Standard Version, second edition (1971); the New English Bible, corrected impression (1972); E. A. Speiser's edition of Genesis (Doubleday, 1964) in the *Anchor Bible* series; and Everett Fox's *Genesis and Exodus: A New English Rendition* (Shocken, 1990).

Finally, I'd like to acknowledge the aid of Hugh Van Dusen and Stephanie Gunning of HarperCollins, the careful copyediting of Erin Clermont, and the support and inspiration of Michael Cader and Catherine Karnow, who made essential contributions to this book in form and content.

Brush Up Your Bible!

The Hebrew Bible
(Old Testament)

The books that now form the Hebrew Bible have an ancient history, stretching back over 3,000 years. But the Jews had no real Bible until about the second century A.D., if we take "Bible" to mean a single and fixed collection of books. It is perhaps better, then, to speak of "Hebrew Scripture" when discussing the original texts and their history, since the Jews' holy books (really scrolls) circulated independently and fluctuated both in form and number until roughly 1,800 years ago.

These books fall into three groups, which vary in importance. The most revered, and those with the oldest components, are the first five—Genesis, Exodus, Leviticus, Numbers, and Deuteronomy, according to their English titles (based on Greek). Jews know these books collectively as the Torah, from the Hebrew for "laws," since they contain, in addition to narratives of primitive Hebrew history, a record of Jewish law as traced back to the great prophet and lawgiver, Moses. (Christians usually refer to these texts as the Pentateuch, from the Greek for "five books.")

The Torah, composed in pieces between about 1000 B.C. and about 400 B.C. (though containing older fragments), was the first collection of holy works accepted as such by the larger Jewish community. Second in importance and acceptance was the collection of books known as the Prophets, which is divided into the Former Prophets and Latter Prophets. The Former Prophets is actually a series of five historical works completed sometime in the sixth century B.C.—Joshua, Judges, Ruth,

Samuel, and Kings (the last two are subdivided in Christian Bibles). They trace the early history of Israel from its establishment through its monarchical period under David and Solomon and its division into two kingdoms (Israel and Judah) to its gradual disintegration. These books are conventionally regarded as "prophetic" because the supporting cast includes prophetic figures such as Deborah, Samuel, and Elijah.

The Latter Prophets comprises books attributed to or written about single figures who claimed to speak for Israel's God, Yahweh. These prophets are called major or minor depending on the importance and length of the writings associated with them. The major prophets are Isaiah (whose book was written between the eighth and fifth centuries B.C.), Jeremiah (seventh to sixth centuries), and Ezekiel (sixth century). The earliest of the twelve minor prophets, Amos and Hosea, preached in Israel in the eighth century B.C.; the latest, such as Zechariah, Malachi, and Joel, prophesied in Judah in the sixth and fifth centuries B.C., after the Persian king Cyrus II had restored exiled Jews to their homeland. The other minor prophets are Micah, Nahum, Zephaniah, Habakkuk, Haggai, Obadiah, and Joshua.

The third grouping of books is called the Writings, a loosely defined collection of works considered sacred by Jews and Christians but which fall outside the other categories. These include the Psalms; books of practical or earthly wisdom (Proverbs, Job, and Ecclesiastes); Chronicles (an abridgment of the history found in the Former Prophets), divided into two books by Christians; the apocalyptic book of Daniel (the newest, dating to the second century B.C.); and miscellaneous texts: The Song of Solomon, Ruth, Lamentations, Esther, and Ezra-Nehemiah (likewise two books in Christian Bibles).

Many other books considered more or less sacred, most now lost, circulated among Jews prior to the establishment of a fixed canon in the second century A.D. Some of these books were preserved in Greek translations of Hebrew Scripture conducted between the third and first centuries B.C. and collectively called the Septuagint (or Seventy, a round figure for the alleged number of translators of the Torah). Since the Septuagint was the unofficial Scripture for the early Christian church, Roman and Orthodox Catholics still accept as sacred most of the texts rejected by Jews and never included in Hebrew Bibles. Protestants, however, stick to the official canon of Hebrew Scripture, which therefore does not differ from what they call the Old Testament, a name retroactively applied once sacred Christian writings were dubbed the New Testament circa A.D. 200.

There are no very old manuscripts of Hebrew Scripture in its official form (which is known as the Masoretic Text after a school of Jewish scribes that flourished in the fifth through ninth centuries A.D.). However, quite old copies or fragments of most books—some dating to the third century B.C.—have been discovered over the last forty-five years or so at sites west of the Dead Sea. These so-called Dead Sea Scrolls, apparently copied and preserved by a Jewish sect known as the Essenes through the first century A.D., prove among other things that the canon of Hebrew Scripture, and even the text of individual books, was still relatively fluid before the birth of Christ. It remains to be seen whether the Dead Sea discoveries significantly influence our understanding of Scripture, but it isn't likely. And in either case the Hebrew canon is fixed, as is of course the King James rendering of it.

Authorship of the Torah

The ancient assumption that the Mosaic Law—or Torah (the first five books of Hebrew Scripture)—was written by Moses himself has not stood up well upon closer inspection. Moses, for example, would probably not have written of himself as a quasi-legendary figure (in the third person, to boot). Among other verses, he certainly didn't compose Deuteronomy 34: 5: "So Moses the servant of the LORD died there in the land of Moab, according to the word of the LORD."

In fact, the numerous redundancies, contradictions, stylistic clashes, differing agendas, and anachronisms contained in the books of Genesis, Exodus, Leviticus, Numbers, and Deuteronomy rule out authorship by any one (or even two) persons. Who exactly did write them will never be known, as the authors took good care to remain anonymous (the more to glorify the words of God). For over a century, however, scholars have generally agreed that whoever compiled the Torah drew on four principal sources, written at various times between the tenth and fifth centuries B.C.

By convention, scholars call the alleged author of the oldest source "the Yahwist," or "J," after the German equivalent. (The name is based on J's consistent use in Genesis of "Yahweh" as the name of the Israelite God.) J most likely lived in Judah, the southern kingdom, sometime between the tenth and eighth century B.C.; his story, which begins in Genesis 2, is the most folkloric, and it treats Yahweh the most anthropomorphically. The author of the most interesting (and ironic) passages in Hebrew Scripture, J is today also the most famous of that text's phantom authors, thanks mostly to Harold Bloom and *The Book of J*. (Bloom's contention that J was female is controversial, to say the least, but that there was such an author as J is not.)

Writing probably a few generations after J, and in Israel (the northern kingdom), was an author or authors known as "the Elohist," or "E," after his name in Genesis for Yahweh (*Elohim*). E's God is a bit less anthropomorphic than J's and not quite so directly involved in human affairs. E also lacks J's literary skills, not to mention his sense of humor, and he appears to have fraternized with a stern circle of prophets. His strand of the Torah, which is the most colorless, begins in Genesis 12 with the story of Abraham.

More important than E is the so-called "Priestly Author," or "P," who most likely represents a centuries-long development of tradition within a priestly circle around the Jerusalem Temple. The P text appears to have been written just after the Babylonian exile in the sixth century B.C. [*see* A VOICE CRYING IN THE WILDERNESS, p. 139]. P is responsible for, among other passages, the famous first chapter of Genesis and nearly all of Leviticus, whose title in fact means "priestly matters." P is the longest-winded and most detail-obsessed of the four, and his purpose is the narrowest: to codify and justify the various ritual laws developed in his circle.

Finally, we have "D," the Deuteronomist, who as you might guess is responsible for large portions of Deuteronomy. He or they also shaped the books of Joshua, Judges,

Ruth, Samuel, and Kings from various documents. Writing in about the seventh century B.C., D had a peculiar view of Jewish history and a polemical intent. Like P, D posits a strict covenant between Yahweh and Israel, and he stresses it wherever possible. In his view, each of Israel's historical misfortunes can be directly traced to some violation of the Mosaic Law; each success, likewise, stems from Israel's obedience. Whenever a king's plots go awry, you can always count on D to inform us that said king "did evil in the sight of the LORD." So fatalistic an attitude would come naturally to someone writing in exile.

In addition to J, E, P, and D, scholars hypothesize a compiler or "Redactor" (known as "R") who gathered the four strands and edited them together, probably sometime in the late fifth century B.C. R clearly shied from tampering too much with his received texts, which is why we find redundancies and contradictions in the whole. On the other hand, he may have excised material which by his day had come to seem embarassing or heterodox. We'll never know if we have all of what J wrote, for example, or if the Bible really begins at the beginning.

In the Beginning

In the beginning God created the heaven and the earth. | And
the earth was without form, and void; and darkness was upon
the face of the deep. And the Spirit of God moved upon the face
of the waters. | And God said, Let there be light: and there was
light. | And God saw the light, that it was good: and God
divided the light from the darkness.

Genesis 1: 1–4

Lots of books claim to begin at the beginning, but the Bible
really means it. Or at least it seems to: we know that before God
began creating, there was no sky ("heaven"), land ("earth"), or
light; many readers imagine that there was no space or time,
either.

Some theologians, in this vein, assert that God conjured the
universe "ex nihilo"—out of nothing—and merely by an act of
supreme will, as embodied in speech ("And God said …"). But
that's not necessarily what the Bible says. While the King James
Version implies that God begins at the absolute beginning, it
misrepresents the Hebrew original. Generally more faithful is
this reading from *The Anchor Bible*: "When God set about to
create heaven and earth— | the world being then a formless
waste, with darkness over the seas and only an awesome wind
sweeping over the water— | God said, 'Let there be light.' And
there was light" (Genesis 1: 1–3).

Some sort of watery, windy "world" already exists as Genesis
opens, as does time ("*When* God set about …"), so the book
doesn't in fact begin at the beginning. On the other hand, the
Hebrew text leaves open the question of whether God also created the "formless waste" and the "seas" out of which he then

shaped "heaven and earth"—which may just be a poetic way of saying "everything else." Either way, in the text as we have it, God doesn't will his creation out of nothing.

It is impossible to know what the author of this passage had in mind, but in any case his account resembles other ancient creation stories—for example, the Babylonian and Greek. In both of these pagan tales, the orderly universe is wrested from a preexisting primeval chaos of darkness and disorganized matter ("chaos" is in fact the Greek term). Furthermore, in the Babylonian account the gods accomplish this by creating the elements of the universe in the same order as in Genesis.

In other words, the author of Genesis 1 probably didn't create ex nihilo either. But he departs from his Near Eastern antecedents in depicting God as virtually omnipotent and certainly unopposed, where the pagans' gods had to struggle with chaotic forces and nasty beasts.

Also novel to Genesis is the idea that God achieved his creation in six days—three days of "separation" and three days of "equipment," to use the theological terms. (On day one he separates light from darkness, and then on day four he equips the sky with lights; the other days follow this pattern.) The author no doubt intended more to sanctify the Israelite six-day work week and Sabbath than to describe reality.

This would all be typical of the author known as P [*see* p. 5], whose purpose here and throughout the Torah is to codify and justify various rituals and laws of his time. P's account of creation, though placed at the beginning of Genesis, was written in about the sixth century B.C. and is thus not really the "beginning" of the Bible. A second creation story, found in Genesis 2, was written by J some three centuries earlier, and it differs in style, detail, and emphasis from the Priestly version [*see* THE BREATH OF LIFE, p. 14].

"In the beginning" is not only one of the most overused titles in English, it's also the Hebrew title for Genesis. Books of the Torah are named after their first words, which in this case is *Bereshit.* The English title "Genesis," like the titles of other Old Testament books, derives from the Septuagint, the third-century-B.C. Greek translation of the Hebrew Bible intended for the Diaspora.

Lesser Light

> And God made two great lights; the greater light to rule the day, and the lesser light to rule the night: he made the stars also.

> Genesis 1: 16

According to P (the source of Genesis 1), God created light, which he called "Day" (1: 5) before he created any heavenly body to supply it. Only on the fourth day did he set "lights" in the skies to "divide the day from the night" and measure time. We don't know how he measured the first three days.

Among these lights two are called "great"—namely the sun and the moon. But rather than say as much, P refers to the sun as "the greater light" and to the moon as "the lesser light." Hebrew, of course, did not lack proper names for these two bodies, but P was not keen to use them. That's probably because the names for "sun" and "moon" were uncomfortably close, and in fact etymologically related, to those of two pagan gods whose Babylonian worshipers had been known to seduce Israelites from their true faith.

Thus we owe the common expression "lesser light" to P's squeamishness and the King James translation. P didn't know that the moon's light was just less of the sun's "greater light," so he couldn't predict how apt his metaphor would prove in modern application. Someone we call a "lesser light" may have his or her own proper talents, but as they are overshadowed by the talents of the "star," they seem only reflected. The Bible probably doesn't mean to be derogatory—moonlight, though less intense, is equally God's creation. But such are the consequences of sun worship.

Be Fruitful and Multiply

And God blessed them, saying, Be fruitful, and multiply, and fill
the waters in the seas, and let fowl multiply in the earth. | And
the evening and the morning were the fifth day.

Genesis 1: 22–23

"Be fruitful and multiply," one of P's favorite formulas, shows
up five times in Genesis. Here, God blesses the living creatures
of the skies and seas, allowing and also requiring them to
propagate his original creation.

The second time, the LORD repeats his order to mankind,
which multiplies, all right, but God doesn't like the taste of this
fruit. Regretting his creation, he floods the earth to wipe it
clean—save for Noah, his family, and some lucky land animals
[see NOAH'S ARK, p. 31]. Once the earth dries, God repeats his
blessing upon the beasts (Genesis 8: 17) and twice later upon
mankind (9: 1 and 9: 7).

Things work out somewhat better the second time, though
good, God-fearing men and women are still in short supply.
Even among the chosen people, corruption and idol worship
become common. Nonetheless, God singles out Jacob to receive
the last of his blessings: "I am God Almighty: be fruitful and
multiply; a nation and a company of nations shall be of thee,
and kings shall come out of thy loins" (Genesis 35: 11).

Jacob's fruitfulness yields the Twelve Tribes of Israel, which,
according to Exodus (1: 7), "were fruitful, and increased abundantly, and multiplied, and waxed exceeding mighty; and the
land [of Egypt] was filled with them"—over a million of them,
if you believe P. This didn't exactly thrill the Egyptians, as we
shall see.

Let Us Make Man in Our Image

> And God said, Let us make man in our image, after our likeness:
> and let them have dominion over the fish of the sea, and over the
> fowl of the air, and over the cattle, and over all the earth and
> over every creeping thing that creepeth upon the earth. | So God
> created man in his own image, in the image of God created he
> him: male and female created he them.
>
> Genesis I: 26–27

As his sixth day of work begins, God announces his plans for his
ultimate creation, mankind. "Let us," he says, "make man in
our image, after our likeness."

"Our" image? Who, you might wonder, is "us"? Perhaps God
is using the royal "we," which would be natural, especially given
that the word the Priestly Author uses for God (*Elohim*) is the
polite plural in Hebrew. Or perhaps the author imagines God
addressing other divine or semi-divine beings, but such beings
haven't been mentioned heretofore in Genesis. (So-called "sons
of God" do show up in Genesis 6—*see* THERE WERE GIANTS IN
THE EARTH IN THOSE DAYS, p. 29).

And the plot thickens. In the very next verse we are told that
God creates man in "his" (singular) image, and the word "likeness" does not appear. Such inconsistencies may mean little, but
the fact that this second verse (27), a hymn, is likely older than
the first (26) suggests more interesting possibilities.

The Hebrew *selem* (translated "image") means something like
"exact duplicate," where *demut* ("likeness") is weaker, implying
only similarity. If "image" is older than "likeness," this may indicate P's attempt to temper the anthropomorphism of the
hymn. If the Israelites once imagined that man actually looked

like God, by the time this chapter of Genesis was written down they (or at least their priests) had changed their minds. Even then, we can't be sure what sort of similarity "likeness" is supposed to suggest, given how most men behave in the Bible.

On top of all that, we're accustomed today to quoting "in his image" or "in our image" without adding "after our likeness," when "likeness" is what we really mean. (The similar expression "after his [own] image" predates the King James Version.) When J. T. Adams wrote in *Harper's Magazine* in 1928 that "the people want officials in their own image," he may have been sarcastic, but he wasn't predicting the cloning of human beings.

The Breath of Life

And the LORD God formed man of the dust of the ground, and breathed into his nostrils the breath of life; and man became a living soul.

Genesis 2: 7

In the middle of Genesis 2, verse 4, begins the second (and older) recounting of the Hebrew creation story, written by J. It differs from the first in many ways; for example, J doesn't begin "in the beginning," but only with the creation of life.

Furthermore, as God creates, he doesn't use speech but his own two hands. For the first man, he takes some dust from the ground and crafts it into human form. He brings this form into life, as "Adam" (the Hebrew for both "man" and "mankind," perhaps derived from *adamah,* "dust," "ground") by blowing into its nostrils "the breath of life." J does not mean that God "breathes" a soul into Adam's lifeless body—since the ancient Hebrews did not really distinguish body from spirit or soul. More precisely, God sparks the flame of a life already potential in Adam's form.

Whatever J meant, we now use "the breath of life" to mean a variety of things—for example, "signs of life," "inspiration," and "the stuff of reality." Some have used it more biblically. "Do you remember the Dying Boar?" queries Oswald Barron in *Day In and Day Out* (1924). "He was a sixpenny toy of the pavement hawkers. You breathed the breath of life into him, filling with air his body that was as an air balloon." It doesn't take much to impress some people.

The Tree of Knowledge

And out of the ground made the Lord God to grow every tree
that is pleasant to the sight, and good for food; the tree of life
also in the midst of the garden, and the tree of knowledge of
good and evil. | … And the Lord God commanded the man,
saying, Of every tree of the garden thou mayest freely eat: | But
of the tree of the knowledge of good and evil, thou shalt not eat
of it: for in the day that thou eatest thereof thou shalt surely die.

Genesis 2: 9, 16–17

Having described Yahweh's creation of Adam, the author of
Genesis 2 moves on to Adam's home, Eden (after the Sumerian
word for "plain"), located roughly in what is now southeastern
Iraq. God equips this primeval paradise with rivers, precious
minerals, and above all lots of pretty fruit trees.

For reasons best known to himself, God singles out one particular tree—called the "tree of knowledge of good and evil"—
whose fruit man is forbidden to eat. This, of course, is the famous "forbidden fruit," though you may be surprised to know
that that phrase appears nowhere in the Bible. (It was coined in
the seventeenth century; "forbidden apple" is even older). And
despite all those pictures of a serpent tempting Eve with an
apple, the Bible never tells us what kind of fruit the tree of
knowledge bears. If anything, it was more likely apricots,
pomegranates, or figs than apples. (Adam and Eve will use fig
leaves to hide their nakedness at Genesis 3: 7; thus the expression "to cover with a fig leaf.")

But the important point about this tree is that if Adam
(meaning "man") eats of it, he shall on that day be "doomed to
death" as the Hebrew says. (The King James rendering—"thou
shalt surely die"—jumps the gun; Adam and Eve live to tell the

tale.) God wouldn't have had to say this, of course, if he didn't know Adam would be sorely tempted, which raises the question of why he put the tree in the garden bible in the first place.

Also puzzling is what the author means by "knowledge of good and evil." In the Hebrew original, the word for "knowledge" also means "knowing," and the entire phrase might be translated as "knowing how to distinguish good from bad"— which Adam presumably wouldn't need to do so long as nothing bad turned up in paradise. But God never promised him that.

As we all know, a serpent does get Eve to eat the forbidden fruit, and she quickly persuades Adam to join her (Genesis 3: 6). Thus "doomed to die," they are expelled from Eden so that they can't get their hands on another magical tree, the "tree of life," mentioned in Genesis 2 as a source of immortality. This one was probably a pomegranate tree, since that fruit was a symbol of eternal life in the Near East.

If you happen to crave the "forbidden fruit" of your forebears, you can still find it today if you live near a good market. The term has been bestowed on a few species of citrus, such as the grapefruitlike shaddock, one variety of which is known as *Citrus paradisi*. Another term for this fruit is "Adam's apple," a name also given to that projection of cartilege in men's throats, on the fanciful assumption that a piece of forbidden fruit stuck in Adam's.

Helpmate AND *Adam's Rib*

> And the LORD God said, It is not good that the man should be alone; I will make him an help meet for him.
>
> Genesis 2: 18

A husband would be best advised not to call his wife a "help-mate" these days, but once upon a time the word was considered a high compliment. The term's prestige derived mostly from its origin in the book of Genesis, where the older form "help meet" is how God describes the mate he creates for Adam.

Actually, though, "help meet" is not an integral phrase in the King James translation, and despite the resemblance "meet"

does not mean "mate," but rather "fitting." What God intends for Adam is a "help" (helper) *meet for him*—in other words, "equal to and appropriate for him." (The oldest English translation, John Wyclif's 1382 version, gives "Make we to hym help like hym.")

The OED calls the word "help-meet" or "helpmeet"—which first appeared in John Dryden's *Marriage à la Mode* (1673)—a "compound absurdly formed by taking the two words help meet" in Genesis "as one word." Absurd or not, the word remained in common usage until the late nineteenth century. By 1715, though, the parallel and more logical term "helpmate" had appeared, and it (barely) survives to this day as an epithet for one's wife.

Now that that's straight, back to the story. If you recall, P told us in Genesis 1 that God created man and woman in a single stroke. In J's version, however, Yahweh first creates Adam but then realizes he is not complete unto himself. God then tries providing various beasts and fowl for company, but among them "there was not found an help meet for him" (Genesis 2: 20).

So Yahweh casts a deep sleep over Adam, opens his flesh, and extracts a rib. From this rib God creates the first woman, who remains unnamed at first but whom Adam calls Eve (*Havva*— "life" in Hebrew, close to the Sumerian for "rib") since, after the fall, she is to be mother of all mankind (Genesis 3: 20). From this story, obviously enough, comes the phrase "Adam's rib," also the title given to a film by George Cukor and to a ski resort in Colorado's White River National Forest.

Even though Eve was created after Adam and from one of his spare ribs, note that the Bible doesn't claim this makes her Adam's inferior. In fact, that's the whole point of the phrase "help meet for him," and of Adam's apostrophe, "bone of my bones, and flesh of my flesh." Women are subjected to men only after Eve takes the lead in defying God—*see* THE TREE OF KNOWLEDGE, p. 15.

Flesh of My Flesh

And Adam said, This is now bone of my bones, and flesh of my flesh: she shall be called Woman, because she was taken out of Man.

Genesis 2: 23

In this passage Adam addresses woman, God's newest creation. Adam, whom God has permitted to name his creatures, lavishes several impassioned epithets on her—among them "bone of my bones" and "flesh of my flesh."

"Bone of my bones" is accurate enough; as Genesis has already told us, God shaped woman from one of Adam's ribs. But a bone is all he uses, so "flesh of my flesh"—the more oft-quoted of these phrases—is just one of Adam's fancies. He probably couldn't have known any better, since he was in a deep sleep during the whole operation.

Equally misguided is the formal name Adam bestows on this charming new creature—"Woman," or *ishsha* in Hebrew—because, he explains, "she was taken out of Man [*ish*]." Actually, the similarity in names is only a pun, having no basis in Hebrew etymology. The English translation works better, since the word "woman" *does* derive from "man"—actually from "wife of man" (the oldest form is *wifmon*). Even so, "woman" does not imply "taken out of man." One wonders how many other creatures Adam misnamed.

Dust to Dust

And unto Adam he said, Because thou hast hearkened unto the voice of thy wife, and hast eaten of the tree, of which I commanded thee, saying, Thou shalt not eat of it: cursed is the ground for thy sake; in sorrow shalt thou eat of it all the days of thy life; | Thorns also and thistles shall it bring forth to thee; and thou shalt eat the herb of the field; | In the sweat of thy face shalt thou eat bread, till thou return unto the ground; for out of it wast thou taken: for dust thou art, and unto dust shalt thou return.

Genesis 3: 17–19

Adam and Eve knew they were doomed to die if they ever ate of the tree of knowledge, but nobody ever explained to them what "dying" would mean—a point exploited by the snake in John Milton's version of the Fall, *Paradise Lost*. In fact, only by eating of the tree would they gain such knowledge, heretofore restricted to what the snake calls "gods" (3: 5). But gods, knowing of death, never need experience it—which is just another ironic twist in J's account.

On top of death, God throws a few other eternal sufferings into the bargain. Since Eve sinned first, women get the worse of the deal, being condemned to suffer giving birth and to find sexual desire painful. Worst of all, they are subjected forevermore to men's rule.

Men, for their part, must now toil to extract grains and herbs from the soil, and they aren't going to enjoy eating them, either. "In the sweat of thy face," God proclaims, "shalt thou eat bread." Following up on this famous line, God drives home the meaning of death: man (*adam* in Hebrew) shall "return unto the ground" (*adamah*) from which he was taken [*see* THE

BREATH OF LIFE, p. 14]. "For dust thou art," says God, "and unto dust shalt thou return." If it's any consolation, the snake doesn't get off too easily, either.

God's sentence is the ultimate source of several English phrases, by way of its quotation or paraphrase elsewhere in the Bible. From various biblical sources comes this line in the Burial section of the first *English Book of Common Prayer* (1548–1549): "Earth to earth, ashes to ashes, dust to dust." Eventually, usage pared this mouthful down to the biblical-sounding "ashes to ashes, dust to dust," which itself never appears in the Bible.

A Flaming Sword AND The Cherubim

And the LORD God said, Behold, the man is become as one of
us, to know good and evil: and now, lest he put forth his hand,
and take also of the tree of life, and eat, and live for ever: |
Therefore the LORD God sent him forth from the garden of
Eden, to till the ground from whence he was taken. | So he drove
out the man; and he placed at the east of the garden of Eden
Cherubims, and a flaming sword which turned every way, to
keep the way of the tree of life.

Genesis 3: 22–24

After Yahweh, jealous of the Tree of Life, banishes Adam and
Eve from Eden, he places guards called "Cherubims" at the
border and somehow or other suspends in the air a "flaming
sword which turned every way."

Nothing more is heard of this sword in the Bible; nonetheless
it would become famous. (The phrase "flaming sword" seemed
the readiest English name for those ceremonial weapons with
wavy edges.) For all its obscurity, the sword—perhaps a poetic
figure for lightning—remains a powerful and intriguing image,
one perhaps ultimately derived from Mesopotamian myths.

More directly linked to ancient Semitic mythology are the
cherubim (now a plural form—the singular is "cherub"; see the
OED for an entire column on the issue). Their name stems
from the Akkadian (*karibu*) for minor Babylonian gods who
guarded threshholds and mediated between the major gods and
mankind.

The cherubim have not been mentioned previously in Genesis, but perhaps they are included among the "us" in such of
God's statements as "let us make man in *our* image." If the
cherubim at all resemble their Babylonian ancestors, they are

creatures like the Greek centaurs, half-human and half-beast. (They are not to be confused with the seraphim, flamelike, winged ministers of God mentioned only in Isaiah, chapter 6.)

Being largely ignorant of Babylonian mythology, Christian artists have tended to represent cherubim as darling little infant creatures with wings—hardly the kind of beings, one would think, fit to guard Eden for an angry God. Whatever, under the influence of such art and its literary equivalent, "cherub" has come to pass as a synonym for "a childlike innocent" and "cherubic" as a metaphor for "angelic."

"Am I My Brother's Keeper?"

> And the LORD said unto Cain, Where is Abel thy brother? And
> he said, I know not: Am I my brother's keeper? | And he [God]
> said, What hast thou done? the voice of thy brother's blood
> crieth unto me from the ground.
>
> Genesis 4: 9–10

Pity poor Eve. Having been expelled with Adam from Eden,
she gives birth twice with great discomfort. On top of that,
now she has to "raise Cain."

Cain, whose name roughly signifies "smith" or "craftsman"
(though he's actually a farmer), turns out to be a rather crafty
fellow indeed, unlike his younger brother Abel, a shepherd,
whose name fittingly suggests "short-lived." Like any first child,
Cain has grown used to special treatment, so when he and his
brother make offerings to God and God pays attention only to
Abel's, Cain is enraged. Thus hatred among men (not to mention sibling rivalry) is born, and it results in another new invention: murder.

How Cain thought he could get away with killing his own
brother is a mystery, and in a flash God is upon him. "Where is
Abel thy brother?" asks Yahweh. "I know not," Cain lies, adding
the retort, "Am I my brother's keeper [guardian]?" Cain's hypocritical (and amoral) denial of responsibility lives on in infamy.

God, of course, has ears to hear the truth, which speaks more
eloquently than Cain. "The voice of thy brother's blood crieth
unto me from the ground," God shoots back, and the word it
speaks is "sin," a word that first appears earlier in this chapter (it
never appears at all in the story of the Fall). Yahweh condemns
Cain not only to labor like his parents, but also to live as a no-

Brush Up Your Bible

mad, ever cheated by the soil of its fullest fruit: "When thou tillest the ground, it shall not henceforth yield unto thee her strength; a fugitive and a vagabond shalt thou be in the earth."

Cain and his progeny are thus relegated to a restless existence in the desert. J, the author of this passage, may have in mind a tribe known as the "Kenites," once thought to be descendants of Cain who subsisted as wandering metalworkers until they settled in Midian on the Sinai peninsula. (Later to be found among the Kenites is Moses' father-in-law—*see* A STRANGER IN A STRANGE LAND, p. 48.)

One problem with this theory is that the Bible will later claim we *all* descend from Cain through his descendant Noah. The other problem is that J is at a loss to explain where, if Cain and Abel are Eve's only children so far, the other men Cain fears come from [*see* the next entry].

The Land of Nod, East of Eden, AND The Mark of Cain

And the LORD said unto him [Cain], Therefore whosoever
slayeth Cain, vengeance shall be taken on him sevenfold. And
the LORD set a mark upon Cain, lest any finding him should kill
him. I And Cain went out from the presence of the LORD, and
dwelt in the land of Nod, on the east of Eden.

Genesis 4: 15–16

Facing the thankless life of a nomad for his treacherous murder
of Abel, Cain declares this "greater than I can bear" (Genesis
4: 13). Not only will he be a "fugitive and a vagabond" upon
the earth, but, according to him, "everyone that findeth me
shall slay me" (verse 14).

Where this "everyone" came from is a mystery, but in any
case Yahweh accepts Cain's complaint at face value. Despite
Cain's horrible crime, God extends him special protection in
the form of a "mark," familiarly known as the "mark [or brand]
of Cain." Though we use this phrase now to mean "the sign of a
murderer," that's not what God had in mind. Cain's mark is
supposed to induce fear in potential enemies, reminiscent of
various tribal symbols common among the peoples of the ancient Near East. In short, anyone who slays a member of Cain's
tribe can expect brutal (and divinely sanctioned) retribution.

Thus shielded, Cain makes his lonely way into a region called
"the land of Nod, on the east of Eden." Wherever Nod is—the
name is from the Hebrew for "wandering"—we are meant to
infer that it's a bleak place indeed, and that east is not the best
direction out of Eden. English punsters ignored these dire facts,
however, when they began using "the land of Nod" as a humor-

ous metaphor for "sleep." (The first to do so was Jonathan Swift.) On the other hand, John Steinbeck's novel of family tragedy, *East of Eden,* is in the right spirit (and is in fact based on Genesis 4).

We hear little more of Cain, except that he went on to build the first city in the world, which he would call Enoch after his eldest son. (The Bible also leaves us guessing where Cain's wife came from.) Enoch, in turn, would beget a certain personage famous for longevity—so read on.

Methuselah

And Methuselah lived an hundred eighty and seven years, and begat Lamech. | And Methuselah lived after he begat Lamech seven hundred eighty and two years, and begat sons and daughters: | And all the days of Methuselah were nine hundred sixty and nine years: and he died.

Genesis 5: 25–27

Though only Methuselah is still renowned in phrase and fable, other prehistoric biblical figures are no slouches, either. Sure, Methuselah lived a stunning 969 years, but a certain Jared racked up 962, and Methuselah's grandson Noah was already 500 when he began fathering offspring. Several other figures lived to be over 900.

It is P who is responsible for calculating these absurd life spans down to the year. He seems to have relied for the purpose on various numerological principles (Enoch lived 365 years, Lamech 777, etc.). Whatever his reasons, P's numbers don't add up at all.

References in English to Methuselah's longevity first appeared in the fourteenth century, while the saying "as old as Methuselah" dates to Thomas Shelton's 1620 translation of Cervantes's *Don Quixote.* But it was only in this century that the name "methuselah" was given to a massive wine bottle, holding eight reputed quarts, or 225 fluid ounces. Put away a couple of those, and you won't even see your next birthday.

(For more on the connection between the Bible and oversize wine bottles, *see* A JEROBOAM, p. 103.)

There Were Giants in the Earth in Those Days

And it came to pass, when men began to multiply on the face of the earth, and daughters were born unto them, | That the sons of God saw the daughters of men that they were fair; and they took them wives of all which they chose. | And the LORD said, My spirit shall not always strive with man, for that he also is flesh: yet his days shall be an hundred and twenty years. | There were giants in the earth in those days; and also after that, when the sons of God came in unto the daughters of men, and they bare children to them, the same became mighty men which were of old, men of renown.

Genesis 6: 1–4

Modern quotations of the biblical expression, "There were giants in the earth in those days"—now meaning roughly, "They don't make men like that anymore"—don't begin to capture the strangeness of the original.

As chapter 6 of Genesis begins, we have just learned the entire genealogy of Noah, grandson of Methuselah, in meticulous detail. In a few verses, we will hear that Yahweh plans to wash mankind (saving Noah's family) off the face of the earth. And here, out of nowhere and seemingly to no end, we learn the entirely unrelated history of peculiar beings called "Nephilim" in Hebrew and "giants" in the King James translation.

According to Genesis, the Nephilim are the offspring by mortal women of so-called "sons of God [*or* gods]." But who are these immortals, what are they doing with desires for women, and how do they consummate their marriages? The Bible never illuminates such questions; as for the giant Nephilim, loosely identified as famous heroes, we never learn their names. Apparently, they drown along with the rest of mankind in the Flood. (Nephilim-like giants are, however, mentioned in Numbers 13: 32–33.)

Wherever this story came from—it does resemble ancient myths—and whatever it's doing in Genesis, it is rather foreboding; it may be meant to exemplify the depraved shennanigans that brought on the Flood. Whoever the "sons of God" are, they clearly have no business mingling with mortals, whether or not great "heroes" are the result.

We also hear, in the middle of all this, that God decides to limit man's life to 120 years, Noah apparently excepted. Whether this is a prediction of the Flood or merely an actuarial statement [*see* METHUSELAH, p. 28], it is not a friendly gesture. Yahweh is running out of patience; the results are described in the next entry.

Noah's Ark

And God said unto Noah, ... | Make thee an ark of gopher wood; rooms shalt thou make in the ark, and shalt pitch it within and without with pitch. | And this is the fashion which thou shalt make it of: The length of the ark shall be three hundred cubits, the breadth of it fifty cubits, and the height of it thirty cubits. | A window shalt thou make to the ark, and in a cubit shalt thou finish it above; and the door of the ark shalt thou set in the side thereof; with lower, second, and third stories shalt thou make it.

Genesis 6: 13–16

Maybe you thought Noah brought a pair of each creature aboard his famous ark. But that's only one of two different stories told in Genesis—P's story. J thought otherwise.

Both authors agree, however, that mankind does not improve with age. With rare exceptions, such as Methuselah's father Enoch (who "walked with God"), men have grown throughly wicked within ten generations. So God the Creator resolves to become God the Destroyer: "I will destroy man whom I have created from the face of the earth; both man, and beast, and the creeping thing, and the fowls of the air; for it repenteth me that I have made them" (Genesis 6: 7). It is not said what the beasts, creeping things, and fowl have done to deserve extinction.

Luckily, one man, Noah, "found grace in the eyes of the LORD" (verse 8); grace enough for Yahweh to revise his plans. Rather than wipe out the entire human race and all those innocent species, he is just going to clean things up a bit with a massive flood. So that Noah and his family might survive the deluge to start up the race from scratch, God directs him to "make an ark of gopher wood."

And God, as is typical in the Priestly strand of Genesis, goes into painstaking detail on the ark's construction, including specifying its exact dimensions in those famous "cubits" (an ancient measurement of somewhere between 18 and 20 inches—this would make the ark between 450 and 500 feet long). God then instructs Noah to bring aboard two of each kind of living creature—or, if you believe J's version of events in Genesis 7, seven pair of each "clean beast" and one of each "unclean." Obedient Noah complies down to the detail—at least, once he's figured out which of God's contradictory orders to obey.

"Ark" is now an uncommon English word reserved almost exclusively for biblical allusions. Besides Noah's flood-worthy vessel, the other famous biblical ark is the so-called "Ark of the Covenant," a mobile chest built to preserve the tablets delivered to Moses on Sinai [*see* THE TEN COMMANDMENTS, p. 64]. In fact "ark" (from the Latin *arca,* "chest," "box") was first used in English, in the ninth century, in reference to this holy Ark. Later the word was put to more general use, meaning either "ship" or "box" (as in the special box built to store copies of the Torah); in the United States it became the specific name of a flat-bottomed riverboat used to transport produce. But such usages virtually perished by the twentieth century, leaving only biblical citations, in particular Noah's ark, on the dry peaks of common parlance.

Forty Days and Forty Nights

> For yet seven days, and I will cause it to rain upon the earth forty days and forty nights; and every living substance that I have made will I destroy from off the face of the earth.

Genesis 7: 4

Besides disputing how many beasts were brought aboard Noah's ark, the two different sources of the story disagree on numerous other points, and it's enough to make your head spin.

J claims, for example, that the floodwaters completely subsided after three weeks, while P claims it took 150 days for the water even to begin receding and over a year for the land to dry. The two do concur on how long God caused rain to fall on the earth: "forty days and forty nights."

This isn't the last time these figures appear in the Bible, though it is the first. Later, Moses will convene with God on Sinai for "forty days and forty nights" (Exodus 24: 18), and the evangelist Mark tells us Christ sojourned in the wilderness for "forty days" (Mark 1: 13; see also Matthew 4 and Luke 4). Thanks to such repetition the phrase has become embedded in English as the most famous statement of duration, saving perhaps for the six days of creation.

Whenever it was that the earth was fit for habitation, Noah disembarks somewhere in the Ararat mountain range with his wife and sons (Shem, Ham, and Japheth), and the beasts. A few of the latter, it turns out, aren't as safe as they might have thought when invited onto the ark, for after piously building an altar to God, Noah fries a few of them up as a sacrifice. "And," J continues (Genesis 8: 21), "the LORD smelled a sweet savour" from the burnt offerings, which prompts him to pledge never

again to "curse the ground ... for man's sake; for the imagination of man's heart is evil from his youth; neither will I again smite any more every living thing, as I have done."

As a token of this promise or "covenant"—in which he seems to resign himself forevermore to human sinfulness—God sets a "bow in the cloud" as a reminder both to man and to himself. (And he's going to need it.) This is the Bible's way of explaining rainbows, though at this remove it would be hard to say how seriously we're supposed to take it. J, at least, seems to know he isn't dealing in facts, but rather in a version of mythology common to the ancient Near East—albeit a version specifically targeted to one group, the Israelites, among the descendants of Noah's eldest son Shem, namesake of the Semites.

For other versions of the Flood myth, you may consult the *Epic of Gilgamesh* or, for the Greek version (starring Deucalion), my book *By Jove! : Brush Up Your Mythology* (HarperCollins).

The Tower of Babel

> So the LORD scattered them abroad from thence upon the face of
> all the earth: and they left off to build the city. | Therefore is the
> name of it called Babel; because the LORD did there confound
> the language of all the earth: and from thence did the LORD
> scatter them abroad upon the face of all the earth.
>
> Genesis 11: 8–9

Interesting parallels and amateur wordplay aside, the word
"babble" does *not* derive from the Tower of Babel, a biblical
emblem for the folly of human ambition.

True, cacaphony and confusion did arise from that abandoned project, as God purportedly split a universal language
into mutually incomprehensible families. But the English
"babble" is related more to babies than to Babylon, the tower's
namesake. "Ba ba" (or "pa pa"), along with "ma ma," is an ex-
clamation common to infants of almost every culture. Thus the
French *babiller* and the Italian *babbolare,* "to act like a baby"—
clear analogues of the English "babble." And thus, incidentally,
the appearance of "papa" and "mama" in so many languages.

As for the legend of the Tower, it is peculiar to the older of the
two strands of primeval history. P tells us that the sons of Noah
begat all the tribes of man, who then dispersed across the earth
and developed independent languages. But J tells us differently.
"The whole world," he begins (11: 1), "had the same language
and the same words." Mankind is still gathered together in the
same place, where the more enterprising begin concocting am-
bitious projects. Among these is the Tower of Babel (Babylon),
intended by its builders to "make a name" for themselves, which
they somehow figure will prevent their being "scattered abroad
upon the face of the whole earth" (11: 4).

The logic of this supposition escapes me, and the plan predictably backfires. Yahweh sees in Babylon the concrete form of human hubris, yet another attempt, parallel to Adam and Eve's, to become more godlike—symbolized by the intent to build a tower "whose top may reach unto heaven" (verse 4).

To the LORD's thinking, this tower is just the beginning. United and monolingual, men could achieve whatever they wished, presumably without consulting him first. To put a stop to this, Yahweh comes down to Babylon to "confound [men's] language" and to scatter them across the face of the earth— precisely the fate they initiated the project to prevent.

"Therefore," goes J's punchline, "is the name of [the city] called Babel; because the LORD did there confound the language of all the earth" (verse 9). J is punning in Hebrew on the word *balal*, "mixed, confused," which actually has nothing to do with the name "Babel" (*Bavel* in Hebrew, from the Akkadian for "gate of the gods"). The English translation is, as we have seen, equally a false etymology, but false or true it would go on to influence the usage of "babble."

If you think about it, though, the pun doesn't really make sense. While God does sow confusion, he doesn't make the tower's builders "babble" (chatter incoherently or foolishly)— he just makes them unable to understand each other's attempts to speak clearly. And another thing: contrary to popular depictions, God doesn't destroy the tower by heaving a thunderbolt. He simply scatters the architects, who "left off to build the city" (11: 8). If the tower ever existed, its ruin would have been more likely due to gradual erosion than to an "act of God."

Sodom and Gomorrah

And the LORD said, Because the cry of Sodom and Gomorrah is
great, and because their sin is very grievous; | I will go down
now, and see whether they have done altogether according to the
cry of it, which is come unto me; and if not, I will know.

Genesis 18: 20–21

Sometimes men just push the LORD too far. This time the evildoers are the denizens of Sodom, a city on the plains of Jordan
near the Dead Sea. We arrive in the neighborhood with Abraham, who, after being chosen by God to beget a "great nation,"
leaves his home in Mesopotamia for a new land to the west
(Genesis 12 and 17). Abraham settles in the hills of Canaan, but
his nephew Lot prefers the urban culture of the plains. So he
pitches his tent in Sodom—a poor choice, as it turns out, since
"the men of Sodom were wicked and sinners before the LORD
exceedingly" (Genesis 13: 13).

Exactly what manner of sinners they were we must infer from
J's hints, which are pretty much limited to one verse (Genesis
19: 5). There, as two visitors (angels in disguise) dine with Lot,
the men of Sodom circle the house. "Where are the men which
came in to thee this night?" they want to know; "bring them out
to us, that we may know them."

Now, we all know what they mean by "know," and so did
Lot. Rather than allow guests to suffer such indignities, he
offers his two virgin daughters in the angels' stead. The mob
isn't having any of this, however; they begin breaking down
Lot's door, until the angels reveal their identity by striking the
perpetrators blind. But Lot's manners do confirm the angels'
opinion of his "righteousness."

From this one incident derives the English usage of "sodomy," "sodomite," etc., although the Bible suggests that the wickedness of Sodom and Gomorrah goes well beyond homosexual rape, which is bad enough. (Inhospitality appears to be a graver sin.) "Sodomy," meaning "unnatural sexual intercourse" dates back to the late thirteenth century, before Genesis had been fully translated into English, and "sodomite" in the sense of "sexual pervert" even predates "Sodomite" in the more primitive sense, "inhabitant of Sodom."

The fascination and disgust embodied through the ages in these words is awesome, as this selection of quotes from the OED demonstrates: "Devil, damned dog, sodomite insatiable"; "that Sodomitical swarm or brood of Antichrist"; "an open Sodomite; a horrible blasphemer"; "Wicked Sodomy, a sin so hateful to Nature itself that she abhors it"; "a filthy Sodomitical schoolmaster"; and so on and so forth.

While it's true that in Genesis we see the wickedness only of Sodom—Gomorrah's is merely reported—it's still strange that the one city should spawn so many terms of opprobrium and the other escape all but direct biblical allusion. Then again, "gomorrhean" and "gomorrhia" don't have the ring that "sodomite" and "sodomy" do, though "gomoria" is in fact one obsolete form of the word "gonorrhea." Whether the biblical city suggested the obsolete spelling, or vice versa, is unknown, but the more etymologically correct form "gonorrhea" derives from Greek, not from the Bible. So you can heave a sigh of relief.

Fire and Brimstone AND *A Pillar of Salt*

> Then the LORD rained upon Sodom and upon Gomorrah
> brimstone and fire from the LORD out of heaven; | And he
> overthrew those cities, and all the plain, and all the inhabitants
> of the cities, and that which grew upon the ground. | But his
> [Lot's] wife looked back from behind him, and she became a
> pillar of salt.
>
> Genesis 19: 24–26

God has finally had it with Sodom, not to mention Gomorrah. But his confidant Abraham hopes to stave off the city's destruction, if only because his nephew Lot is still living there.

Applying all the rhetoric he can muster, Abraham persuades the LORD to spare Lot and his family, but not the city. So on the eve of destruction, the LORD dispatches two angels to get them out while the getting's good. But the angels attach a few strings to the rescue: "Escape for thy life," one says; "look not behind thee, neither stay thou in all the plain; escape to the mountain, lest thou be consumed" (Genesis 19: 17).

So you can't say they weren't warned. On schedule, Yahweh rains down his famous "fire and brimstone"—a phrase dating in English to a rendering of this passage circa 1300. But, if just to prove that warnings can backfire, Lot's wife lets curiosity get the better of her: looking back on the horrible destruction, she is instantly turned to a pillar of salt. And that's the last we hear of her.

Why salt? you ask. Why *not* look back? you might reasonably inquire. What the heck is "brimstone"? you've always wondered. Let's try answering these in reverse order.

"Brimstone," simply put, used to be the common name for sulphur, but its meaning was refined under biblical influence (the influence more of Revelation 19: 20, which speaks of a hellish "lake of fire burning with brimstone," than of this passage). The word is employed today almost exclusively in allusions to God's fiery wrath, especially when channeled by righteous mouthpieces. ("Fire and brimstone," by the way, is most likely a poetic way of saying "sulphurous fire," the translation given by *The Anchor Bible*.)

Why not look back? Well, why not eat of the tree of knowledge? Because Yahweh says so, that's why. Beyond that, it seems that viewing the cities' destruction would be more than man or woman could bear—turning to stone being perhaps a concrete metaphor for terror. (Compare the Greek myth of the Gorgons, and think of common metaphors like "scared stiff" and "petrified.") In short, as E. A. Speiser puts it, "God's mysterious workings must not be looked at by man."

Why a pillar of salt? Because mineral pillars abounded in the region around Sodom and Gomorrah, and as we shall see salt was to the Jews a most notable mineral [*see* THE SALT OF THE EARTH, p. 172]. In other words, J describes the origins of these strange pillars with a folktale related to other ancient myths in which various individuals turn to pillars of salt when they see a god.

Jacob's Ladder

And he [Jacob] dreamed, and behold a ladder set up on the earth, and the top of it reached to heaven: and behold the angels of God ascending and descending on it. | And, behold, the LORD stood above it, and said, I am the LORD God of Abraham thy father, and the God of Isaac: the land whereon thou liest, to thee will I give it, and to thy seed....

Genesis 28: 12–13

You may know the flower Jacob's Ladder, with its long, delicate pistil and bluish petals. But did you know that the original Jacob's ladder, which reached to heaven, wasn't a ladder at all?

As we pick up the story, Jacob's mother Rebekah has sent him to seek a wife in Paddan-aram, the land of her father. This mission, partly intended to keep Jacob from falling in love with a pagan, also gets him out of the way of Isaac (his father) and Esau (his elder brother), both of whom he's cruelly tricked.

Jacob, you see, is not a very nice fellow. So it would seem strange that God should elect him as the next in the line of Hebrew patriarchs (after Abraham and Isaac). But the ways of Yahweh are mysterious, and so is the method he chooses to tell Jacob the news.

In a verse composed by the Elohist (E), when an exhausted Jacob stops to rest on the first night of his journey, he dozes off on a stone pillow and begins dreaming. In a vision, he beholds "angels of God" mounting and descending a stairway or ramp, in Hebrew *sullam* and improbably translated as "ladder" in the King James Version. The angels, imagined to be roughly the size and shape of human beings, would have had a hard time climbing up and down a ladder all at once, as they are described doing. More likely, *sullam* refers to a stone-cut stairway (a common sight in the ancient Near East), or perhaps even to the graduated face of a ziggurat.

Since the E narrative breaks off here, we hear nothing more about the angels or the stairway. Though the King James rendering suggests that Jacob sees God standing "above" the "ladder," in the original verse by J, Jacob is not dreaming, and Yahweh appears right beside him. This is when the LORD informs Jacob that he and his "seed" (descendants) shall inherit "the land whereon thou liest," including not only the precise spot (which Jacob names Beth-el, "house of God") but the expanse of territory surrounding it. This is the so-called "promised land," which has in fact already been promised to Abraham and will later be promised to Moses. (The phrase "promised land" never appears in the King James Version.)

The upshot of all this is that the image of "Jacob's ladder," confined to one verse, is never properly explained or interpreted. It is most likely, once again, an allusion to Babylonian myth, in which the gods were said to appear atop ziggurat temples. As such, the tale may prefigure the building of a temple at Beth-el, a place sacred to the northern tribes of Israel (Jacob calls it the "gate of heaven" in verse 17; "heaven's gate is not in the Bible).

In any case, this passage is so obscure that English speakers have been able to apply the phrase "Jacob's ladder" to a wide variety of items, none of them having anything to do with Jacob or even the Bible. The first beneficiary, *Polemonium caeruleum,* was the plant mentioned above, a garden variety whose leaves arrange themselves in a vaguely ladderlike pattern. By the mid-nineteenth century, "Jacob's ladder" had also become the name of rope ladders with wooden steps used to climb from the deck of a ship up its rigging. Steep flights of steps, for example at Oxford and on St. Helena, also took the phrase as a proper name, as did a now-obsolete sort of industrial elevator. Finally, and most whimsically, the English once called stocking-runs "Jacob's ladders"—perhaps after the fancy that the original mounted to heaven.

If you're interested in knowing how Jacob fares in wife-hunting, he does find a spouse among Rebekah's kin—in fact, he finds two, Leah and Rachel. But that's another story. More pertinent is that, on his way home fourteen years later (Genesis 32), Jacob once again has a roadside dream; in this one he wrestles with an adversary, who turns out to be Yahweh himself. By staying in the game until morning, Jacob displays his newfound moral strength, and earns from God the new name "Israel," which the Bible claims is derived from "striven [*sarita*] with gods [*elohim*]." But more likely "Israel" is from the Hebrew for "may God preserve."

Onanism

> And Er, Judah's firstborn, was wicked in the sight of the LORD;
> and the LORD slew him. | And Judah said unto Onan, Go in
> unto thy brother's wife, and marry her, and raise up seed to thy
> brother. | And Onan knew that the seed should not be his; and it
> came to pass, when he went in unto his brother's wife, that he
> spilled it on the ground, lest that he should give seed to his
> brother. | And the thing which he did displeased the LORD:
> wherefore he slew him also.
>
> Genesis 38: 7–10

As a favored son of God's chosen patriarch, Jacob (a.k.a. Israel),
Judah should have been sitting pretty. But in fact his family life
is miserable. Judah's first son, Er, turns out to be "wicked in the
sight of the LORD"; so God kills him. Judah's second son, Onan,
likewise "displease[s] the LORD," so God kills him, too. But at
least in Onan's case we're told why.

You might think Onan's sin was "onanism," an eponymous
English term for masturbation. But such is not exactly the case.
True, Onan "spills his seed on the ground," but he doesn't do it
all by himself. Jacob has put him on the spot, by means of a
peculiar tribal law: though Er is dead, if Er's brother impreg-
nates Er's widow (Tamar), then any resulting son will be taken
as Er's. It's bizarre enough that Onan could father Er's son if
he wanted to. What's more, since primogeniture (succession
through the first-born son) was of supreme importance at this
stage of Israelite society, he's compelled by duty to do so.

But Onan, rebelling at the idea that his own child will be
credited to Er, tries to pull a fast one. He "goes into" Tamar, all
right—to use the biblical expression—several times, in fact. But

every time he does he "comes out" at the crucial moment. It is this outrageous shirking of duty that so displeases Yahweh, not the method Onan uses to spill his seed—which is technically coitus interruptus.

Nonetheless, when "onanism" first appeared in English (in the eighteenth century), it was quaintly defined as "the crime of self-pollution." Occasionally, the term has been employed with slightly more fidelity to the Bible; A. K. Gardner, for example, referred in his 1892 work *Conjugal Relations* to "the best-calculated refinements of conjugal onanism." In a more recent development, "onanism," once virtually restricted to private activities by men, has been given wider application, as when George Steiner refers in *Language and Silence* (1967) to some "recent university experiment in which faculty wives agreed to practice onanism in front of the researchers' cameras."

The Fat of the Land

And Pharaoh said unto Joseph, Say unto thy brethren, This do ye: lade your beasts, and go, get you unto the land of Canaan; | And take your father and your households, and come unto me: and I will give you the good of the land of Egypt, and ye shall eat the fat of the land.

Genesis 45: 17–18

Diet-conscious modern readers may have some trouble with the concept of "fat of the land," which in the Bible means "the earth's choicest produce." But in those leaner times, fat was harder to come by than it is in the modern West. It's a sign of the times that this sense of "fat" is now obsolete, except in the expression "fat of the land."

Dietary evolution aside, there's another reason the phrase might be confusing. Biblical Pharaohs are generally quite evil; so, reading out of context, you're likely to interpret this one's offer of the "fat of the land" as some kind of threat. But it's not: not only is this Pharaoh a soft-hearted sort, he's got good reason to put himself at the disposal of Joseph, Jacob's penultimate son and the last of the Hebrew patriarchs.

Joseph, though brought to Egypt as a slave, has risen to a high position in government, second only to Pharaoh, by interpreting a few of Pharaoh's strange dreams and thus correctly forecasting a prolonged regional drought. By overseeing the storage and distribution of the "fat" of Egypt, Joseph saves the people from starvation.

At this point in the story (the second year of the drought), Joseph's brothers journey to Egypt from the equally drought-stricken Canaan to seek food. Joseph, whom they don't recognize, might easily turn them back empty-handed, since it was they who sold him into slavery (so J tells us at Genesis 37: 27–28, though E demurs). Nonetheless, after putting his brothers through a few tests, Joseph reveals himself and embraces them, and he even goes so far as to offer them a new home in Goshen, on the Nile delta.

What pleases Joseph pleases Pharaoh, who seconds the invitation and promises the entire house of Israel that they shall "eat the fat of the land"—while back home the Canaanites starve. Actually, in the Hebrew text Pharaoh doesn't say "fat," just "best": the phrase was doubled and "fat" introduced by the King James translators. Thus "fat" must already have meant "the good bit" before 1611, and indeed, "fat of the soil" was in circulation by the 1570s. Nevertheless, "fat of the land" per se is first found in the Authorized Version, and it is only biblical usage that preserves the phrase, despite the best efforts of modern translators, who have some sort of obsession with accuracy.

A Stranger in a Strange Land

And Moses was content to dwell with the man [Reuel]: and he
gave Moses Zipporah his daughter. I And she bare him a son,
and he called his name Gershom: for he said, I have been a
stranger in a strange land.

Exodus 2: 21–22

Generations pass, and the Israelites, obeying God's command to
"be fruitful and multiply" [*see* p. 11], grow numerous in Egypt.
At the same time, Joseph's erstwhile service to the state is forgotten. A new Pharaoh, ignorant of Egypt's historical debt to Israel,
finds little comfort in the immigrant nation's increasing prosperity and power; indeed, he views Israel as an enemy within.

So Pharaoh subjects the Israelites to slavery, hoping to
humble them. But he doesn't succeed in crushing their spirit,
even as he makes their tasks more onerous. Angry and frus-
trated, Pharaoh ultimately commands that all the Israelites'
male children be thrown in the Nile.

This tactic proves unsuccessful, of course, through both
Egyptian resistance and Israelite cleverness. For example, when
a baby boy named Moses (*Moshe* in Hebrew) is born to the Israelite tribe of Levi, his mother builds a small papyrus ark,
places the boy inside, and floats it down the Nile where she
hopes it will be discovered by a sympathetic Egyptian. As luck
would have it, Moses is claimed by Pharaoh's daughter, whose
tender feelings shield him from death.

So Moses grows to manhood in Pharaoh's palace—that is,
right in the enemy's bosom. As was bound to happen, Moses
eventually runs afoul of Pharaoh and is forced to flee the country. He soon finds a home among the Kenites, a Semitic people,

in Midian (now in Saudi Arabia, on the east bank of the Gulf of Aqaba). And when Moses one day comes to the aid of some lovely maidens, he finds among them a wife as well—Zippora, daughter to a Midian priest variously named "Reuel" and "Jethro."

Nature takes its course, and Zippora gives birth to a son, whom Moses names Gershom, after the Hebrew *ger,* "alien, sojourner, refugee." In case his in-laws haven't caught the reference, Moses provides this gloss: "I have been a stranger (*ger*) in a strange land (*nakhor*)"—that is, Midian. The line is more beautiful in the King James translation than in the original, which Everett Fox more faithfully renders thus: "A sojourner have I become in a foreign land." The King James Version is not, however, all that far off, given that "stranger" and "alien" were once synonymous in English (compare the French *étranger*), as were "strange" and "foreign." A later rendering of the same phrase as "an alien in a strange land" (Exodus 18: 3) is less misleading to the modern reader, but at the expense of the poetry.

In fact, the former translation is much better remembered—thanks in part to science-fiction author Robert Heinlein's bestowing the title *Stranger in a Strange Land* (1961) on what became his best-known novel. Deservedly forgotten, however, is Margaret Mitchell's pun "stranger in a strange town," from her wildly popular *Gone with the Wind* (1936).

The Burning Bush

Now Moses kept the flock of Jethro his father in law, the priest
of Midian: and he led the flock to the backside of the desert, and
came to the mountain of God, even to Horeb. | And the angel of
the LORD appeared unto him in a flame of fire out of the midst
of a bush: and he looked, and, behold, the bush burned with fire,
and the bush was not consumed.

Exodus 3: 1–2

One day, wandering absent-mindedly with his father-in-law's
sheep, Moses happens upon Mount Horeb (Mount Sinai),
which the Bible knows as "the mountain of God."

Moses is startled to find a bush that, while aflame, doesn't really "burn," because it isn't consumed. Even more startling, the
bush calls out to him, insisting that he take off his shoes, because "the place whereon thou standest is holy ground." The
voice is Yahweh's, though the fire is just one of his angels.

Yahweh isn't just calling for a friendly chat: he's got plans for
Moses. God has heard the cries of his people suffering in Egypt
and has finally decided to honor his promise of a happier future.
Moses shall be his instrument in bringing the Israelites into
their promised "land of milk and honey" [see the next entry].

The burning bush has long been a staple of literary allusion,
but it wasn't often used humorously until another Bush started
burning. Looking ahead to his speech at the 1992 Republican
National Convention, the former president promised that "if it
catches fire, it may give a whole new meaning to the burning
Bush." "A humorous remark," mused Norman Mailer in *The
New Republic,* "but a vain hope. He was too angry within: the
delegates instead were treated to the smouldering Bush."

A Land of Milk and Honey

And I am come down to deliver them out of the hand of the
Egyptians, and to bring them up out of that land unto a good
land and a large, unto a land flowing with milk and honey: unto
the place of the Canaanites, and the Hittites, and the Amorites,
and the Perizzites, and the Hivites, and the Jebusites.

Exodus 3: 8

Addressing Moses from the burning bush, Yahweh announces
his plan to bring Israel out of Egypt to a "land flowing with milk
and honey." God means Palestine, the land he promised to
Abraham (Genesis 12) and again to Jacob (Genesis 28).

He doesn't mean, though, that milk and honey wash over the
land—as "flowing" might suggest—but rather that his people
can look forward to a booming economy. (They could also look
forward to unfriendly natives, but that's another story.) Milk
and honey were dietary staples for the semi-nomadic Israelites
of biblical times, so Palestine would indeed be a promising
home, abounding in goats and swarming with bees. The soil
would be fertile, too, nourishing grapevines and date trees,
whose syrup was also called "honey" in Hebrew.

Though the medieval British diet must have differed consid-
erably from the ancient Israelites', the phrase "land of milk and
honey" is one of the earliest biblical expressions to have made its
way into English (ca. A.D. 1000), via Ælfric's rendering of
Numbers 16: 13. "Flowing with milk and honey," however, had
to wait for Wyclif's 1382 translation of Ezekiel (20: 6). The
phrase had apparently embedded itself in English speech by the
time William Tyndale used it in translating the present passage,

for he claimed never to have glanced at Wyclif or any other English version of the Bible.

As you might imagine, writers have seized upon Ælfric's phrase and wrested it out of context to describe whatever locale happened to catch their enthusiasm, whether or not goats and date trees abounded. Once upon a time Englishmen viewed America in particular as a "land of milk and honey," but all that has changed, even for Americans. John Steinbeck captured the native disillusionment in *The Grapes of Wrath* (1939), where a once-hopeful immigrant to California wryly observes that "this ain't no lan' of milk an' honey like the preachers say" (chapter 20).

To Harden Your Heart

And the LORD said unto Moses, When thou goest to return into
Egypt, see that thou do all those wonders before Pharaoh, which
I have put in thine hand: but I will harden his heart, that he shall
not let the people go.

Exodus 4: 21

The good news: the LORD has promised to deliver Israel from its
sufferings in Egypt. The bad news: it's not going to be easy.

Here's how God sees it: Moses shall return to Egypt and rally
the elders of Israel behind him. They shall then approach Pharaoh to demand a three-day vacation in the wilderness, to make
sacrifice to their God; but "the king of Egypt will not let you go,
no, not by a mighty hand" (Exodus 3: 19).

But there's more good news: Yahweh will then smite Egypt
with his "wonders" (verse 20), namely plagues, and in the end
Pharaoh will gladly let Israel go. More bad news: Yahweh plans
to stiffen Pharaoh's resistance, or "harden his heart," so that a
few mere disasters won't make him loosen his grip. Moses will
have to threaten, and God produce, ever more drastic calami-
ties, culminating in the death of all Egypt's first-born sons, before Pharaoh relents. So while God will free his people through
Moses, he will lengthen their bondage through Pharaoh.

It's been said before, but mysterious are the ways of the LORD.
The point the author (E) wants to make, however, is that all the
crucial events in Israel's history, both successes and failures, have
ultimately been orchestrated by God. Why God might want to
work at cross-purposes in freeing his people is never explained,
but it is probably to prolong the Egyptians' humiliation.

Note that in Exodus hardening the heart is something *God* does to *you,* not something you do to yourself. Our usage takes a cue from the book of Psalms, where the phrase "Harden not your heart" appears (95: 8). This is the unique reference in the Bible to self-inflicted hardening.

"Let My People Go"

And afterward Moses and Aaron went in, and told Pharaoh,
Thus saith the LORD God of Israel, Let my people go, that they
may hold a feast unto me in the wilderness.

Exodus 5: 1

You may think that the oft-quoted phrase, "Let my people go,"
is Moses' one classic line in the Bible. But not only is this demand borrowed from Yahweh (the "my" of "my people"), it is
spoken to Pharaoh by Moses' elder brother Aaron, a high priest
of Israel and a much more dynamic orator.

Moses himself admits to God (Exodus 4: 10) that "I am not
eloquent, neither heretofore, nor since thou hast spoken unto
thy servant: but I am slow of speech, and of a slow tongue"—a

The Hebrew Bible

roundabout way of putting it, which proves the point. So God commisions Aaron to deliver the line—not that he succeeds any better in persuading Pharaoh. "I know not the LORD," Pharaoh retorts, "neither will I let Israel go" (5: 2).

In fact, Pharaoh imposes new sufferings on the enslaved Israelites. Moses promptly complains to God, who of course already knows that the brothers have failed. And this time the gloves are off: "Now shalt thou see," Yahweh says, "what I will do to Pharaoh: for with a strong hand shall he let them go, and with a strong hand shall he drive them out of his land."

Yahweh's device is a series of brutal plagues, ten according to Exodus but only seven according to two different Psalms (78 and 105). The description in Exodus of these plagues is actually a composite, with the older narrative (J's) also listing seven plagues—of blood, frogs, flies, death of cattle, hail, locusts, and death of first-born boys. The Priestly Author adds plagues of gnats, boils, and darkness.

Whether or not these plagues have a basis in history—and it's possible to ascribe them to natural causes—there was no doubt some good reason Egypt let go of Israel, even if it wasn't Moses' eloquence. But once the Hebrews discover that freedom does not end their troubles—far from it—they begin to wish Pharaoh would take God's people back [see FLESHPOT, p. 62].

Incidentally, it is from Yahweh's promise that, while killing Egypt's first-born sons, he shall "pass over" the Hebrews (Exodus 12: 13) that we take the name "Passover." To this day Passover, a feast commemorating the Hebrews' deliverance from slavery, is the most widely celebrated of Jewish holidays.

Jehovah ("I Am That I Am")

And God spake unto Moses, and said unto him, I am the LORD:
| And I appeared unto Abraham, unto Isaac, and unto Jacob, by
the name of God Almighty, but by my name JEHOVAH was I not
known to them.

Exodus 6: 2–3

You may wonder, as you read along in the Hebrew Bible, why
God has so many names. To the polite plural *Elohim* ("gods") of
Genesis 1, Genesis 2 adds the "tetragrammaton" (four-letter
name) YHWH or YHVH, rendered as "the LORD" in the Au-
thorized Version. Later we find other designations, such as
Eloah ("God"), *El Shaddai* ("God of the Mountains"), *El Elyon*
("God Most High"), and so on.

The reason for this confusing plenitude is that some of the
Bible's authors have a problem with the proper name YHWH,
pronounced as "Yahweh." J is not one of them, as he uses it
consistently from the start, and he tells us in Genesis (4: 26) that
men first called God YHWH in the days of Seth, the third son
of Adam and Eve.

J is contradicted, however, in Exodus, where God tells Moses
that he "appeared unto Abraham, unto Isaac, and unto Jacob,
by the name of God Almighty [*El Shaddai*], but by my name
JEHOVAH [YHWH] was I not known to them" (Exodus 6: 3).
Perhaps God forgets that Abraham "called upon the name of
the LORD [YHWH]" at Genesis 12: 8; that Isaac "called upon
the name of the LORD [YHWH]" at Genesis 26: 25; and that he
himself (Genesis 28: 13) announced to Jacob that "I am the
LORD [YHWH] God of Abraham thy father, and the God of
Isaac." If so, God has a mighty short memory.

The truth, however, is that P wrote chapter 6 of Exodus, and P (like E) had different ideas than J about the use of God's proper name. So in Genesis he and E use *Elohim* and *El Shaddai* and so forth, since according to them God's name was unknown to men until he revealed it to Moses.

I'm sure all that's now crystal clear, but there remain the questions of what "Yahweh" means and how it came to be Anglicized as "Jehovah." Yahweh has already explained to Moses, in a passage by E (Exodus 3: 14), that his name means "I am that I am"—*ehyeh asher ehyeh,* an obscure statement that might also be rendered "I will be what I will be" or "I cause that which is to be." (Yahweh probably means both that he is a completely self-sufficient being, and that he is the ultimate source of all other beings.) Transposed into the third person—"he is who is" or "he who causes what is to be"—God's statement would read *Yahweh asher yihweh,* Q.E.D. The form YHWH itself is the standard Hebrew spelling, which only renders consonants.

As for the English spelling, we owe that to William Tyndale's 1530 translation of this passage, where "Jehovah" (old spelling "Iehoua") replaces the term "Adonai" ("My Great Lord"), which is found in Wyclif's translation. Yet does not entirely replace it: in fact, "Jehovah" is compounded from the sacred consonants YHVH and the vowels of Adonai.

This is where the plot really thickens. It turns out that the "false" vowels of Adonai had already been added to YHWH in "pointed" versions of the original Hebrew text, which, for purposes of reading aloud, subscribed vowels to the consonants as found in the original. But YHWH was marked with the vowels of Adonai precisely in order to remind readers to say "Adonai" rather than utter the sacred name itself, which was the subject of increasing awe and superstition. (After about 300 B.C., Jews almost entirely ceased pronouncing the name "Yahweh.")

Tyndale was not the first to blunder in adding false vowels to Yahweh's name, but he was the first to do so in English. Not only did he obscure the true pronunciation of the divine name, his version is furthermore apt to recall the pagan deity Jove, whose name is not at all related to God's, but which would occasionally serve as a euphemism among reverential Englishmen. And because "Jehovah" was mistaken as authentic, Tyndale and later translators wished to avoid using it except when absolutely necessary—which is why it is represented as "LORD" in the King James text. It turns out, of course, that they could have gone right ahead and used "Jehovah."

As for "I am that I am" or whatever the name means, Yahweh probably wouldn't sanction most of the quotations in his honor, since presumably human beings *aren't* "that they are"—that is, not the source of their own being. But the narrator of Aldous Huxley's story "After the Fireworks" (in *Brief Candles,* 1930) mistakes Yahweh to mean "I am *what* I am," which is of course always literally true as it is spoken. "They behave as they do," he opines, "because they can't help it; that's what they happen to be like. 'I am that I am'; Jehovah's is the last word in realistic psychology."

On the other hand, if we take "I am what I am" figuratively, it needn't be true, as Iago realizes in Shakespeare's *Othello* (1604). At one point he announces to Roderigo that "I am not what I am" (Act 1, scene 1), which means "I am not as I appear" but also much more. Iago is the closest we come in Shakespeare to the devil.

The Parting of the Waters

> And the LORD said unto Moses, Wherefore criest thou unto me? speak unto the children of Israel, that they go forward: | But lift thou up thy rod, and stretch out thine hand over the sea, and divide it: and the children of Israel shall go on dry ground through the midst of the sea. | And I, behold, I will harden the hearts of the Egyptians, and they shall follow them: and I will get me honour upon Pharaoh, and upon all his host, upon his chariots, and upon his horsemen.
>
> Exodus 14: 15–17

If "parting of the waters" calls to mind Moses waving his rod and dividing a vast sea into two huge walls of water, forget it. What is called the "Red Sea" in Exodus is almost certainly not what we call the Red Sea today, but rather a much humbler body of water.

Parting the Red Sea would indeed be a feat, since it is 150 miles wide on average (not to mention 1,450 miles long). It is highly unlikely, though not completely out of the question, that this is the sea the LORD has in mind; none of the probable Exodus routes takes the Israelites anywhere near it at this stage of their journey. The Hebrew term *yam suph,* which is used for the Red Sea and its two gulfs, literally means "Sea of Reeds," and so probably refers here to a freshwater marsh on the border between Egypt and the Sinai Peninsula. Such a lake, while no pushover to cross at high water, might easily be "parted" for passage by a good drought, or even, as the Bible suggests, by a "strong east wind" (verse 21).

So while one needn't deny God's hand in parting the waters, he might have been able to do it by natural means. In any case, the rest of the story does suggest that what happened at *yam suph* was extraordinary at least in its timing. Though the lake was passable by the Israelites, who crossed on foot, it foiled the Egyptians, sent in pursuit by the hard-hearted Pharaoh. The wheels of their chariots got stuck in the muddy marsh-bed, and thereupon the waters returned to drown the whole lot of them, along with their horses.

That's the last the Israelites heard of Egypt, and their miraculous delivery had the side effect of striking the fear of God (and Moses) into them—at least for a while. The whole episode, among others, suggests that in Moses' time Yahweh was thought of primarily as a warrior-god, personally involved in his worshipper's battles. Though in later books the LORD is often given the credit for Israel's military victories and defeats, he is less and less directly involved. By the time Israel and Judah are established as states, Yahweh is principally a god of law—a role he first assumes by issuing Moses the Ten Commandments [*see* p. 64].

Fleshpot

And the children of Israel said unto them, Would to God we had
died by the hand of the LORD in the land of Egypt, when we sat
by the flesh pots, and when we did eat bread to the full; for ye
have brought us forth into this wilderness, to kill this whole
assembly with hunger.

Exodus 16: 3

At first the Israelites welcomed their delivery from slavery in
Egypt, but hunger in the wilderness isn't quite what they expected. As the previous verse puts it, "The whole congregation
of the children of Israel murmured against Moses and Aaron,"
their deliverers. In retrospect, slavery doesn't seem so bad at all:
at least the Israelites had their fill of the famous "flesh pots" of
Egypt.

"Flesh pot"—the phrase is from Miles Coverdale's 1535
translation—refers to a large metal caldron used by luxuriating
Egyptians to boil meat. For centuries writers used "flesh pot"
exclusively with reference to this passage. And since the author
of Exodus clearly looks askance at the Israelites' yearnings, the
phrase has always signified decadent temptation. But it's only in
this century that the "flesh" of "fleshpot" has come to mean
human flesh, and the luxury become carnal. Those who wish to
be more precise use the derivative term "sexpot," which gets
right to the point.

Manna from Heaven

And when the dew that lay was gone up, behold, upon the face
of the wilderness there lay a small round thing, as small as the
hoar frost on the ground. | And when the children of Israel saw
it, they said one to another, It is manna: for they wist not what it
was. And Moses said unto them, This is the bread which the
LORD hath given you to eat.

Exodus 16: 14–15

After the Israelites have complained long and hard about the
scarcity of food in the wilderness, Yahweh promises to "rain
bread from heaven" upon them (Exodus 16: 4) and even throws
quail meat into the bargain. The birds he delivers are the standard variety, but the bread is like nothing they've ever seen.
"What is it?" they ask one another—"*Man hu?*" in Hebrew—
and thus, by their puzzlement, they name the bread *man*.

But the Israelites are puzzled only because they've been
cooped up in Egypt too long. Manna—known as *mann* to this
day—is a delicious, sugary derivative of the tamarisk bush, native to the Sinai peninsula. Knowing how it's produced, however, may blunt your appetite. Manna is a crystallized form of
tamarisk sap, excreted in drops (like honeydew) by insects. It
falls from the bushes in the morning, thus symbolically "raining
from heaven." Being round, white, and flaky, this manna does
indeed have the appearance of hoarfrost (verse 14).

The Israelites aren't much interested in finding out how God
produced this miracle. They had better things to do—like
gather up the manna before ants got to it and think up new
complaints against Moses.

The Ten Commandments

I am the LORD thy God, which have brought thee out of the
land of Egypt, out of the house of bondage. | Thou shalt have no
other gods before me. | ... Thou shalt not bow down thyself to
[strange gods], nor serve them: for I the LORD thy God am a
jealous God, visiting the iniquity of the fathers upon the children
unto the third and fourth generation of them that hate me; | And
shewing mercy unto thousands of them that love me, and keep
my commandments.

Exodus 20: 2–3, 5–6

The Hebrews, having had a taste of the LORD's power, would
rather not have anything directly to do with him. "Let not God
speak with us," they plead to Moses, "lest we die" (verse 19).

So it is Moses' job to parley with Yahweh whenever the LORD
has a message for his people. And in this case the message is
crucial: God has decided to spell out the laws to which he intends to hold his chosen people, at least if they want to make it
to the Promised Land in one piece.

The first (and most important) table of laws is known as the
"Decalogue" or "Ten Commandments" (and there are hun-
dreds more). Jews, Catholics, Protestants, and Eastern Orthodox Christians alike accept these names for the laws, but they
disagree on how to number them. Jews, for example, traditionally regard verse 2 as the first commandment (or "utterance"
in Hebrew), though it's really a self-proclamation rather than a
commandment: "I am the LORD thy God." They then group
together what Protestants take to be the first and second commandments, the prohibitions against other gods and against
graven images [see the next entry]. But the Jews' second com-

mandment is the Catholics' first, and as you can see trying to sort all this out quickly becomes a nightmare.

For the sake of convenience, I'll list the remaining eight commandments in the order favored by Jews and Protestants:

3. "Thou shalt not take the name of the LORD thy God in vain" (Exodus 20: 7)—in other words, you shall not employ the divine name for base or trivial purposes, such as swearing falsely or performing magic;

4. "Remember the sabbath day, to keep it holy" (verse 8)—no working allowed on Saturday (Christians, believing Christ died on a Sunday, made that their holy day);

5. "Honour thy father and thy mother" (verse 12)—on penalty of death (Exodus 21: 15–17);

6. "Thou shalt not kill" (Exodus 20: 13)—except those who break the law;

7. "Thou shalt not commit adultery" (verse 14)—broadly intepreted in some quarters as condemning all extramarital sex;

8. "Thou shalt not steal" (verse 15)—self-explanatory;

9. "Thou shalt not bear false witness against thy neighbour" (verse 16)—don't make up mean lies about other people;

10. "Thou shalt not covet thy neighbour's house, thou shalt not covet thy neighbour's wife, nor his manservant, nor his maidservant, nor his ox, nor his ass, nor any thing that is thy neighbour's" (verse 17)—which could have been put more concisely.

Once he's through delivering these laws to Moses, God puts on a little show for the Hebrews: "And all the people saw the thunderings, and the lightnings, and the noise of the trumpet, and the mountain smoking: and when the people saw it, they removed, and stood afar off" (verse 18). I don't blame them; God clearly means business.

So that they don't forget any of these laws—say, the seventh—God proceeds to etch them out on two tablets for Moses (Exodus 24: 12). This takes quite a while, though, which understandably gives the Hebrews the jitters. Who knows what God is prohibiting, if it's taking him forty days and forty nights to write it all down.

A Graven Image

Thou shalt not make unto thee any graven image, or any likeness
of any thing that is in heaven above, or that is in the earth
beneath, or that is in the water under the earth.

Exodus 20: 4

The Israelites were perhaps the least visual people in the ancient
world, as they showed little interest in painting, decoration, or
representations of any sort. Above all, they shunned depicting
their God Yahweh in drawings or statues, thus obeying the
commandment (quoted here) against "graven images."

Despite what God seems to say in the King James translation,
he is not really forbidding representational art—just represen-
tation of divine things. Among all ancient deities, Yahweh is
uniquely abstract, and the most insistent not only on his
ineffability but also on his singularity (all other gods are "false").
As he famously puts it in verse 5, "I the LORD thy God am a
jealous God"—a claim he will prove over and over again in the
Hebrew Bible.

Other passages in Exodus (15: 11; 18: 11; and 32: 4, for example) suggest that the Israelites acknowledged pagan gods as
real. Yet they saw Yahweh as a greater god and were monotheists
in the practical sense, worshiping only him—except, that is, on
those all-too-frequent occasions when heathens enticed them
into their loose rituals. And on the matter of "graven images"—
carved statues—they were absolutely rigorous; no archeologist
has ever excavated a statue of Yahweh.

Such rigor indicates not only a powerful sense of difference
from other Near Eastern cultures (in which idol worship was
widespread) but also a somewhat more interior notion of God

(which, however, did not preclude sacrifices and burnt offerings to him). As time went on, the Israelite image of Yahweh grew even more abstract and less anthropomorphic, and those portions of the Hebrew Bible written later reflect a special contempt for pagan idols—typical epithets, as listed in *Harper's Bible Dictionary,* include "powerless ones," "pellets of dung," and "shameful things." The relatively tame English phrase "graven image" dates to the 1388 revision of Wyclif's translation of Exodus (the original, from 1382, read "graven thing").

Eye for Eye, Tooth for Tooth

And if any mischief follow, then thou shalt give life for life, | Eye
for eye, tooth for tooth, hand for hand, foot for foot, | Burning
for burning, wound for wound, stripe for stripe.

Exodus 21: 23–25

Law-and-order types are fond of citing the Israelite penal code,
which is indeed no day at the beach. This passage quoting God's
instructions to Moses (along with its restatement in Leviticus
24) is a particular favorite, especially among advocates of the
death penalty. But it's never quoted in full—it does get out of
hand—and nobody really follows through on the logic, which
seems to demand stealing from thieves and raping rapists.

In fact, Yahweh isn't averse to such sentences, if they are
practical—something many people would like to forget or explain away. Nor does he object to capital punishment, which he
demands not just for murder but for striking a parent or stealing
a slave (but not for killing one of your own). In general the law
seeks parity and restitution: what you take from a man, you
must replace or else forfeit, be it an eye, a tooth, an ox, or a life.

It is a mistake to read the present verses too figuratively, as a
poetic version of Cicero's "Let the punishment fit the crime."
Yahweh means what he says—he's talking about real eyes and
teeth and hands and lives. The problem is that we now use the
phrase "eye for eye, tooth for tooth" *only* metaphorically and
would condemn as barbaric its literal observance. So whatever
the justifications for capital punishment, it's unwise to quote
them from the Bible, which can be a real Pandora's box. Besides, Jesus will have a few things to say about "eye for eye, tooth
for tooth" [*see* TO TURN THE OTHER CHEEK, p. 176].

One should not be too horrified by what one finds in this chapter of Exodus, which forms part of the so-called "Book of the Covenant," a collection of divinely sanctioned laws. In certain respects Yahweh's code is much less harsh than many others prevailing at the time it was formulated. Manslaughter, for example, is distinguished from murder and punished differently; causing a woman to miscarry, furthermore, does not call for death, as it apparently did elsewhere. Finally, you only had to lose an eye if you put out someone else's—which, believe it or not, was getting off easy.

Speaking of getting off easy, Ernest S. Bates shows us how to interpret Exodus in a truly Christian manner in his *American Faith* (1940). "Immorality and crime may be expiated by finite punishments: an eye for an eye and a tooth for a tooth," he hopefully begins; "but sin demands an infinite punishment."

The Golden Calf

And he [Aaron] received them [the golden earrings] at their
hand, and fashioned it with a graving tool, after he had made it a
molten calf: and they said, These be thy gods, O Israel, which
brought thee up out of the land of Egypt.

Exodus 32: 4

Encamped at the base of Mount Sinai, the Israelites grow nervous as eight chapters go by and Moses is still missing. The last
they knew, Yahweh had whisked him up the mount for a summit, and they've begun to feel abandoned by both.

They begin to question the prohibition against "graven images," which was fine as long as Yahweh kept in touch directly
or through Moses. Turning to their chief priest, Aaron, they
demand that he "make us gods, which shall go before us," that
is, lead them through the wilderness (Exodus 32: 1).

That the people have yet to shake the Egyptian proclivity for
idols is bad enough; worse is that Aaron goes along with them.
He melts down their gold earrings to form a "calf" or, according to the Hebrew, a bullock. Aaron then somewhat illogically
proclaims the idol (singular) the "gods" (plural) who had delivered Israel from Egypt, and the people promptly begin making
sacrifices to it/them.

Aaron's imagery is no accident; various major pagan gods
were represented as virile calves. Furthermore, scholars detect in
this passage veiled criticism of Jeroboam [*see* p. 103], who had
set up statues of bulls at the chief Israelite shrines. The austere
author (E) likely found such iconography both disgusting and
heretical; if so, his judgment is shared by both Yahweh and
Moses, as we shall see.

A Stiff-Necked People

And the LORD said unto Moses, I have seen this people, and,
behold, it is a stiffnecked people: | Now therefore let me alone,
that my wrath may wax hot against them, and that I may
consume them: and I will make of thee a great nation.

Exodus 32: 9–10

The adjective "stiff-necked" was coined by William Tyndale for
his 1526 translation of the Acts of the Apostles (7: 51), but the
phrase "stiffnecked people" (sans hyphen) first appears here, and
it will be applied again and again to the obstreperous Israelites.

Their necks are called "stiff" because they won't bend to
God's will, in this case his commandment against graven images. As he sees the Israelites eat, drink, and make merry in the
company of their new golden god, Yahweh cuts short his con-
ference with Moses and vows to wipe out the entire crew.

But Moses defends his people, despite God's offer to make a
"great nation" of his progeny. He argues that Israel's destruction
will only comfort Yahweh's Egyptian enemies and reminds him
of his promises to Abraham, Isaac, and Jacob. The LORD listens
to reason and "repents" of "the evil which he thought to do unto
his people" (Exodus 32: 14).

But Moses is almost as angry with his people as Yahweh was.
When he witnesses their vile behavior with his own two eyes, he
flies into a rage, smashing the two tablets on which God had
inscribed the Ten Commandments—thus symbolically breaking the whole of the covenant his stiff-necked people partly
violated in the golden calf incident.

Then, as his anger "waxe[s] hot" (verse 19), Moses seizes the
golden bull and tosses it in a fire, which seems to char rather

than melt it, since Moses then grinds it into powder. Mixing the powder with water, he forces the sinning Israelites to drink the potion, which I expect made them thoroughly sick.

Even this, however, isn't enough for Moses. Calling out to the camp, he demands to know who is with the LORD and who is against him. Only the priestly tribe of Levi pledges their allegiance, and when they have gathered around, Moses orders them to "slay every man his brother, and every man his companion, and every man his neighbor" (verse 27), which they promptly do. Three thousand Israelites die.

As a reward, Moses confers Yahweh's blessing upon the Levites and then returns to Mount Sinai. There, Yahweh promises to send an "Angel" before the people so that they'll have no further use for idols. But he also vows to be revenged upon any future stiffnecked sinners. He won't have long to wait.

Long-Suffering

And the LORD passed by before him [Moses], and proclaimed,
The LORD, The LORD God, merciful and gracious, longsuffering,
and abundant in goodness and truth....

Exodus 34: 6

The compound "long-suffering" debuted in William Tyndale's 1526 translation of the Epistle to the Galatians (5: 22), where it is used as a noun. Much more common today is the adjective (as in "my long-suffering accountant"), also a biblical coinage, tracing to Miles Coverdale's 1535 translation of this passage.

If you had to define the term from its context, you might mistake its meaning, considering Yahweh's temper. Yet the LORD knows that he is a jealous God, so in renewing his covenant with Israel after the golden calf debacle he pledges to rely more often on his better qualities of graciousness and mercy (Exodus 33: 19).

This doesn't mean, however, that all the Israelites' sins will be forgiven. In the same breath as he declares himself "merciful and gracious, longsuffering, and abundant in goodness and truth," Yahweh also notes that his patience and mercy will "by no means clear the guilty," and that a father's sin will be paid back upon four generations of his offspring (Exodus 34: 7)—a sentence later reversed after the Babylonian exile.

In short, "long-suffering" did not originally imply meek or all-forgiving, as it tends to do today. More faithful to the original phrase is an implied breaking point: one may suffer long, but not forever, and the longer the suffering, the more violent the backlash.

A Scapegoat

And he [Aaron] shall take of the congregation of the children of Israel two kids of the goats for a sin offering, and one ram for a burnt offering. | … And he shall take the two goats, and present them before the LORD at the door of the tabernacle of the congregation. | And Aaron shall cast lots upon the two goats; one lot for the LORD, and the other lot for the scapegoat. | And Aaron shall bring the goat upon which the LORD's lot fell, and offer him for a sin offering. | But the goat, on which the lot fell to be the scapegoat, shall be presented alive before the LORD, to make an atonement with him, and to let him go for a scapegoat into the wilderness.

Leviticus 16: 5, 7–10

The Priestly Author of Leviticus (whose title means "priestly matters") details the rituals to be observed on the annual Jewish "Day of Atonement," or Yom Kippur. (Though P claims such rites were handed down to Moses by God, in actuality Yom Kippur was not celebrated before the sixth century B.C.) Among these is the ritual sacrifice of a bullock, two rams, and a goat as "sin offerings," in symbolic atonement for the people's sins.

The poor bullock and rams never had a chance, but the goat was chosen from two candidates, so had a fifty-fifty chance of escaping the blade. Which of the two wound up a "sin offering" was determined by lottery, with the high priest (here, Aaron) casting the lots—"one for the LORD," as the text says, "and the other lot for the scapegoat (*Azazel*)."

The word "scapegoat" is a piece of patchwork by William Tyndale, who translated this passage in 1530. The Hebrew *Azazel* confused him; following the Latin (Vulgate) Bible, he figured that it must refer to the goat that "lost" the lottery and so was let loose the wilderness. For *Azazel*, therefore, Tyndale forged a compound from "goat" and the Renaissance word "scape," an obsolete form of "escape."

But it turns out that Azazel is no goat; Tyndale and later translators missed the whole point. In fact, Azazel is an evil demon or "angry god," which is approximately what the Hebrew name means. And the losing goat was not really permitted to "scape"; rather, it was sent, bearing the communal sins, into the wilderness to meet an unknown fate at Azazel's hands. (This demon and his devices are never again mentioned in the Bible.)

Though the translation was botched, the basic idea of the ritual is clear. The burning of offerings was meant to solicit God's forgiveness and to cleanse symbolically the holy places of Israel. Afterward, the high priest laid hands on the "scapegoat" to transfer to it all the people's sins and thus banish them from the community.

The idea that sins or crimes can be collectively cast onto an innocent animal lies behind modern usage of "scapegoat." The metaphorical sense dates to 1824, when Mary Russell Mitford asserted, in a series entitled *Our Village,* that "Country-boys are patient ... and bear their fate as scape-goats (for all sins whatsoever are laid as matters of course to their door ...) with amazing reservation." That Mitford had to explain what she meant by "scape-goat" implies its novelty. The indefatigable correspondent and fourth earl of Oxford, Horace Walpole, however, had already exploited Tyndale's mistake some fifty-nine years earlier when in a letter to the Earl of Hertford he referred to the apparently feckless Lord Halifax as a "scape-goose."

Love Thy Neighbor

Thou shalt not hate thy brother in thine heart: thou shalt in any
wise rebuke [reason with] thy neighbour, and not suffer sin upon
him. | Thou shalt not avenge, nor bear any grudge against the
children of thy people, but thou shalt love thy neighbour as
thyself: I am the LORD.

Leviticus 19: 17–18

You may think that Jesus invented the phrase "Love thy neighbor as thyself" (Matthew 5: 43, etc.), but like the rest of us he
actually quotes the Hebrew Bible.

So to say that Jesus replaced the harsh and rigorous Torah of
Judaism with a new covenant of Love is to oversimplify—and to
insult Hebrew culture. True, Yahweh demands "eye for eye,
tooth for tooth" [*see* p. 69], but he also insists that his people
respect and forgive their neighbors. On the other hand, he
means "neighbors" more literally than Jesus does. He himself
hardly "loved" the Egyptians who held his people captive, nor
will he object as the Israelites wage bloody war against their
neighbors, the Canaanites, in the Promised Land.

In short, by "neighbors" the LORD *means* neighbors—that is,
other Israelites, and more specifically members of one's own
community or tribe. Nonetheless, he originates a powerful idea:
that you should treat your fellow as you yourself would be
treated. This is perhaps the oldest definition of empathy, and it
marks the Israelites as a people capable of introspection.

If we cannot credit Jesus with the words themselves, we at
least owe him their modern meaning. The phrase is usually
quoted today—often in an irritating fashion—to mean "love

thy (potential) enemy" as well as "love thy kith and kin." Such usage is faithful to the New Testament if not to Leviticus.

But the teachings of Jesus have often proved too difficult for most mortals, and his expansion of "love thy neighbor" would later be greeted skeptically. In 1640 George Herbert recorded as a proverb this qualified version: "Love your neighbor, yet pull not down your hedge"—in short, "No Tresspassing." (Ben Franklin liked the new version, incorporating it into his 1754 edition of *Poor Richard's Almanac*.) Woodrow Wilson likewise spoke practically during a 1912 speech in New York: "No one can love his neighbor on an empty stomach." Playwright Eugene O'Neill went furthest of all in *The Great God Brown* (1926), penning the warning, "Fear thy neighbor as thyself" (Act 2, scene 3).

Jubilee

And thou shalt number seven sabbaths of years unto thee, seven
times seven years; and the space of the seven sabbaths of years
shall be unto thee forty and nine years. | Then shalt thou cause
the trumpet of jubile [*sic*] to sound on the tenth day of the
seventh month, in the day of atonement shall ye make the
trumpet sound throughout all your land. | And ye shall hallow
the fiftieth year, and proclaim liberty throughout all the land
unto all the inhabitants thereof: it shall be a jubile unto you.…

Leviticus 25: 8–10

For the Israelites, good things came in sevens, so all the better in
seven times seven. Each seventh year was a "sabbatical" year
when, according to various and contradictory accounts, either
debts among the Jews were canceled, field-workers were released
from labor, the poor were granted special dispensation, Jews
enslaved to other Jews were freed, or mortgages were dissolved.

In any case, "Jubilee" was occasion for all of the above, being
the sabbath of sabbaths, the seven times seventh year. The
phrasing here is unclear—does Jubilee happen during the forty-

ninth year, during the following year, or both? The Bible may use "fiftieth" as a round figure, but in the matter of such laws it is rarely ambiguous. The latest theory is that Jubilee happened every fifty years before the fall of Jerusalem, and every forty-nine years later.

According to the OED, the Hebrew word for Jubilee (*yobel*) seems to have originally meant "ram" but was then applied to the ram's horn used as a trumpet to proclaim the Jubilee year. In St. Jerome's Latin (Vulgate) Bible, *yobel* becomes *jubilaeus* by way of association with the roughly homonymous Latin verb *jubilare*, to shout or to rejoice—whence our word "jubilation." This mixing up of senses accounts for our own use of "jubilee," via Wyclif's fourteenth-century translation of this passage. (His "jubilee" became "jubile" in later translations, such as the King James, but the two words were pronounced alike.) Thereafter, "jubilee" could refer to a fiftieth anniversary, a period of freedom from duties and debts, a season of celebration, a general rejoicing, or any bang-up affair at which one can gratify indulgences and maybe even wear silly hats.

Aaron's Rod

And the LORD spake unto Moses, saying, | Speak unto the children of Israel, and take of every one of them a rod according to the house of their fathers, of all their princes according to the house of their fathers twelve rods: write thou every man's name upon his rod. | And thou shalt write Aaron's name upon the rod of Levi: for one rod shall be for the head of the house of their fathers.

Numbers 17: 1–3

All is not well in the wilderness, even as the tribes of Israel near the end of their forty-year journey to the promised land. First, a faction among the Levite tribe rebels against Moses and Aaron. When the LORD causes the ground to swallow up these malcontents, a larger group, blaming their leaders, mounts a second rebellion. This time God unleashes a plague, which Aaron halts by burning some incense, but not before 14,700 Israelites die.

The LORD, aware of how short his temper can be, advises Moses to settle the question of authority once and for all, lest the people be tempted to another suicidal uprising. He instructs Moses to gather from each of the twelve tribes a "rod" or staff inscribed with the name of that tribe's "prince" (chieftain)—in the case of the Levites, Aaron. These rods are to be laid overnight before the tabernacle, and by morning one will have blossomed to signify the LORD's choice of a leading clan and ultimate authority. Naturally, it is "Aaron's rod" that blossoms, budding with almonds.

This story inspired the familiar English name "Aaron's rod" for several plant species, for example the Great Mullein and Goldenrod (but not almond trees). Most literary references, though, hark back to the rod's appearance in Exodus 7, where Aaron casts it before Pharaoh. Upon striking the ground, it turns into a serpent, devouring the serpents Pharaoh's court magicians had likewise produced. James T. Adams, in *Our Business Civilization* (1929), blames Alexander Hamilton for creating in America "a vast manufacturing nation with its Federal government eating up all the state governments like an Aaron's rod." If he'd thought about it, he'd have realized this is a compliment.

What Hath God Wrought!

Surely there is no enchantment against Jacob, neither is there
any divination against Israel: according to this time it shall be
said of Jacob and of Israel, What hath God wrought!

Numbers 23: 23

As the Israelites make their way up the west bank of the Jordan,
preparing to enter the promised land of Canaan, they find it
necessary to dispatch a few recalcitrant native tribes. So when
they reach the land of Moab and camp on the plains, across the
Jordan from Jericho, the Moabite people are understandably
anxious.

Their chieftain Balak summons an Eastern wizard, or professional curser, named Balaam, to put the kibosh on the Israelites.
But Balaam has consulted various oracles and chatted directly
with the LORD, only to discover that he will in no way be permitted to curse Israel.

Nonetheless, encouraged by God, Balaam makes the trip to
Moab, where Balak trots him off to three different mountain
tops overlooking the Israelites' encampment. From each peak
Balaam, divinely inspired, actually blesses rather than curses the
Hebrews. The second time, from the prospect of Pisgah [*see*
p. 346], he utters the lines quoted here, which mean in effect
that nobody but God himself can curse "Jacob" or "Israel" (the
names are synonymous), and that all exotic magics are useless.
He sums all this up with the memorable line, "What hath God
wrought!"—that is, "Behold what a mighty people the LORD
has made of Israel!"

(Ironically enough, the Israelites, rather than laying waste to
Moab, will embrace its naughty rituals, which include "sacred

prostitution" and the worship of the heathen fertility god Baal. Some conquerors.)

The line "What hath God wrought!" is remembered today thanks as much to Samuel Morse as to Balaam. Having just invented the telegraph, Morse was searching for an appropriate first message when the daughter of a U.S. patent official suggested the biblical phrase. He sent it on May 24, 1844, humbling his own role while aggrandizing the invention. I don't know if other inventors have lifted the phrase, but we more often quote it now with fear or horror than reverence. Perhaps we're just cynical about what technology has wrought.

A Thorn in Your Side

And the LORD spake unto Moses, … saying, | Speak unto the children of Israel, and say unto them, When ye are passed over Jordan into the land of Canaan; | Then ye shall drive out all the inhabitants of the land from before you, and destroy all their pictures, and destroy all their molten images, and quite pluck down all their high places: | … But if ye will not drive out the inhabitants of the land from before you; then it shall come to pass, that those which ye let remain of them shall be pricks in your eyes, and thorns in your sides, and shall vex you in the land wherein ye dwell.

Numbers 33: 50–52, 55

Before drawing a detailed map of the Israelites' "promised land"—that is, the coastal territory of Canaan—the LORD first instructs them, through Moses, on how they should behave when they first arrive. Rather than love their Canaanite neighbors, they are told to drive them (and their hideous gods) clean out of the land. Otherwise, God warns, the natives shall be "pricks" in the Israelites' eyes, and "thorns in your sides."

Yahweh's metaphorical admonition was certainly prophetic. As the books of Joshua and Judges describe the situation, Canaanite tribes made for quite a collection of pricks and thorns, since it proved more difficult than God lets on to uproot them. Joshua himself—Moses' successor and leader of the Israelites into Canaan—admits that the struggle will be long, and he warns in a valedictory speech never to accommodate their heathen enemies. Otherwise, "The LORD your God will no more drive out any of these nations from before you; but they shall be snares and traps unto you, and scourges in your sides, and thorns in your eyes …" (Joshua 23: 13).

Joshua muffs the quote, and the generations have preferred Yahweh's original coinage, "thorns in your sides," rendered as such into English by the King James team. (The more commonly quoted phrase "a thorn in the flesh" is also from the King James Bible—St. Paul coins it at II Corinthians 12: 7.) "Thorns in your eyes" is just a bit too improbable, though "prick" and "eye" are joined in motherhood's collective unconscious.

Oddly enough, Numbers has also influenced China's disaffected youth, who for about a month in 1991 sported T-shirts emblazoned with rebellious slogans. In addition to such cynical phrases as "Aren't you witty!," "I'm terribly depressed! Keep away from me!," and "Chinese the world of evil beasts," teenagers proclaimed, "I've never been a thorn in anybody's side" with their casual wear. These, along with other shirts, were promptly banned by the government.

Man Does Not Live by Bread Alone

And thou shalt remember all the way which the LORD thy God
led thee these forty years in the wilderness, to humble thee, and
to prove thee, to know what was in thine heart, whether thou
wouldest keep his commandments, or no. | And he humbled
thee, and suffered thee to hunger, and fed thee with manna,
which thou knewest not, neither did thy fathers know; that he
might make thee know that man doth not live by bread only,
but by every word that proceedeth out of the mouth of the LORD
doth man live.

Deuteronomy 8: 2–3

Moses is rehearsing for the Hebrews their history of hardships
during the exodus from Egypt. According to him, the main
purpose of their trials was to humble them and test their com-
mitment to the covenant struck on Mount Sinai [*see* THE TEN
COMMANDMENTS, p. 64].

And what's a little hunger, Moses goes on, when the LORD
offers relief in the form of manna from heaven [*see* p. 63] that is
much better than anything the Israelites could have produced
on their own? On bread alone they would have starved, and no
human skill could have saved them. Extrapolating a lesson,
Moses concludes that earthly sustenance and man's own knowledge is not enough to survive on without God's help, advice,
and laws (his "words"). What's more, if you disobey those, you
will die (8: 14).

The phrase "Man doth not live by bread only" is one of many
from the Torah that Jesus quotes in the New Testament, though
he changes "does" to "shall" and "only" to "alone" (Matthew 4: 4
and Luke 4: 4). Thus the familiar "man does not live by bread
alone" is a hybrid of two versions; the equally familiar "man

cannot live" is simply a corruption. But the phrase hardly ever escapes violence in quotation. George Macaulay Trevelyan said of the book market in the early eighteenth century that "the reading public was still so small that authors could not live by their sales alone" (*England under Queen Anne*, 1930–1934). G. B. Harrison likewise punned, re: Shakespeare, that "poetry does not live by sound alone" (*Introducing Shakespeare*, 1939). Hardly words that passed out of the mouth of the LORD.

To Heap Mischief

> For a fire is kindled in mine anger, and shall burn unto the
> lowest hell, and shall consume the earth with her increase, and
> set on fire the foundations of the mountains. | I will heap
> mischiefs upon them; I will spend mine arrows upon them.

> Deuteronomy 32: 22–23

These dire words, quoting the LORD, are found in the so-called "Song of Moses," one of the leader's last lectures to what he calls a "perverse and crooked generation" of Israelites. Moses recalls their complacency and their embracing "strange gods" in the face of God's good deeds toward them.

He then warns of God's promised reaction. The LORD will turn away from Israel and inflict it with foreign enemies, who will by proxy unleash the fires of hell (*sheol* in the Hebrew) and various other mischiefs. They can expect famine, plague, and pestilence, the ravages of wild beasts and the poisons of "serpents of the dust"—in short, "The sword without, and terror within" (verse 25).

Sinners in the hands of an angry God, indeed. But the LORD will stop short of letting any enemy destroy Israel entirely, lest such enemies get the wrong idea that it was all their doing. And in any case, the LORD pledges to one day show up all the foreign gods, thus disposing with any cause for future jealousy. In other words, Israel faces a terrifying future if it remains disobedient, but it will at least survive. And Moses goes on to pull a velvet glove over the LORD's stark fist in chapter 33 of Deuteronomy, in which each of the twelve tribes of Israel receives a blessing and a promise. This will be Moses' last address to the people.

The Way of All Flesh

> And, behold, this day I am going the way of all the earth: and ye know in all your hearts and in all your souls, that not one thing hath failed of all the good things which the LORD your God spake concerning you; all are come to pass unto you, and not one thing hath failed thereof.

Joshua 23: 14

For once, the Authorized Version loses. "The way of all the earth," its translation of Joshua's phrase, is much less popular than "the way of all flesh," which comes from the English Catholic Bible of 1609, by way of various medieval texts.

Either way you like it, what the aged Joshua means is that he must die, and this is his swan song. But over the years his words came to mean something else altogether. Perhaps influenced by Jesus' saying, "The spirit indeed is willing but the flesh is weak" (Matthew 26: 41), pious Englishmen began using the present phrase to mean "the way the flesh desires," which wasn't thought terribly godly.

An early example is to be found in the play *Westward Ho!* (1605) by Shakespeare's contemporaries Thomas Dekker and John Webster. "I saw him even now going the way of all flesh," says Mistress Birdlime, explaining, "(that's to say) towards the kitchen." By 1668 the phrase was used to allude to sex, following in "fleshpot's" footsteps [*see* p. 62]. In any case, it would rarely be used thereafter to mean "to die"; Joseph Conrad didn't mean to contradict himself when he wrote in *The Rescue* (1921) that "His flesh had gone the way of all flesh, his spirit had sunk in the turmoil of his past, but his immense and bony frame survived as if made of iron."

A Shibboleth

And the Gileadites took the passages of Jordan before the
Ephraimites: and it was so, that when those Ephraimites which
were escaped said, Let me go over; that the men of Gilead said
unto him, Art thou an Ephraimite? If he said, Nay; | Then said
they unto him, Say now Shibboleth: and he said Sibboleth: for
he could not frame to pronounce it right. Then they took him,
and slew him at the passages of Jordan: and there fell at that time
of the Ephraimites forty and two thousand.

Judges 12: 5–6

Whenever no idol-worshiping enemy is handy for a fight, the
tribes of Israel kill time by bickering among themselves. This
time Hebrew settlers in Gilead, west of the Jordan and famous
for its balm, have angered the tribe of Ephraim by pounding on
a mutual enemy without consulting them. Hotheads on both
sides provoke a civil war, and the Ephraimites launch an incur-
sion across the river.

But they're no match for the Gileadites, who block passage
back across the Jordan and kill any foe who falls into their
clutches. If an Ephraimite attempted to pass himself off as a
friend, the Gileadites would make him pronounce the word
Shibboleth—Hebrew for "flooding stream." Each Ephraimite
victim, ignorant of his comrades' fate, would lapse into his dia-
lect, in which initial *sh* sounds were pronounced *s,* yielding
"*Sibboleth.*" And that was the last word he ever spoke.

This charming tale has, of course, left its mark on everyday
English. "Shibboleth," in line with the biblical story, now
means primarily "password" or "distinguishing trait," though
what it distinguishes is not limited to one's tribe. In the sense of

"peculiar language or habit revealing ties to a party, sect, or subculture," shibboleth may also mean "slogan" and "catchphrase." ("Tubular," for example, is a shibboleth of surfing culture.) This is how Sir Walter Scott used the word when he asserted in one of his letters that "Knaves and fools invent catchwords and shibboleths" to keep honest, plain-speaking folk like himself "from coming to a just understanding." Much the same has been said by distressed commentators about the current academic scene.

Philistine

And Samson said unto her [Delilah], If they bind me with seven
green withs [boughs] that were never dried, then shall I be weak,
and be as another man. I Then the lords of the Philistines
brought up to her seven green withs which had not been dried,
and she bound him with them. I Now there were men lying in
wait abiding with her in the chamber. And she said unto him,
The Philistines be upon thee, Samson. And he brake the withs,
as a thread of tow is broken where it toucheth the fire. So his
strength was not known. I And Delilah said unto Samson,
Behold, thou hast mocked me, and told me lies....

Judges 16: 7–10

Always thorns in the Israelites' sides, the Philistines here make
yet another bid to foil Samson, the current Jewish champion
and Judge. In this effort they have a handy ally: Samson's wife,
Delilah, herself a Philistine. Here she attempts to carry off an
ambush but is foiled—at which point she has the gumption to
accuse Samson of tricking *her*!

Though the Philistines appear throughout the Hebrew Bible,
this passage was singled out for comment in a late-17th-century
German sermon, in which local anti-intellectuals were likened
to the Philistines. This usage caught on in Germany and then
eventually in England, where "Philistine" had earlier meant
simply "enemy" or on occasion "drunkard."

Thomas Carlyle, for example, referred in 1851 to "Philistines
... what we would call bores, dullards, Children of Darkness."
More famously, Matthew Arnold, that self-appointed champion of culture, warned in his *Study of Celtic Literature* (1867)
that "We are imperilled by what I call the 'Philistinism' of our
middle class," who are characterized by "vulgarity," "coarse-

ness," and "unintelligence." Is it a surprise that Arnold was the son of an English headmaster?

Originally, "Philistine" derived from *p'lishtim*, the Hebrew name for the so-called "sea people" (perhaps from Crete) who had settled in Palestine. (The place name in fact derives directly from the Hebrew term.) John Wyclif, in his 1382 translation of Amos (9: 7), actually calls the people "Palistens," even while he uses "Philistynes" elsewhere.

The legend of Samson and Delilah, by the way, though well known, has lent no memorable phrases to English.

God Save the King

And Samuel said to all the people, See ye him whom the LORD hath chosen, that there is none like him among all the people? And all the poeple shouted, and said, God save the King.

I Samuel 10: 24

Before there were kings of Israel there were Judges, ad hoc leaders who rose to meet the latest crisis. In the time of the last Judge, Samuel, the Israelites found their theocracy inadequate in the face of constant conflict with the Philistines. They yearned for a true ruler to unite them once and for all against the enemy. Neither God nor Samuel is entirely happy about this, but the people persist. Reluctantly, Samuel seeks out a man fit to be king, and with God's help he selects Saul—"him whom the LORD hath chosen."

The people shout "God save the King," which is the King James Bible's translation of what in Hebrew is closer to "long live the King." (The English version is unintentionally ironic—Saul loses God's support rather early.) But the translation stuck and became the title and theme of a tune composed by John Bull in the early seventeenth century and later adopted as the British national anthem. Americans know the tune better as the setting for "My Country 'Tis of Thee."

A Man after His Own Heart

And Samuel said to Saul, thou hast done foolishly: thou hast not kept the commandment of the LORD thy God, which he commanded thee: for now would the LORD have established thy kingdom upon Israel for ever. | But now thy kingdom shall not continue: the LORD hath sought him a man after his own heart, and the LORD hath commanded him to be captain over his people, because thou hast not kept that which the LORD commanded thee.

I Samuel 13: 13–14

Well, Saul has gone and done it—ignored a divine commandment, and Samuel takes this opportunity to remind him, several times. Saul's crime is hard to explain in a few words, but suffice it to say that, in the heat of a desperate battle against the Philistines, he made a burnt offering before Samuel allowed it.

Naughty, naughty, naughty. As the price of this infraction, and a few more like it, Saul is going to lose his crown. As Samuel speaks, God is already casting about for someone more suitable—"a man," as Samuel puts it, "after his own heart." What he means, of course, is someone whose heart is more Godly—someone more apt to behave himself; that someone will be David.

We use the phrase now to mean more or less the same thing: someone like-minded, or whose feelings are gratifyingly like one's own. Not that we always mean it sincerely; take the character Jones in William Faulkner's novel *Soldier's Pay* (1925). "Old fool, thought Jones, saying: 'marvelous, magnificent! You are a man after my own heart, Doctor.'"

David and Goliath

> And there went out a champion out of the camp of the Philistines, named Goliath of Gath, whose height was six cubits and a span. I … And he stood and cried unto the armies of Israel, and said unto them, Why are ye come out to set your battle in array? am not I a Philistine, and ye servants of Saul? choose you a man for you, and let him come down to me. I If he be able to fight with me, and to kill me, then will we be your servants: but if I prevail against him, and kill him, then shall ye be our servants, and serve us.
>
> I Samuel 17: 4, 8–9

This is a tale very dear to the hearts of modern Israelis, who often compare their state to a tiny David set against the hostile Goliath of its Arab neighbors. Their hero, the shepherd David, is the archetypal underdog, cunning and brave but far outmatched in physical stature by his Philistine opponent, whom the King James Version describes as "six cubits and a span" (9 feet, 9 inches) in height.

The setting is another episode in the continuing face-off between Israel and its Philistine neighbors [see p. 93]. The Philistines have set up battle camp in territory claimed by the tribe of Judah, and they send out their biggest bully to challenge a man of Israel's choosing. The Hebrews' first reaction is something short of glorious: "And all the men of Israel, when they saw the man [Goliath], fled from him, and were sore afraid" (verse 24).

Enter David, who's indignant that an "uncircumcised Philistine" should "defy the armies of the living God" (verse 26). Presenting himself to Saul as a volunteer, David dons sword and armor, and for good measure stashes five stones in his shepherd's sack. When Goliath spies his puny challenger approaching, he has a good laugh; but he doesn't laugh long. The defiant David pulls a stone from his sack, loads his sling, and "smit[es] the Philistine in his forehead, that the stone sunk into his forehead; and he fell upon his face to the earth" (verse 49). He then finishes the job by cutting off Goliath's head.

This is the tale with which almost everyone is familiar—and it has served countless times as an analogy for any mismatch in which the little guy overcomes heavy odds. Unfortunately, many of its details were apparently absent from the original text, which some later author or authors saw fit to enhance. The name Goliath, for example, seems to have been borrowed from another story, reported in II Samuel 21, where someone named Elhanan slays "Goliath the Gitite" (verse 19). The King James translators, confused, inserted the phrase "the brother of"— yielding "Elhanan ... slew the brother of Goliath the Gittite." And Hebrew texts older than that used by the King James folks report that the Philistine challenger—whatever his name—was a mere "four cubits and a span" tall (six foot nine). There weren't exactly giants in the earth in those days.

One of These Days

And David said in his heart, I shall now perish one day by the hand of Saul: there is nothing better for me than that I should speedily escape into the land of the Philistines; and Saul shall despair of me, to seek me any more in any coast of Israel: so shall I escape out of his hand.

                                                                    I Samuel 27: 1

The King James Version of the Bible has contributed so many words and phrases to English that it can be forgiven for occasionally trying to subtract one. In Miles Coverdale's 1535 translation of this verse, what David says in his heart is that "One of these days shall I fall into the hands of Saul." The 1611 rendition "one day," though more to the point, lacks Coverdale's *je ne sais quoi*.

In whichever version, David has more on his mind than future quotation—namely, his own hide. Through ineptitude and insubordination Israel's first king, Saul, has severely alienated Yahweh, who transfers his spirit into a newly anointed leader, the shepherd David. At first, David acts to shore up Saul's power and mental health, but as David's power and renown increase over time, Saul grows madly jealous and ultimately murderous.

Through a series of dodges and ruses, David manages to escape his intended doom and even spares Saul when offered the chance to do away with him. But this cannot go on forever: "one of these days" Saul might catch up with him, so David resolves to flee into exile among his former enemies, the Philistines. Needless to say, he outsmarts them, too.

Even while "one of these days" has been a vaguely threatening catchphrase since Coverdale's day, the exasperated "one of those days" is of more recent vintage. It seems to have first appeared in writing in 1936, when Robert Peter Fleming, in *News from Tartary: A Journey from Peking to Kashmir,* described arriving at an inn after a hard day's trek, only to see the building next door collapse: "It was one of those days."

How the Mighty Are Fallen!

And David lamented with this lamentation over Saul and over Jonathan his son: | … The beauty of Israel is slain upon thy high places: how are the mighty fallen! | Tell it not in Gath, publish it not in the streets of Askelon; lest the daughters of the Philistines rejoice, lest the daughters of the uncircumcised triumph.

II Samuel 1: 17, 19–20

The last thing we want, of course, is for the daughters of the uncircumcised to go around triumphing! What David, who sings this hymn, doesn't say is that lately he could have been found fighting on the side of the Philistines—the very uncircumcised dogs who have just defeated Saul, king of Israel, and his sons. (The Philistines kill the sons; Saul falls on his sword.)

David is apparently of two minds on these events. While Saul pursued him, he was a loyal Philistine ally, but with Saul safely dead, David laments Israel's humiliation. The threat removed, David can now fondly laud the greatness of his erstwhile enemy, celebrating qualities not so apparent while Saul was alive. The king and his sons—especially Jonathan—were the "beauty of Israel" (verse 19), "lovely and pleasant in their lives," "swifter than eagles," and "stronger than lions" (verse 23). They were, in short, "mighty," and now they have fallen.

That David's line is a bit opportunistic hasn't stopped anybody from solemnly quoting it when allegedly great leaders bite the dust. Also occasionally cited is the bonus phrase "tell it not in Gath"—Gath being a chief Philistine city—which is now an (often humorous) synonym for "keep it hush-hush."

To Put Words in One's Mouth

Now Joab the son of Zeruiah perceived that the king's heart was toward Absalom. | And Joab sent to Tekoah, and fetched thence a wise woman, and said unto her, I pray thee, feign thyself to be a mourner, and put on now mourning apparel, and anoint not thyself with oil, but be as a woman that had a long time mourned for the dead: | And come to the king, and speak on this manner unto him. So Joab put the words in her mouth.

II Samuel 14: 1–3

Joab, King David's nephew and Israel's commander-in-chief, is currently basking in his uncle's favor. Joab is a ruthless character, but in this he is matched by David's son Absalom, who has just murdered his brother Amnon for raping his sister Tamar. Though Absalom is the apple of his father's eye, the king is understandably upset. And when Absalom flees without a word of explanation or apology, David is paralyzed with grief and anxiety. Joab, seeing this, sets in motion a plot to reconcile the two. His agent in this is a nameless woman of Tekoah; Joab puts the appropriate words in her mouth.

Wyclif coined this figure for manipulation in his 1382 translation, and it remains popular. Strangely, though, the reverse expression, "to take the words out of one's mouth," of sixteenth-century origin, was much more common before the eighteenth century. Since it is better to give than to receive, one would think that Wyclif's coinage should have prevailed earlier on.

A Jeroboam

And the man Jeroboam was a mighty man of valor: and Solomon
seeing the young man that he was industrious, he made him
ruler over all the charge of the house of Joseph.

I Kings 11: 28

If you run into a jeroboam at a New Year's Eve party, it won't be
an Israelite king but rather a wine bottle (used mostly for cham-
pagne) holding three liters, roughly four-fifths of a gallon.
These jeroboams bring much joy, unlike their namesake, who
"made Israel to sin" (I Kings 14: 16).

How and when Jeroboam lent his name to the container is
unknown, though the fact that he was "mighty" and inspired sin
must have had something to do with it. The biblical story is of
little help, being fragmentary, obscure, and contradictory. In
simplified form, it goes something like this: after having
achieved a position in King Solomon's government, the ingrate
Jeroboam mounted an unsuccessful coup. He then fled to
Egypt, where he remained until Solomon's death and the succession of his son Rehoboam. When Rehoboam insulted the
northern Israelite tribes (promising to chastise them with "scor-
pions"), they seceded from the unified kingdom and chose
Jeroboam as their leader.

Bad move. Jeroboam proved insufficiently attentive to God's
laws as set forth in the Torah, in particular to Yahweh's desig-
nation of Jerusalem (in Judah, the southern kingdom) as his
sole legitimate shrine. Jeroboam not only built new sanctuaries
in the north, at Dan and Bethel, but revived the now-repudi-
ated practice of setting up idols of Yahweh—golden calves, no
less [see p. 71].

A Jezebel

And Ahab the son of Omri did evil in the sight of the LORD
above all that were before him. | And it came to pass, ... that he
took to wife Jezebel the daughter of Ethbaal king of the
Zidonians, and went and served Baal, and worshipped him.

I Kings 16: 30–31

The First Book of Kings forms part of a larger biblical strand,
stretching from Deuteronomy to Second Kings, known as the
"Deuteronomistic history." By and large the moral of these
books is that the Israelites and their rulers repeatedly "did evil
in the sight of the LORD," which explains various historical
tragedies.

Even the wise Solomon strayed from the true path by tolerat-
ing the gods of his many heathen wives. Far more brazen, however, the apostate Ahab, ruler of the Northern Kingdom of
Israel in the ninth century B.C., "did more to provoke the LORD
God of Israel to anger than all the kings of Israel that were before him" (I Kings 16: 33).

Ahab's father Omri, seeking an alliance with the Phoenicians,
had married him to Jezebel, princess of Tyre. Soon after, Jezebel
set about perverting both Ahab and Israel to the worship of
Baal, the storied Canaanite thunder god. Ahab even built an altar to the god in Samaria, while Jezebel "cut off [that is,
slaughtered] the prophets of the LORD" (18: 4). And that was
just for starters.

Nonetheless, a few godly men did survive her murderous
campaign, including the prophet Elijah. He colorfully ex-
pressed the LORD's disgust by predicting that "The dogs shall eat
Jezebel by the wall of Jezreel" (21: 23), site of Ahab's palace. Sure

enough, Jezebel met her fate at the hands of the Baal-hating king, Jehu, who had her thrown out a high window (II Kings 9: 33). And when Jehu's men went to collect Jezebel's remains, they found only her skull, her feet, and the palms of her hands (verse 35). Elijah's prophecy had been fulfilled.

Jezebel—whose name means "Where's the prince?" in Hebrew—has gone down in history as the most wicked woman in the entire Bible. In the New Testament, she is the archetype of the evil temptress; God himself vilifies her in Revelation (2: 20). In later times, she would serve as a metaphor for a wicked and corrupting woman, especially one who wore lots of makeup. (Jezebel had attempted to hide from Jehu by painting her face—thus the intensified insult is "painted Jezebel.")

To Gird Your Loins

And it came to pass in the mean while, that the heaven was black
with clouds and wind, and there was a great rain. And Ahab
rode, and went to Jezreel. | And the hand of the LORD was on
Elijah; and he girded up his loins, and ran before Ahab to the
entrance of Jezreel.

I Kings 18: 45–46

Although "to gird your loins" sounds racy to the modern reader,
all Elijah is doing is pulling in his pants. "Gird"—actually "gird
up" in the original—means "tighten with a belt" or "put on a
girdle." Elijah does not, as modern usage might suggest, fortify
his thighs—"loin" may rhyme with "groin," but this sense is
relatively new.

Kind of brings you down, but that's what the Hebrew says—
or, in the words of the New English Bible, "he tucked up his
robe." Equally disappointing is that Elijah does not "gird up his
loins" to rush into battle. Rather, after slaughtering the false
prophets of King Ahab's adopted god Baal, he simply wants to
be the first to tell the town of Jezreel the news. So he pulls in his
petticoats the better to outpace Ahab, which is no small feat
since the king's got a chariot. Once Queen Jezebel hears Elijah's
news, she vows to pay the prophet back in kind; this time he
girds his loins to make a hasty exit out of Israel.

A Still Small Voice

> And he [the LORD] said, Go forth, and stand upon the mount
> before the LORD. And, behold, the LORD passed by, and a great
> and strong wind rent the mountains, and brake in pieces the
> rocks before the LORD; but the LORD was not in the wind: and
> after the wind and earthquake; but the LORD was not in the
> earthquake: | And after the earthquake a fire; but the LORD was
> not in the fire: and after the fire a still small voice.

I Kings 19: 11–12

The prophet Elijah, fleeing Israel to escape Jezebel's wrath, doesn't stop running until he reaches Beer-sheba in the Kingdom of Judah. Exhausted and dispirited, he then heads out into the wilderness to pray for death.

After several hours, Elijah falls into a deep sleep, which is Yahweh's cue. An angel appears, forcing the prophet to eat and drink, and then to set out on a forty-days' journey to Mount Horeb, also known as Mount Sinai. If you recall the episode of the burning bush [*see* p. 50], it's no surprise that a mysterious voice calls to Elijah, ordering him to "stand upon the mount before the LORD" (I Kings 19: 11).

What follows is a rather drawn-out introduction, in which God first teases the prophet with wind, an earthquake, and a fire before finally manifesting himself in a "still small voice"—Renaissance English for "a soft, whispering murmur"; that is, a breeze. Since this voice argues Elijah out of his mood and sets him back on a holier track, some commentators have identified it with "the voice of conscience." Indeed, the message of these verses seems to be that God need not appear to men embodied in great natural forces—though he certainly can do this—but may also reveal himself directly, softly, and personally, like a voice in the mind.

The authors probably wish to make a special point of this here in light of recent events [*see* A JEZEBEL, p. 105], since Baal, like the Yahweh of the Pentateuch, liked to announce himself with lots of sound and fury. The LORD may have found such methods necessary in primitive times, but in his fight against pagan heresies he now chooses the more discreet and verbal medium of quietly inspiring prophecy.

The first writer to use "still small voice" in the sense of "conscience" seems to have been poet William Cowper in *The Task* (1784). Thomas Grey had another idea in his "Ode for Music" (1769), where we find the line, "the still small voice of gratitude." Lord Byron took up Cowper's tune in *The Island* (1823), where there "still whispers the still small voice within." Further down the line, the phrase became useful as a handy piece of lofty rhetoric good for sprucing up indignant letters.

To Take Root

> ... Ye shall eat this year such things as grow of themselves, and in the second year that which springeth of the same; and in the third year sow ye, and reap, and plant vineyards, and eat the fruits thereof. | And the remnant that is escaped of the house of Judah shall yet again take root downward, and bear fruit upward.
>
> II Kings 19: 29–30

This passage, set in the context of a face-off between the Kingdom of Judah and Assyrian invaders circa 700 B.C., purports to transcribe a letter sent by the prophet Isaiah to the Judean king Hezekiah.

Isaiah's rebuke of the blaspheming Assyrians contains a number of difficult and curious passages. But the basic message is that while Assyria has subjected most of the kingdom, a "remnant" of Jews shall "take root" again in the soil of Jerusalem and "bear fruit" as holy warriors against the infidels.

Of this rhyming pair of predicates, "bear fruit" had been an English phrase since the late thirteenth century, but "take root" was coined only in 1535 when Miles Coverdale translated this passage. In this case, it means something like "stand one's ground" or "cling tenaciously," and Isaiah extends the metaphor by predicting the "fruit" of resistance to foreign uprooting. Although we still sometimes speak of a community "taking root," the phrase now more often refers to an idea that implants itself in the mind. The phrase was first used this way in the same poem, William Cowper's *The Task* (1784), that lent us the modern sense of "still small voice." Cowper wrote that "Prejudice in men of stronger minds / Takes deeper root, confirm'd by what they see." How true.

Put Your House in Order

In those days was Hezekiah sick unto death. And the prophet
Isaiah the son of Amoz came to him, and said unto him, Thus
saith the LORD, Set thine house in order; for thou shalt die, and
not live.

II Kings 20: 1

The prophet Isaiah can sure pack a lot of quintessentially biblical phrasing into one verse. Here the Judean king Hezekiah is
"sick unto death," so Isaiah advises him to "Set thine house in
order."

The idea isn't novel to Isaiah—we've been told in Second
Samuel that Ahitophel "put his household in order" before
hanging himself. But Isaiah's hortatory version is the better remembered—"put your house in order" is almost always a piece
of advice, not a description. What Isaiah means, roughly, is
"make sure your property will be properly disposed of when you
die." What we mean today is more figurative: "your life is a
mess, so do something about it."

As it turns out, the LORD hears Hezekiah weeping and wail-
ing and allows him another fifteen years to live, mostly so that
he can continue resisting Assyrian assaults on Jerusalem.
Granted this respite, Hezekiah foolishly neglects to put his
house in order. So, as Isaiah correctly foresees, the Babylonians
and not Hezekiah's sons will inherit the king's treasures. Worse,
those sons "shall be eunuchs in the palace of the king of Babylon" (II Kings 20: 18). Rather harsh punishment for bad household management, you'd think.

Satan

And Satan stood up against Israel, and provoked David to number Israel.

I Chronicles 21: 1

The Satan of the Hebrew Bible—who appears briefly in Job, Zechariah, and Chronicles—is not the "fallen angel" or "prince of Hell" we find in Christian tradition. Rather, he is in literal Hebrew an "adversary" in the LORD's service whose job is to provoke proud mortals to overplay their hands.

If the serpent who tempts Eve is really Satan, it never says so in Genesis. In fact, there is no "devil" at all in the Hebrew Bible,

though we do meet a few threatening spirits and curious demigods, Azazel for example [*see* A SCAPEGOAT, p. 75].

What's more, it's possible that in this passage from Chronicles the Hebrew *satan* refers not to an entity but to David's own initiative, which turns out to have evil consequences. In an earlier rendition (II Samuel 24: 1), God himself "moved David" to take a census of Israel, which God, for some unstated reason, in fact resented. (The basic idea is that David was beginning to think too independently.) This paradox proved too much for the author of Chronicles, who thus ascribed the motivation to "Satan."

This substitution still didn't solve the problem, however; Satan, whether impulse or persona, was still the LORD's servant. Not until the second century B.C., at the earliest, did some Jews develop a dualistic conception of the universe, in which God is a source only of good, evil being an independent force. By the time of Jesus, the name "Satan" had come to designate the brains behind evil in the world; this Satan, who ruled over a kingdom of demons, was then also identified with the serpent of Genesis (see Revelation 12: 9).

Though Satan appears only three times in the Hebrew Bible, in the book of Isaiah we meet another character called Lucifer, depicted as a "son of the morning" who has "fallen from heaven" (14: 12). Despite the fancies of such writers as John Milton, who in *Paradise Lost* (1667) identified Lucifer with Satan, in Isaiah "Lucifer" is merely a metaphor. The name comes from a Latin rendition of the Hebrew for "morning star" (Venus), which Isaiah compares to a Babylonian king who had been brought down by the Medes. Jesus does report in the Gospels that he "saw Satan fall like lightning from heaven" (Luke 10: 18), but he, unlike later interpreters, never equated Satan with Isaiah's heavenly object.

The Lord Gave, and the Lord Hath Taken Away

> Then Job arose, and rent his mantle, and shaved his head, and fell down upon the ground, and worshipped, | And said, Naked came I out of my mother's womb, and naked shall I return thither: the LORD gave, and the LORD hath taken away; blessed be the name of the LORD.
>
> Job 1: 20–21

You will not find the phrase, "The Lord giveth, and the Lord taketh away" in the King James Bible—nice try with the Renaissance conjugations, but still a misquotation.

It's not even clear Job intended to make the sweeping generalization we do. The Hebrew verb translated as "gives" might really mean "gave," in which case Job is talking about only one particular incident, though admittedly it's a doozy.

What happens is that one day the LORD casts his eye upon the earth and notes with satisfaction how godly and upright his "servant" Job is. But among the "sons of God" there is a dissenter: the "adversary" Satan [see p. 112]. He cynically attributes Job's piety to prosperity and dares the LORD to deprive Job of everything. Then, Satan predicts, Job "will curse thee to thy face."

The Book of Job presents us with several challenges and mysteries, among them who the "sons of God" are, what Satan's role is in the heavenly court, and why God takes up the dare when he should already know the outcome. Whether to see for himself or only to prove to his "sons" Job's faith, God destroys Job's livestock, servants, house, and family. But rather than curse God to his face, Job stoically notes that he was born with nothing ("naked") and is content to die with nothing; the LORD, after all, gave him all he has, and it was the LORD's right to take it away. (The bit about nakedness shows up again in Ecclesiastes and in Cervantes's *Don Quixote*.)

If Job is really speaking in the past tense, he may think he's suffered all he can, but if so he's wrong. Satan isn't satisfied yet, so he dares the LORD to keep trying—this time by smiting Job's person. God rises to the challenge by afflicting Job with boils from head to toe. This prompts Job's wife to utter her one, infamous, line: "Curse God, and die" (Job 2: 9). Job refuses to bite, though he ends up cursing almost everything else.

The resulting ranting and raving has convinced at least the pundit and language columnist William Safire that Job was *The First Dissident* (1992). Perhaps he's right, if you don't count the serpent of Genesis, or Satan for that matter.

The Skin of Your Teeth

> Yea, young children despised me; I arose, and they spake against me. | All my inward friends abhorred me: and they whom I loved are turned against me. | My bone cleaveth to my skin and to my flesh, and I am escaped with the skin of my teeth. | Have pity upon me, have pity upon me, O ye my friends; for the hand of God hath touched me.

Job 19: 18–21

Job complains to three "friends"—a pitiless bunch—about his recent troubles, which have reduced him to skin and bones, and bad skin at that. He has only "escaped with the skin of his teeth"—that is, his gums are about the only flesh he has left.

The phrasing is the work of the Geneva Bible translators (1560), who much improved on the earlier version by Miles Coverdale (1535): "My bone hangeth to my skin, and the flesh is away, only there is left me the skin about my teeth." The Geneva translation, besides being more elegant, is also more suggestive. Job not only has little flesh left "about" him, he has also escaped death by just the measure of that flesh. We now push the metaphor to its absurd limit, taking "the skin of your teeth" to mean the skin *on* your teeth (which is nonexistent), rather than the gums around them.

Such absurdity has made the phrase accommodating to humorists. Mark Twain, for example, noted with delicate contempt that "I made up my mind that if this man was not a liar he only missed it by the skin of his teeth" (*Roughing It*). On a darker note, Thornton Wilder used the line as the title of one of his plays, the upshot of which is that the human race has survived only by the skin of its teeth.

The Root of the Matter

But ye should say, Why persecute we him, seeing the root of the
matter is found in me? | Be ye afraid of the sword: for wrath
bringeth the punishments of the sword, that ye may know there
is a judgment.

Job 19: 28–29

For sixteen chapters, Job has had to endure the accusations and
mockery of his so-called friends, whose theme is that, since God
is just, Job must have done something to deserve his affliction.
Here Job warns his accusers to look to themselves and to fear the
"punishments of the sword."

Unfortunately, the King James Version makes a hash of Job's
comeback. A better rendering of verse 28 (admittedly confusing
in Hebrew) is, "My heart failed me when you said, 'What a train
of disaster he has brought upon himself! The root of the trouble
lies in him'" (New English Bible). Job, in short, laughs bitterly
once more at the notion that he has provoked his own suffering.

Whatever their failings, the King James translators at least
gave us "root of the matter," which is more faithful to the Hebrew than "root of the trouble." In either case Job does seem to
mean "the source of my afflictions," so current usage is less
faithful. By "root" we usually mean "true basis" or "key" rather
than "origin," though in practice the distinction may be hard to
draw.

Eyes to the Blind

I was eyes to the blind, and feet was I to the lame. | I was a father
to the poor: and the cause which I knew not I searched out. |
And I brake the jaws of the wicked, and plucked the spoil out of
his teeth.

Job 29: 15–17

Anything would look good compared to Job's present misery,
but he does go overboard in praising his past. Rivers of oil once
poured forth to him from rocks; young men feared him, and the
old revered him; he struck awe in princes and noblemen and
drew blessings from every mouth. All this was because he was
superhumanly good—a deliverer of the miserable, fatherless,
and abandoned; a comforter of the widowed; a font of righteousness and justice; "eyes to the blind," "feet to the lame,"
"father to the poor," and so on and so forth.

Job's high opinion of the man he used to be may partly explain why God has singled him out for disaster. As a supremely
proud, if pious, man, Job could probably benefit from a lesson
in the mysteriousness of God's ways—success, as well as failure,
may have very little to do with just desserts. And if this is part of
the message, then the Book of Job presents an argument very
different from that of the preceding books, in which the LORD
rewards those who obey his laws and afflicts those who ignore
them.

In any case, we have only Job's word for it that he was "eyes to
the blind"—which he probably means more literally than we do
in quoting him. Today the phrase most often refers to intellec-
tual, not literal, blindness and its putative remedies.

Behemoth AND *Leviathan*

Behold now behemoth, which I made with thee; he eateth grass
as an ox. | Lo now, his strength is in his loins, and his force is in
the navel of his belly.

Job 40: 15–16

Canst thou draw out leviathan with an hook? or his tongue with
a cord which thou lettest down? | Canst thou put an hook into
his nose? or bore his jaw through with a thorn? | Will he make
many supplications unto thee? will he speak soft words unto
thee?

Job 41: 1–3

God has had enough of Job's moaning and his friends' smug re-
joinders. Addressing Job "out of the whirlwind" (38: 1), God
demands to know where any of these people got the idea they
could fathom his motivations. "Where wast thou," God queries
sarcastically, "when I laid the foundations of the earth? declare if
thou has understanding" (38: 4).

God continues by citing a string of his awesome deeds and
by posing a series of withering puzzles—"Hast thou entered
into the springs of the sea?" "Where is the way where light
dwelleth? and as for darkness, where is the place thereof?"
"Hath the rain a father? or who hath begotten the drops of
dew?" Et cetera. All of these are versions of "What makes you
think *you're* so smart?"

God wants to make another point: not only is mankind ignorant, but it tends to take a grandiose view of its importance.
Within nature—over which the God of Genesis had given man
dominion—there are creatures who fear no man, and forces
only God can control. Among these are the fearsome "behemoth" (40: 15) and "leviathan" (41: 1). Some literal-minded

readers of the Bible have equated these mighty creatures with actual animals—surmising, for example, that Behemoth is a hippopatomus or elephant and Leviathan a crocodile or whale.

But scholars now believe that Leviathan is based on a seven-headed sea monster named "Lothan" found in Canaanite myths. This Lothan is a primordial enemy of the thunder god Baal, who ultimately destroys it, even as God in Psalm 74 "breakest the heads of leviathan in pieces, and gavest him to be meat to the people inhabiting the wilderness" (verse 14). Lothan/Leviathan is also paralleled in Greek myth, where Zeus faces down a many-headed dragon named Typhon.

No similar parallel, however, has been discovered for the randy Behemoth. The OED speculates that the Hebrew *b'hemoth* may derive from the Egyptian *p-ehe-mau*, "water ox," which certainly accords with its description in Job. Many scholars still maintain that it was originally a hippo, though it likely also had some mythical aspect. In any case, "behemoth" has come to be used in English to describe any huge and fearsome beast.

"Leviathan," on the other hand, while also signifying "huge monster," has proved a more versatile metaphor. When Lord Byron spoke of an "oak leviathan" in 1818, he was referring to a boat; Edmund Burke meant that the Duke of Bedford was a mighty man, not a fire-breathing monster, when he called him "the leviathan among all the creatures of the crown"; and Thomas Hobbes in *Leviathan* (1651) considered the commonwealth a "great Leviathan," by which he meant "a mortal god," granted us by the immortal one for our common defense. Far be it from me to accuse Hobbes of misreading the Bible, but I don't think he expected God to crush England to pieces.

Out of the Mouths of Babes

O LORD our Lord, how excellent is thy name in all the earth!
who hast set thy glory above the heavens. | Out of the mouth of
babes and sucklings hast thou ordained strength because of thine
enemies, that thou mightest still the enemy and the avenger.

Psalm 8: 1–2

"Out of the mouths of babes," we now say (slightly misquoting), come the darndest things. Children sometimes speak, in their simplicity, more wisely than their elders.

But adults will notice that, in coining this phrase, the author of Psalm 8 (allegedly David) isn't talking about darling little remarks or amusing notes. What he is talking about depends on the translation. In the King James Version, the LORD "ordains strength" (issues strong words) against his enemies, even through "babes and sucklings." In the New English Bible, babes likewise "rebuke the mighty." But in the Revised Standard Version and in the Jerusalem Bible, the little ones chant the glory and majesty of the LORD.

Though translators can't agree on whether the Psalmist's babes spout fighting words or waft hosannas—either way it's a miracle—Jesus preferred the latter. When the chief priests and scribes of the Jerusalem Temple cringe at the din of children crying "Hosanna to the son of David," Jesus scolds them: "Yea, have ye never read, Out of the mouth of babes and sucklings thou hast perfected praise?" (Matthew 21: 16). Jesus' quote, or rather paraphrase, is the main reason "out of the mouths of babes" became a popular catchphrase. But it didn't ensure the phrase would be well employed.

Tender Mercies AND *Loving-Kindness*

> I have called upon thee, for thou wilt hear me, O God: incline thine ear unto me, and hear my speech. | Shew thy marvelous lovingkindness, O thou that savest by thy right hand them which put their trust in thee from those that rise up against them.
>
> Psalm 17: 6–7

> Remember, O LORD, thy tender mercies and thy lovingkindnesses; for they have been ever of old.
>
> Psalm 25: 6

Though their emphases differ, Psalms 17 and 25 share a common theme: the LORD is loving and merciful to those who trust and obey him. The Psalmist—both poems are attributed to David—cries unto God to show him "tender mercies" and "lovingkindness," both by pardoning his lapses and by protecting him against the wickedness of his enemies, who "are inclosed in their own fat" (Psalm 17: 10).

Both "tender mercies" and "loving-kindness" (now hyphenated) were coined by Miles Coverdale for his 1535 rendition of the Psalms and then adopted by the King James translators. The former phrase still has the whiff of the Authorized Version about it, Hollywood and ironic quotation notwithstanding. But "loving-kindness" had by the nineteenth century settled into a more generic and secular usage, as in Washington Irving's reference to a "lady of unbounded loving-kindness" (*Salmagundi*).

While Jeroboam was sinful, the Bible never accuses him of drunkenness, so the modern history of his name doesn't make a whole lot of sense. In any case, the term had come into use before 1816, when Sir Walter Scott recorded it in *The Black Dwarf,* and it inspired bottle-makers to turn to other biblical figures to name even mightier vessels.

Here is a complete list of wine-bottle names, and their capacities according to modern reckoning:

- BOTTLE: 75 centiliters (about 25 ounces).
- MAGNUM: two bottles, or 1.5 liters.
- JEROBOAM: four bottles, or 3 liters.
- REHOBOAM: six bottles, or 4.5 liters.
- METHUSELAH: eight bottles, or 6 liters; named after the longest-lived man in Genesis [*see* p. 28].
- SALMANAZAR: twelve bottles, or 9 liters; named after Salmanazar V (or Shalmanezer), the Assyrian king who, according to II Kings 17–18, conquered Samaria before his death in 722 B.C.
- BALTHAZAR: sixteen bottles, or 12 liters; named after the king of Babylon (sixth century B.C.) who appears in the book of Daniel as a great partier who "drank wine before the thousand" [*see* FEET OF CLAY, p. 152].
- NEBUCHADNEZZAR: twenty bottles, or 15 liters; named after the Babylonian king (early sixth century B.C.) who toppled Jerusalem and destroyed the Temple of Solomon.

A Two-Edged Sword

For the lips of a strange woman drop as an honeycomb, and her
mouth is smoother than oil: | But her end is bitter as wormwood,
sharp as a twoedged sword. | Her feet go down to death; her
steps take hold on hell. | Lest thou shouldest ponder the path of
life, her ways are moveable, that thou canst not know them.

Proverbs 5: 3–6

The "two-edged (*or* double-edged) sword" of Proverbs has very
little to do with today's metaphor. A father is advising his son to
resist the temptations of a loose woman, whose enticing words
may sound sweet, but who will taste bitter in the end, truly
"sharp as a two-edged sword"—that is, really, *really* sharp.

But that's not what we mean. Today's "two-edged sword" is
something that "cuts both ways" and is as harmful as helpful.
The author (said to be Solomon), however, thinks a loose
woman is only harmful and walks in only one direction: down
the twisted path to *sheol* (translated "hell"), the Hebrew under-
world. To take her apparent pleasures as the other "edge" is to
misread the proverb.

Though this is the earliest passage in the Bible in which "two-
edged sword" appears, the phrase was originally coined by William Tyndale in 1526 as he translated the New Testament
epistles, specifically Hebrews 4: 12: "For the word of God is
quick, and powerful, and sharper than any twoedged sword."
This is even less ambiguous than Proverbs.

Early figurative applications were more or less faithful to the
biblical sense, but by the late seventeenth century the phrase
was already on the path to distortion. The famous chemist Robert Boyle, in *Some Considerations Touching the Style of Holy*

Scriptures (1661), referred for example to certain notions as "two-edg'd Weapons" that "are as well applicable to the service of Falsehood, as of Truth."

"Double-edged" is now commonly substituted for "two-edged," so it's even more false to the Bible. We owe the change, it seems, to John Dryden, who wrote in *The Hind and the Panther* (1687) of a "double-edged" sword that "cuts on either side." James Martineau virtually quoted Dryden verbatim in his *Essays Philosophical and Theological* (1866–1869): "The charge … is double-edged, and cuts both ways." At least this piece of boilerplate has a distinguished history.

To Spare the Rod

He that spareth his rod hateth his son: but he that loveth him chasteneth him betimes.

Proverbs 13: 24

Most biblical proverbs go something like this: "A faithful witness will not lie: but a false witness will utter lies" (14: 5). In other words, they're hard to argue with. But this one is different, especially in this age of competing child-rearing philosophies.

In point of fact, while the Bible is high on having children, it doesn't have much to say about the proper way to raise them. This verse is about all we get, and it advocates periodic "chastening" (beating) with a rod. The author liked the idea so much he repeated it ten chapters later: "Withhold not correction from the child: for if thou beatest him with the rod, he shall not die. | Thou shalt beat him with the rod, and shalt deliver his soul from hell" (23: 13–14). Of course, these were the days when you might be put to death for striking a parent [*see* EYE FOR EYE, TOOTH FOR TOOTH, p. 69], so you might take the Bible's advice with a grain of salt.

Shakespeare, however, seems to endorse Proverbs' sentiment when he has Duke Vincentio, in *Measure for Measure* (1604), call for strict enforcement of the law: if authorities merely brandish laws as threats—as "fond [doting] fathers" might stick bundles of twigs in their children's faces, "For terror, not to use"—then "in time the rod / Becomes more mock'd than fear'd" (Act 1, scene 3). Later poets, such as Samuel Butler, were less serious. In the satiric *Hudibras* (1663–1678), Butler jokes that if, as poets would have it, "Love is a boy," then we ought to "spare the rod, and spoil the child."

Butler's paraphrase is now more famous than the original, but the irony has been bled out of it, so there isn't much difference in meaning between the two. "Spare the rod and spoil the child" is certainly less harsh than Proverbs' talk of death and hell, but tell that to a schoolboy who's just been whipped.

Pride Goes before a Fall

Pride goeth before destruction, and an haughty spirit before a fall. | Better it is to be of an humble spirit with the lowly, than to divide the spoil with the proud.

Proverbs 16: 18–19

Though one of the creakiest pieces of ancient wisdom, the idea that "pride goes before a fall" (an abridgment of Proverbs 16: 18) often bears repeating. Certain high flyers of the 1980s, for example, might profitably have brushed up their Bible.

We tend to think pride is dangerous because it plays with the mind, leading us to overreach ourselves or to offend the wrong people. But the author of Proverbs is less interested in psychology or ethics than in power, namely God's. Our comparative insignificance is something we forget at our peril, because "Every one that is proud in heart is an abomination to the LORD" (verse 5), who tends to the jealous side.

Such notions were also shared by the Greeks, whose goddess Nemesis took care of mortals who thought themselves too godlike. But the Greek notion of cosmic balance was alien to Hebrew thought, just as Hebrew ideas of religious duty and sin were alien to the Greeks. We all know who won the contest for the heart of Western ethics.

The phrasing "pride goeth before destruction" is perhaps a bit confusing; what "goeth before" means here is "leads to" ("go" was a much more versatile verb in the Renaissance than it is now). Yet "goeth" does suggest that pride is a force capable of moving on its own and of leading us by the hand to our doom, which is both more vivid and truer to Hebrew psychology.

Vanity of Vanities

Vanity of vanities, saith the Preacher, vanity of vanities; all is vanity.

Ecclesiastes 1: 2

Right at the beginning of his book, Ecclesiastes—called "the Preacher" here but whose name really means "assembler"—sets forth his theme: "vanity of vanities: all is vanity." In other words, "human endeavor is vain and empty." Writing books excepted, of course.

The King James rendition, which borrows from the Geneva Bible of 1560, preserves a peculiar Hebrew method of forming superlatives. "Vanity of vanities" (meaning "vain beyond belief") is a memorable example, as are "king of kings" (meaning "supreme king") and "song of songs" [*see* p. 134]. Though this "X of Xs" structure is not native to English, Ecclesiastes' denunciation made it fashionable for a time in the Renaissance. "Give me that man / That is not passion's slave, and I will wear him / In my heart's core, ay, in my heart of heart," says Hamlet (Act 3, scene 2). This is not quite faithful to the Hebrew form, but then again Hamlet does have only one heart. Though the modern phrase "in my heart of hearts" (which seems to trace to William Wordsworth's "Intimations of Immortality," 1806) recalls Ecclesiastes more exactly, it is both a misquotation of Shakespeare and an offense to logic.

There Is Nothing New under the Sun
AND *Eat, Drink, and Be Merry*

> The thing that hath been, it is that which shall be; and that
> which is done is that which shall be done: and there is no new
> thing under the sun.

Ecclesiastes 1: 9

Ecclesiastes never foresaw the hydrogen bomb, tabloid journalism, or the Lambada when he opined that "there is no new thing under the sun." On the other hand, he would probably have called such inventions "novelties," not "new," because they wouldn't change anything important.

This is because Ecclesiastes takes a grand view of things, to say the least. Nothing we do or make matters because his context is the sweep of history and the totality of nature. But this leaves him stating the perfectly obvious: day after day, "the sun also ariseth, and the sun goeth down"; the winds blow as they always do, and rivers continue to run; men keep working, but remain unsatisfied.

Ecclesiastes isn't tearing down human creativity out of spite. In fact, his ultimate message is "Don't worry, be happy"—since you can't do anything new or significant, you might as well just enjoy yourself. "There is nothing better for a man," he advises, "than that he should eat and drink, and that he should make his soul enjoy good in his labour" (2: 24; compare 3: 13). And later: "a man hath no better thing under the sun, than to eat, and to drink, and to be merry" (8: 15). If you're tempted to add, "for tomorrow he dies," that part of the proverb is supplied by Isaiah (Isaiah 22: 13) in one of his merrier moods.

A Season for Everything

To everything there is a season, and a time to every purpose under the heaven: | A time to be born, and a time to die; a time to plant, and a time to pluck up that which is planted; | A time to kill and a time to heal; a time to break down, and a time to build up....

Ecclesiastes 3: 1–3

If you're humming "Turn Turn Turn" and wondering how all this talk of killing and breaking got into a song by the peacenik Pete Seeger, meet Ecclesiastes, biblical tunesmith. Though Seeger did do a little embellishing ("A time for peace, I swear it's not too late"), to his credit he preserved some of Ecclesiastes' rawer sentiments, which are central to the meaning of the book. Ecclesiastes did really mean that there is a "season" (proper time) for everything—death as well as birth, destruction as well as creation, hate as well as love.

Unfortunately, you're never going to be able to predict the right season for anything. It is God who disposes time, and it is beyond man to know its pattern, either in the past or in the future: "no man can find out the work that God maketh from the beginning to the end" (3: 11). That God creates a season for evil as well as for good is another mystery, and it's no use blaming him if you think the season of your reward, or your enemy's punishment, is long past due. Ecclesiastes harps on his theme: you can't know anything important, and you can't do anything to secure your future. So relax.

This text was apparently dear to President John F. Kennedy, as it was read at his funeral—though most Americans felt that event came out of season.

Two Are Better than One

There is one alone, and there is not a second; yea, he hath neither child nor brother: yet is there no end of all his labour; neither is his eye satisfied with riches.... | Two are better than one; because they have a good reward for their labour. | For if they fall, the one will lift up his fellow: but woe to him that is alone when he falleth; for he hath not another to help him up. | Again, if two lie together, then they have heat: but how can one be warm alone?

Ecclesiastes 4: 8–11

Ecclesiastes' formula "two are better than one" (the phrasing is from Miles Coverdale's 1535 rendition) strikes the ear as lacking a certain rhythm. But it's hard to know whether that's because we're used to hearing "two heads are better than one" or if the more specific form became proverbial (by 1546) because it trips more nicely on the tongue.

In either case, Ecclesiastes isn't concerned with problem-solving, virtually the only topic to which we apply his words today. What he means is "two *bodies* are better than one"—the better to plow fields, recover from accidents, fend off enemies, and keep warm at night. He's talking about physical challenges, not opinions, and it's easier to agree with his advice than with the more familiar proverb. Especially as we grow older and more dependent, we value more the helping hand, while growing more fixed in our ideas. Ecclesiastes is a book of aged wisdom, and its author, though he seeks no second opinion on the vanity of ambition, knows it is not good to be lonely and defenseless.

A Fly in the Ointment

Dead flies cause the ointment of the apothecary to send forth a stinking savour: so doth a little folly in him that is in reputation for wisdom and honour.

Ecclesiastes 10: 1

I don't know about ointment, but I do know that one little fly can really spoil a good potato salad. Ecclesiastes' vivid phrasing—the fly causes not just a "bad smell" but a "stinking savour"—emphasizes how catastrophically, and how quickly, a relatively minor flaw may ruin the best of things. (In English, Ecclesiastes speaks of "dead flies"; we've dropped "dead" from our usage, which is no great loss, because in the Hebrew the phrase is closer to "deadly flies.") And the better something is, the smaller need be the flaw to spoil it.

Here, the author speaks of how damaging one miscue may be to the person of high repute. Today, "a fly in the ointment" generally refers to less consequential disappoint-ments—the one sour note, the one bad joke. P. G. Wodehouse proposed this nice equation: "one flaw, one fly in the ointment, one individual caterpillar in the salad" (*The Indiscretions of Archie,* 1921).

To Cast Bread upon the Waters

Cast thy bread upon the waters: for thou shalt find it after many days. | Give a portion to seven, and also to eight; for thou knowest not what evil shall be upon the earth.

Ecclesiastes 11: 1–2

As Ecclesiastes nears the end of his sermon, his writing becomes more lofty and poetic, and thus more obscure. These verses are a case in point: the business about giving a portion to seven and also to eight has left many a reader scratching his head.

I'll leave that one to the exegetes, who say the basic idea is that you should hedge your bets. A bit more manageable is the preceding verse: "Cast thy bread upon the waters: for thou shalt find it after many days." Though the first half of the clause is often used now as a call for charity—with "bread" standing, as in slang, for wealth and "waters" for an ocean of need—Ecclesiastes had something more self-serving in mind.

Borrowing his imagery from Egyptian lore, he depicts the world of business as an ocean upon which your "bread" (again, wealth) may multiply, but only if you're willing to take the risk of tossing it out there and waiting for the profits to float back. (He may refer to trading grain by sea, but then again the Hebrews were never great merchant mariners.) Quite the opposite of charitable giving, in which nothing returns from the waters except perhaps gratitude, or inner satisfaction.

The Song of Songs

The song of songs, which is Solomon's.

The Song of Solomon 1: 1

If Solomon had actually written the biblical books wholly or partly ascribed to him (Proverbs, Ecclesiastes, The Song of Solomon, and the Apocryphal Wisdom of Solomon), he wouldn't have had much time to govern Israel, let alone attend to his thousand wives.

But the first verse of this book—which is actually a superscription or title—boldly proclaims that this "song of songs" is indeed the king's work, a claim virtually no scholar credits today. The Song of Solomon, while occasionally referring to the king, appears rather to be an anthology of popular Hebrew love lyrics, sung and then written down over a period of centuries.

The construction "song of songs" is a Hebrew superlative, meaning "supreme song," as I explain elsewhere [see VANITY OF VANITIES, p. 128]. This description, and the book's acceptance into both the Jewish and Christian canons, has led some to read its lyrics as metaphors of divine love. On the other hand, there are many overt references to sex, and not one to God.

Whatever motivated the compilers of the Bible to include this book, it does help balance out some of the drier material—the books of Chronicles, for instance. Among the lovely phrases still occasionally quoted are:

- "I am black, but comely" (1: 5)—the "I" cannot be Solomon, since a woman is singing and "black" refers to the dark complexion of a field-laborer;

Brush Up Your Bible

- "I am the rose of Sharon, and the lily of the valleys" (2: 1)—a verse which, via the Latin Bible, lent the name "lily of the valley" to the *Convallaria majalis,* an especially beautiful springtime flower;
- "Stay me with flagons, comfort me with apples: for I am sick with love" (2: 5)—actually "Sustain me with raisins, refresh me with apples," etc., in the Hebrew. Raisins and apples were apparently considered mild aphrodisiacs;
- "the voice of the turtle" (2: 12)—referring to the sweet song of the turtledove in springtime; and,
- "our vines have grown tender grapes" (2: 15)—namely, the fruits of passion.

Beyond these lines, which testify to the popularity of chapter 2, the entire Song of Solomon has remained over the centuries a rich source of allusions and quotations in Hebrew poetry. Some Jews, too, still sing its verses on the eve of the Sabbath, especially during Passover. This tradition seems to have less to do with the book's holiness than with its beauty, which is undeniable.

White as Snow

Come now, and let us reason together, saith the LORD: though your sins be as scarlet, they shall be as white as snow; though they be red like crimson, they shall be as wool. I If ye be willing and obedient, ye shall eat the good of the land: I But if ye refuse and rebel, ye shall be devoured with the sword: for the mouth of the LORD hath spoken it.

Isaiah 1: 18–20

The prophet Isaiah has an important message for the people of Judah, who face invasion by the Assyrians: their troubles stem from their own evildoing. Yahweh personally condemns them through his prophet, but he speaks more in sorrow than in anger: there is almost a pleading tone in his call, "Come now, and let us reason together." (This famous line, taken out of context, would become a favorite of President Lyndon B. Johnson.) In other words, let's argue the pros and cons of sin and obedience.

If the Judeans were reasonable, God says, they would abandon their hateful ways and "Learn to do well; seek judgment, relieve the oppressed, judge the fatherless, plead for the widow" (verse 17). If they heed his call, their "scarlet" sins will be washed clean, "white as snow," and they will once again enjoy prosperity; otherwise, they can only look forward to being "devoured" by the swords of their enemies.

The phrase "white as snow" appears several times in the Bible, but Isaiah's line is the most famous, and furthermore he is the first to actually say "white as snow" in Hebrew. Isaiah refers, of course, to purity and innocence, which he compares to the spotless whiteness of wool. Any child, thanks to the song about Mary's little lamb, would make the same connection today.

Brush Up Your Bible

To Beat Swords into Plowshares

And it shall come to pass in the last days, that the mountain of the LORD's house shall be established in the top of the mountains, and shall be exalted above the hills; and all nations shall flow unto it. | And many people shall go and say, Come ye, and let us go up to the mountain of the LORD, to the house of the God of Jacob; and he will teach us of his ways, and we will walk in his paths: for out of Zion shall go forth the law, and the word of the LORD from Jerusalem. | And he shall judge among the nations, and shall rebuke many people: and they shall beat their swords into plowshares, and their spears into pruninghooks: nation shall not lift up sword against nation, neither shall they learn war any more.

Isaiah 2: 2–4

If you've always wondered what a "plowshare" is and how you could beat a sword into one, I can save you a trip to the dictionary. A plowshare, also known as a "share," is simply the sharp blade of a plow, which you might indeed fashion by beating an old straight sword into a new curved shape. Good, sharp metal was hard to come by in the Judea of Isaiah's time, still an essentially agrarian society living at subsistence levels. Nothing could be wasted, and every hand not raised in defense of the land would be required to cultivate it. Think of beating swords into plowshares as converting defense industries to domestic production.

If you find that prospect a bit utopian, so is Isaiah's vision, which looks ahead to the "last days," meaning here the distant future. Isaiah foresees a time when Jerusalem's sacred Mount Zion will become a mecca for all nations. The whole world will finally bow to the God of Jacob and flock to Zion for instruc-

tion and worship; at one in faith, nations will submit to the LORD's arbitration and cease to war among themselves. In this era of universal peace, men shall "beat their swords into plowshares, and their spears into pruninghooks" (also sharp, curved tools, signifying horticulture as the plowshares signify agriculture).

Obviously, we have yet to see these "last days," though that hasn't stopped politicians from citing Isaiah's words in their periodic pleas for peace. (They completely ignore Joel's warmongering inversion, "Beat your plowshares into swords, and your pruninghooks into spears"—Joel 3: 10.) We can probably count on being asked to beat swords into plowshares a whole lot more before anybody actually does it. So don't hold your breath for the "peace dividend."

A Voice Crying in the Wilderness

> Comfort ye, comfort ye my people, saith your God. | Speak ye
> comfortably to Jerusalem, and cry unto her, that her warfare is
> accomplished, that her iniquity is pardoned: for she hath re-
> ceived of the LORD's hand double for all her sins. | The voice of
> him that crieth in the wilderness, Prepare ye the way of the
> LORD, make straight in the desert a highway for our God.

Isaiah 40: 1–3

What we mean by "a voice crying in the wilderness" today is "a
warning voice no one heeds"—the wilderness is metaphorical, a
lack of sense or reason. What no one seems to have heeded in
early translations of Isaiah, however, is that the voice doesn't cry
in the wilderness at all. In Hebrew, the voice instructs some
unnamed prophet to prepare a "highway" *through* the wilderness. The line was botched both in the Greek Septuagint and
the Latin Vulgate, and the King James Version follows suit.

In truth, these verses are pretty confusing, so we shouldn't
blame the translators too much. After all, the authors of the
Gospels, citing Isaiah, made the same mistake (John the Baptist
is the "voice crying in the wilderness" at Matthew 3: 3, etc.—*see*
LOCUSTS AND WILD HONEY, p. 168). Other problems with the
passage are harder to deal with—for example, identifying the
"ye" whom God commands to comfort Jerusalem.

Whoever the speaker and whoever the audience, the message
is clear. This portion of the Book of Isaiah—from chapter 40 to
chapter 55—is called "Second Isaiah" because it is unquestion-
ably of a different period from chapters 1 to 39 ("First Isaiah")
and by a different author or authors. (Chapters 56 to 66 are
different still and are known collectively as "Third Isaiah.")

Where First Isaiah addresses the Judeans in their plight at the turn of the seventh century B.C., Second Isaiah addresses Jews who had been exiled to Babylon after Jerusalem fell to Nebuchadnezzar in the sixth century B.C.

Anticipating the exiles' return home under the guidance of Cyrus II, Persian conqueror of Babylon, the author of these verses harks back to the Hebrews' escape from Egypt to the promised land of Canaan some seven centuries before. Then as now, Yahweh's people had to pass through a "wilderness," but this time the Jews, better supplied and trained, will build in advance a path or "highway" through the rocky desert.

Whoever cried out, the people listened, returning to Jerusalem and rebuilding Solomon's temple, which had been leveled by Babylon. (The result is known as the Second Temple.) So the phrase was not only mistranslated, it's almost always quoted out of context. But to try changing that would be crying in the wilderness.

A Drop in the Bucket

> Behold, the nations are as a drop of a bucket, and are counted as the small dust of the balance: behold, he taketh up the isles as a very little thing. | And Lebanon is not sufficient to burn, nor the beasts thereof sufficient for a burnt offering. | All nations before him are as nothing; and they are counted to him less than nothing, and vanity.
>
> Isaiah 40: 15–17

Here the author of Second Isaiah reminds the exiled Jews of the mysterious wisdom and awesome power of the LORD. Hostile nations are to him "as a drop of a bucket," a mere trifle.

Yes, "a drop *of* a bucket" is the original phrase, coined by the translator Wyclif in the fourteenth century. Though we've changed one word, the meaning is essentially the same: a drop is inconsequential, whether it's added to, subtracted from, or left in the bucket. What matters more is how big a bucket you're talking about—which is why legislators, for example, can speak of huge sums of money as merely "a drop in the bucket" of a mind-boggling budget.

"Drop of" was the standard phrasing for centuries. But perhaps under the influence of such later expressions as "a drop of water in the ocean" (from Charles Dickens's *A Christmas Carol,* 1844) and "a drop in the sea" (coined nine years later), "drop of" quietly gave way to "drop in." The latter and now familiar version has been traced to a letter of Hart Crane's, written in 1921, in which the poet cites "Sara Teasdale, Marguerite Wilkinson, Lady Speyer, etc." as "a few drops in the bucket of feminine lushness."

To See Eye to Eye

How beautiful upon the mountains are the feet of him that
bringeth good tidings, that publisheth peace; that bringeth good
tidings of good, that publisheth salvation; that saith unto Zion,
Thy God reigneth! | Thy watchmen shall lift up the voice; with
the voice together shall they sing: for they shall see eye to eye,
when the LORD shall bring again Zion.

Isaiah 52: 7–8

We don't really mean "see eye to eye," and neither did the author of Isaiah. The Hebrew "eye to eye" actually means "right
before the eye" and doesn't necessarily involve a second party,
despite the way we use it today. And it has nothing to do with
equality of views.

Here the author imagines the happy day when Yahweh will
humiliate the oppressors of Israel by returning with his liberated
people to the holy hill of Zion. As they witness these develop-
ments "eye to eye" (that is, plainly), sentries and heralds will
shout the good news that Israel is free and that God the King
has returned. These joyous events are supposed to bring har-
mony and peace among all the peoples of Palestine—or make
them see "eye to eye" in the modern sense, which appears to
date to the 1870s.

A Lamb to the Slaughter

All we like sheep have gone astray; we have turned every one to his own way; and the LORD hath laid on him the iniquity of us all. | He was oppressed, and he was afflicted, yet he opened not his mouth: he is brought as a lamb to the slaughter, and as a sheep before her shearers is dumb, so he openeth not his mouth.

Isaiah 53: 6–7

The book of Isaiah sometimes has been called "the Gospel in the Old Testament" because of chapters like this, which greatly influenced the depiction of Jesus in the New Testament. Christians see in Isaiah, especially in the latter books, prophecies of their messiah, on whom "the LORD hath laid … the iniquity of us all" and who let himself be led uncomplaining to his death.

This particular passage is cited in the Acts of the Apostles (8: 32), where Jesus is identified with Isaiah's "suffering servant." We don't know exactly whom the author of Isaiah really had in mind, though—perhaps a prophet, or a king, or a personification of the faithful, or indeed the Messiah. Though his identity is a mystery, the servant's task is clear: to lead the LORD's people from exile back to Zion. But first he must take upon himself the iniquity of Israel, suffering the hardships of exile as just punishment for his people's sins. He, and those he represents, will not complain of their hardships but will be mute when brought like a "lamb to the slaughter."

We're probably not talking about actual death here, though certainly some resistant Jews did perish in exile. "Lamb to the slaughter" is more likely just a metaphor for an acceptance of fate and a docility in the face of God's judgments. We distort Isaiah's phrase by implying that the lamb is innocent and defenseless, its fate cruel and undeserved. The suffering servant accepts that he is sinful, so accepts his punishment, too.

Modern usage, however, is supported elsewhere: Jeremiah, reporting a plot on his life that was foiled by God, compares himself to "a lamb or an ox that is brought to the slaughter; and I knew not that they had devised devices against me" (Jeremiah 11: 19). On the other hand, Jeremiah has already launched an attack on the treacherous and wicked, praying that the LORD will "pull them out like sheep for the slaughter, and prepare them for the day of slaughter" (12: 3). So he's really no help at all.

Holier than Thou

I have spread out my hands all the day unto a rebellious people,
which walketh in a way that was not good, after their own
thoughts; | A people that provoketh me to anger continually to
my face; ... | Which say, Stand by thyself, come not near to me;
for I am holier than thou. These are a smoke in my nose, a fire
that burneth all the day.

Isaiah 65: 2–3, 5

"Holier than thou": sanctimonious, arrogant, superior, smug—
for once, we use a biblical phrase to express the same attitude as
the Bible.

What angers God is the hypocrisy of claiming to be holy
while abusing holy rites. Not only do some self-styled seekers
flirt with strange gods, sacrifice in profane places, burn incense
on bad altars, seek prophecies from the dead, eat swine's flesh,
and so forth, they also feel superior for doing so and sneer at
humble but true believers for not joining in their rituals. All this
is as "smoke" in Yahweh's nose, and it doesn't smell very good at
all. He vows to "recompense, even recompense into their bosom" (verse 6)—in other words, do some serious smiting.

Even today, "holier than thou" still seethes with God's sar-
casm. You might think it would have come in handy during the
contentious early days of the Reformation, but in fact it wasn't
quoted in writing until this century. The American novelist
Theodore Dreiser referred in *The Financier* (1912) to the "'holier
than thou' attitude" as "quite the last and most deadly offense
within prison walls," where nobody likes a wise guy. Sancti-
mony isn't popular anywhere, of course, so be careful not to let
reading this book make you too much holier.

A Leopard Can't Change Its Spots
AND *Jeremiad*

And if thou say in thine heart, Wherefore come these things
upon me? For the greatness of thine iniquity are thy skirts
discovered, and thy heels made bare. | Can the Ethiopian change
his skin, or the leopard his spots? then may ye also do good, that
are accustomed to do evil.

Jeremiah 13: 22–23

Once again, the LORD is fuming over the sins of Judah and
Jerusalem, and once again he has chosen a prophet to predict
vengeance—which will arrive when Babylon conquers the kingdom and sacks the Jerusalem temple.

The warnings, accusations, and condemnations occupy a
long series of chapters. On top of these Jeremiah adds his own
complaints against his society, which are so bitter and proved
so unpopular that we've coined the word "jeremiad"—meaning
"lamentation" or "tirade"—in his honor. The term first appeared in 1780, when Hannah More accurately observed that "It
has long been the fashion to make the most lamentable
Jeremiades on the badness of the times." There's certainly never
been a lack of social critics with dire views of the state of
affairs—people President George Bush fondly referred to as the
"doom and gloom crowd."

Jeremiah, however pessimistic, did have a way with words.
Here he's in the middle of rebuking those who would presume
to object when God rightly punishes them for their pride,
drunkenness, and assorted other sins. (Among other things, the
LORD will "discover their skirts," which doesn't mean that he'll
rummage through their closets, but rather that he will tear off

their clothing, in other words strip them of their defenses.)

God, whom Jeremiah now quotes, doesn't offer them much hope of escape, for he sees that their evil is dyed in the wool. With one powerful rhetorical question—"Can the Ethiopian change his skin, or the leopard his spots?"—he justifies his forthcoming punishments on the grounds that these sinful Jews are incorrigibly perverse. The leopard never questions the rightness of his appearance, just as these people, schooled in sin, are complacent in their evil. Just as a leopard can't change his spots, neither can they suddenly do good. Which of course puts Jeremiah's whole enterprise in question—why warn them if they're already doomed?

"A leopard can't change its spots" is now the regular form of the proverb, though in its source it is phrased as a question. P. G. Wodehouse's Bertie Wooster got this much right when, apropos of an unmanageable young monster named Master Thomas, he noted, "Once a Thos., always a Thos. Can the leopard change his spots or the Ethiopian his what-not?" (*Very Good Jeeves*, 1930).

Set Your Teeth on Edge

Behold, the days come, saith the LORD, that I will sow the house of Israel and the house of Judah with the seed of man, and with the seed of beast. | And it shall come to pass, that like as I have watched over them, to pluck up, and to break down, and to throw down, and to destroy, and to afflict; so will I watch over them, to build, and to plant, saith the LORD. | In those days they shall say no more, The fathers have eaten a sour grape, and the children's teeth are set on edge. | But every one shall die for his own iniquity: every man that eateth the sour grape, his teeth shall be set on edge.

Jeremiah 31: 27–30

Though Jeremiah's bitter prophecy has come true and Judah has fallen to Nebuchadnezzar, here he preaches a message of hope. Just as the LORD has presided over his people's punishment, he will nurture them as they rebuild their kingdom.

When, furthermore, the kingdom of Judah returns from exile to its liberated land, the people shall no longer say "the fathers have eaten a sour grape, and the children's teeth are set on edge." Jeremiah's interesting phrase seems to have two meanings. On one level, he refers only to the returned exiles, who will no longer be able to sit around blaming the previous generation for their predicament. On a higher level, though, he's promising a new covenant between God and his chosen people that will extend into the future. No longer will Jews suffer for the sins of their ancestors; now, only the sinner—the grape-eater himself—must face the music.

But that doesn't answer the question of what "teeth ... set on edge" means. The Hebrew phrase is unclear, and the Latin Vulgate rendered it as "teeth are numbed." The English phrasing suggests otherwise. Wyclif gives "teeth waxen on edge" for the same Hebrew at Ezekiel 18: 2; he probably drew on the older expression "to edge one's teeth," which means something like "to put a tingle in one's mouth," as sour fruit and chalk were said to do, and as certain brands of chewing gum boast of doing today. Someone else will have to explain what people were doing eating chalk.

Wheels within Wheels

Now as I beheld the living creatures, behold one wheel upon the earth by the living creatures, with his four faces. | The appearance of the wheels and their work was like unto the colour of a beryl: and they four had one likeness: and their appearance and their work was as it were a wheel in the middle of a wheel. | When they went, they went upon their four sides: and they turned not when they went.

Ezekiel 1: 15–17

We now use "wheels within wheels" to mean "devices within devices," or "multilayered plots" with intricate, hidden motions. But what the prophet Ezekiel sees in his strange "visions of God" (1: 1) is something more mysterious.

As Ezekiel, an exile in Babylon, hears of the fall of Judah to the forces of Nebuchadnezzar, he wonders why this calamity strikes both the wicked and the obedient. As he ponders the mysteriousness of God's ways, the heavens open before him and out of a whirlwind emerges a great cloud flashing a "fire infolding itself."

In its amber glow he sees four figures, resembling men but each with four faces (those of a man, a lion, an ox, and an eagle) and four wings, all joined together in a circle, moving in whichever of the four directions they choose without turning. At each figure's feet is a wheel, fiery gold, that has the shape and motion of a "wheel in the middle of a wheel," with eyes ringed about it. As these wheels moved, "they turned not when they went"— which may mean that they didn't turn at all or, as the New English Bible has it, that they "never swerved in their course." According to Ezekiel, "the spirit of the living creatures was in the wheels" (verse 20).

What Ezekiel describes, if it isn't some real device, is probably his idea of an ideal foundation for the throne of God, which he soon sees suspended above the four interlocked figures. As God is both mysterious and never-changing, so the creatures and their wheels—a kind of living platform—are mysteriously constructed and never-turning. All this is lost on most people who quote from Ezekiel today. While he claims to have seen God eye to eye, we refer to what is hidden rather than revealed.

Feet of Clay

Thou, O king, sawest, and behold a great image. This great
image, whose brightness was excellent, stood before thee; and the
form thereof was terrible. | This image's head was of fine gold,
his breast and his arms of silver, his belly and his thighs of brass,
| His legs of iron, his feet part of iron and part of clay.

Daniel 2: 31–33

Reminiscent at turns of the dream-interpreting Joseph [*see*
p. 46] and of the visionary prophet Ezekiel [*see* p.150], Daniel is
a learned Jewish exile at the court of the Babylonian king
Nebuchadnezzar. As we join the story, Nebuchadnezzar has
been having strange and troubling dreams, which stymie his
court astrologers and sorcerers—not least because he refuses to
tell them what actually goes on in the land of Nod. The enraged
king orders that all his so-called wise men be torn into pieces.

But Daniel, taking pity on them and fearing for his own skin,
resolves to crack Nebuchadnezzar's riddle. On cue, God sends
Daniel a vision by night, which he relays to the king. Declaring
that the dreams are images of "what shall come to pass" (2: 29),
Daniel describes what Nebuchadnezzar saw: a towering figure
with a golden head, a silver torso, a brass midsection, iron legs,
and "feet part of iron and part of clay." Somehow, a stone cut
from a mountain by no visible hand is hurled at the grotesque
figure, which is shattered, and its fragments scattered by the
wind. Thereupon the stone grew into a new mountain, so great
that it "filled [covered] the whole earth" (verse 35).

Daniel then offers the stunned monarch his interpretation:
by God's will, Nebuchadnezzar has become a "king of kings"
over a vast territory, and Babylon is represented in the dream-

figure's golden head. Each of the other metal sections, in descending order, represents a succeeding and weaker kingdom—after Babylon, scholars surmise, the Median, Persian, and Macedonian empires. The fourth kingdom, represented as iron legs, will break the whole world into pieces and subdue it—not too far from what Alexander the Great actually did.

But this last kingdom will eventually be divided, as the figure's feet are into iron and clay, partly strong and partly weak, constitutionally unstable. (The Macedonian empire did come apart at the seams, and Daniel may be thinking in particular of its Egyptian and Syrian components.) It is in the era of this divided kingdom, Daniel predicts, that God shall "set up a kingdom, which shall never be destroyed," though it will itself shatter all other kingdoms (verse 44). This is the great stone in the dream, which grows into a worldwide mountain, and which represents an impending utopia.

Daniel's virtuoso exposition earns him a high government position, and it earned the phrase "feet of clay" an enduring place in English. Of course, our catchphrase distorts Daniel's text, where the colossus has feet "part of iron and part of clay," though it does preserve the basic meaning, namely "apparently strong in substance but weak in foundation." The phrase is most often applied to a seemingly admirable person with a crippling character flaw or moral weakness. "Feet of clay" in this metaphorical sense was first used by Lord Byron in his "Ode to Napoleon Buonaparte" (1814), and it was picked up by a string of notable literary figures. Call the *Oxford English Dictionary* if you ever find a reference to "feet of iron."

The Writing on the Wall AND *Weighed in the Balance*

> In the same hour came forth fingers of a man's hand, and wrote over against the candlestick upon the plaister of the wall of the king's palace: and the king saw the part of the hand that wrote. | Then the king's countenance was changed, and his thoughts troubled him, so that the joints of his loins were loosed, and his knees smote one against another. | The king cried aloud to bring in the astrologers, the Chaldeans, and the soothsayers....
>
> Daniel 5: 5–7

When you "see the writing on the wall," you have no doubt that you're doomed: the message has become crystal clear. Such is not the case with the original writing (or "handwriting") on the wall, which is found in the book of Daniel though the actual phrase is not.

In this chapter we find Nebuchadnezzar's successor, King Belshazzar, carousing with his court and sipping wine from golden goblets purloined from the Jerusalem Temple. Suddenly a mysterious, detached hand appears in the air to write on his chamber walls. Belshazzar, so terrified that his knees start knocking, promises great power and wealth to whoever can interpret the writing.

Once again, the assorted astrologers and soothsayers are at a total loss. So Daniel is summoned for a repeat performance. The prophet warns Belshazzar to stop profaning the holy objects of the LORD's temple and to give up his idol worship. The hand that appeared in his chamber was that of the one true God, who holds the king's "breath" in his hands (5: 23–24).

As for the message, it reads, in Aramaic, "MENE, MENE, TEKEL, UPHARSIN." In slightly garbled form, these are the names of various coins, listed according to descending value (a *pharsin* is two *pheres*, which make a *tekel*; sixty *tekels* made a *mene*). There are five coins in all (two *menes*, one *tekel*, two *pheres*), and these perhaps represent five successors of Nebuchadnezzar, each less substantial than his predecessor.

But Daniel knows there's more to this list than pocket change. Each of the three names is similar and perhaps etymologically related to an Aramaic verb, so that the entire phrase might be translated as "numbered, numbered, weighed, and divided." Daniel transforms each verb, in turn, into a sentence, in both senses of the term. From *mene* ("numbered") Daniel extrapolates: "God hath numbered thy kingdom, and finished it." From *tekel* ("weight"): "Thou are weighed in the balance, and art found wanting." Finally, from *pheres* ("halved" or "divided," with a pun on "Persian"): "Thy kingdom is divided, and given to the Medes and Persians" (verses 25–27). It doesn't take long for Daniel's predictions to come true: that very night, Belshazzar is slain and his kingdom overrun by King Darius of Media.

This whole strange episode has not only lent us "writing on the wall" but is also the primary source of our phrase "to be weighed in the balance." The image, as a metaphor for judgment, dates in English at least to the fourteenth century, but Daniel made the precise wording famous and fixed the phrase with its ominous overtones.

To Reap the Whirlwind

Thy calf, O Samaria, hath cast thee off; mine anger is kindled
against them: how long will it be ere they attain to innocency? |
For from Israel was it also: the workman made it; therefore it is
not God: but the calf of Samaria shall be broken in pieces. | For
they have sown the wind, and they shall reap the whirlwind: it
hath no stalk: the bud shall yield no meal: if so be it yield, the
strangers shall swallow it up.

Hosea 8: 5–7

It's been over 640 pages in the standard King James Version
since God laid down his commandment against "graven images," and 628 since the unfortunate incident of the original
golden calf [*see* pp. 67 and 71]; yet here we are again, with Israel
setting up a golden calf in Samaria.

The prophet Hosea had his work cut out for him, since he
preached in the Northern Kingdom of Israel, where graven images were both more plentiful and better tolerated than in
Judah. Idolatry, just one of Israel's many sins, comes sharply
into focus in this passage from chapter 8, in which Yahweh,
speaking through Hosea, declares his anger suitably kindled.
He pledges to smash the calf into pieces and cause Israel to be
swallowed up by its enemies. The Israelites' actions call forth
an opposite and much greater reaction: they have, in Hosea's
memorable phrase, "sown the wind, and they shall reap the
whirlwind."

Israel, in other words, has planted the seeds of its own destruction by worshiping false gods, who will bring only grief,
barenness, and conquest. Hosea's proverbial metaphor stresses
both Israel's responsibility for its fate and its pathetic igno-

rance—the idolators think their sins merely a puff of wind, and they have no idea what a whirlwind these will yield.

Though Wyclif first planted the phrase into English in the fourteenth century, it didn't yield a whirlwind of quotations until the nineteenth, after Sir Walter Scott revived it in his novel *The Black Dwarf* (1816). (In 1857, Henry Buckle coined an eloquent variant: "to see whether they who raised the storm could ride the whirlwind.") By the turn of this century, the phrase had become a certified cliché, with little of its original force, meaning something like "to get more than you bargained for," but that's rarely of whirlwind proportions.

Jonah and the Whale

Now the LORD had prepared a great fish to swallow up Jonah. And Jonah was in the belly of the fish three days and three nights.

Jonah 1: 17

There are several surprises to the story of Jonah. First, not a single English proverb or catchphrase derives from it; and, second, despite its fame it is only four short chapters (forty-eight verses) long. Third, the text never—in Hebrew, Greek, Latin, or English—refers to a "whale." Perhaps there's no other candidate for the "great fish" mentioned here in the King James Version, but those who remember Leviathan [*see* p. 119] will avoid drawing hasty conclusions.

Whatever the fish, the LORD means to teach the coward Jonah a few lessons. At the beginning of the tale, God calls Jonah to go condemn the evils of "Ninevah, that great city" (Jonah 1: 2; Ninevah, located on the Tigris River, was once the capital of Assyria and had probably fallen into Persian hands by the time of Jonah's call). Jonah, however, isn't one bit interested in the job, and to escape from "the presence of the LORD" he hops a ship going the other way—namely, to Spain.

Unamused, Yahweh harries the vessel with winds and tempests, until its terrified crew hauls Jonah from his hiding place and forces him to confess. Suitably impressed by the power of Jonah's God, they decide the best way to save their ship is to toss Jonah overboard. This is where God steps in with his "great fish," in whose belly Jonah cowers three days and three nights.

This gives Jonah sufficient time to pen a hymn of thanksgiving to Yahweh, which he recites from the belly of the fish. Hearing this, "the LORD spake unto the fish, and it vomited out Jonah upon the dry land" (2: 10)—in other words, right back where he started from. Only this time he does go to Ninevah, prophesying the city's imminent doom, which for once causes the people to repent. As far as God is concerned, that's the happy ending to the whole business.

Here things take a surprising turn: Jonah is actually *angry* that his preaching has worked, and that God has spared the city despite its history of wickedness. Clearly, Jonah has learned nothing about mercy from his experience in the fish's belly, and God has to teach him another lesson—this time with a gourd and a worm. To make a long story short, it repeats the lesson of the first: that God values his creations and doesn't destroy them easily.

The New Testament

Christians take their name from "Christ" (in Greek, "annointed one" or "chosen one"), a title bestowed after his death on the central figure in their religious history, Jesus. A Palestinian Jew born within a year or so of 4 B.C. (not in A.D. 1—*see* p. 167), Jesus was considered by many who heard him a very great prophet, or at least a very great teacher with a radically new, populist view of Scripture. In citing Scripture, Jesus used what he considered important texts in Hebrew, among them the Torah and the Major Prophets [*see* pp. 1–2]. It was his new reading of these old texts that came to be known as "gospel," or "good news."

Late in Jesus' life, or shortly after his death (ca. A.D. 30), his disciples came to believe he was more than a great prophet. He was their "Messiah," chosen by God to herald a new age that would spell the end of the profane world and to lead Israel into the coming divine kingdom. The disciples became apostles, bearers of this news to the world; they proselytized among Jews and Gentiles alike, through personal contacts and through letters. One late convert to the cause was Saul of Tarsus—better known as Paul—whose letters to various Gentile Christian communities, written in the 50s and 60s, are the oldest documents in what would come to be called, circa A.D. 200, the "New Testament."

Christian writings were not required so long as most Christians lived close by Jerusalem and so long as Jesus' disciples were still alive to attest directly to his words and deeds. But as new communities sprang up in Syria, Greece, Asia Minor, and Italy, and as the original disciples died—many of them executed—

there grew a demand for written records of Jesus' "gospel." Four such records were eventually preserved in the Christian Bible, in which they would be considered as sacred as the Hebrew Scriptures. These are the Gospels according to Mark, Matthew, Luke, and John, written probably in that order between A.D. 60 and 100.

I treat the Gospels at length on page 163. Suffice it to say here that out of the many oral and written records of Jesus' life, only these four were widely circulated and accepted among Christians. Likewise, several of Paul's "epistles" (formal, public letters) were circulated widely and preserved, and they, like the Gospels, eventually came to be regarded as divinely inspired Scripture. They include Galatians, First and Second Corinthians, Romans, First and Second Thessalonians, Ephesians, Colossians, Philemon, and Philippians.

Besides the four Gospels and the ten letters generally accepted as Paul's, thirteen other texts or "books" would join the Christian canon. Three (First and Second Timothy and Titus) are letters alleged to be by Paul; one (Hebrews) is a sermon in letter form once also thought to be Paul's; seven more are epistles allegedly composed by other apostles; one (Acts) is a historical work by the author of Luke; and the last is an apocalyptic book (Revelation) written by someone influenced by John.

All these texts became part of the Christian canon by their supposed apostolic origin and/or their use in Church liturgy. That these twenty-seven, and only these, made up the "New Testament" of specifically Christian Scripture was not formally decided by the Catholic Church before the sixteenth century, though for all practical purposes the canon was fixed by the fifth, and so it is common both to Catholics and Protestants.

Why Four Gospels?

The word "Gospel" is from the Old English for "good news," a translation of the Greek *euangelion,* after which the authors of our four Gospels are called "evangelists." Originally, "Gospel" simply referred to the teachings of Jesus; later it was applied to the four different narratives of those teachings; and even later (in the thirteenth century) it took on the figurative meaning, "an authoritative account."

But why do we need four records of one life and one body of teaching—the Gospel "according to" four different writers? The answer is that we don't, or wouldn't if one of the accounts were complete and truly authoritative. Each evangelist—called Matthew, Mark, Luke, and John—tells part, but not all, of the story. More important, each has a particular view of Jesus' mission and status, and each, writing for a different community, has his own agenda. No one should mistake any of the Gospels for "gospel truth," since each author chose to include and omit different sayings and stories, which themselves have no real claim to historical accuracy. Drawing from a body of oral traditions and written records, each evangelist put his own spin on the material, which sometimes required invention as well as transcription.

Most scholars agree that Mark's Gospel is the oldest. It was written after A.D. 60—that is, at least thirty years after Jesus' death (it is thus also later than Paul's epistles); the anonymous author is sometimes (but not plausibly) identified with a companion, also named Mark, of the apostle

Peter. The language and general outlook of this Gospel point to an author who lived outside Palestine and who wrote for Gentiles.

Mark's account, the rawest, most dramatic, and least kind to the disciples, would form the basis for two others—Matthew's and Luke's. These three Gospels are collectively known as the "Synoptic Gospels," after the title of a nineteenth-century text that printed them side by side for comparison. The best-known and most widely quoted Gospel of the three is Matthew's, which was always the Catholic Church's favorite because it is the only one to even mention a church [*see* THE KEYS OF THE KINGDOM, p. 209]. Because this Gospel is traditionally the most prominent (and is printed first in all Christian Bibles), I will cite from Matthew even when the same phrase appears in Mark and/or Luke.

Matthew's concern with Jewish law and his numerous "fulfillment citations" (references to passages in Hebrew Scripture that Christ "fulfills") make it likely that he himself was a Jewish Christian. His Gospel was probably written circa A.D. 90 in Syria; his sources included not only Mark but also, apparently, a collection of Jesus' sayings (also used by Luke) and another written account only he had access to. Though some of Matthew's sources were written in Hebrew or Aramaic, he, like all the evangelists, wrote in Greek.

More elegant than either Mark's or Matthew's Gospel is Luke's, which continues in The Acts of the Apostles. Luke, who probably wrote between A.D. 80 and 85, may or may not have been a companion of St. Paul (modern scholars doubt it). Luke is distinguished not only in style but in approach; he is socially concerned where Matthew is theologically oriented, and he seems less inclined than the other evangelists to believe that the End is at hand.

Separate from the Synoptic Gospels is the Gospel according to John, which represents an entirely different tradition. Though John is aware of many of the incidents related in the other Gospels, his Jesus is a different person altogether—a man who tells no parables and who makes few witty comebacks, but who delivers long discourses on his own divinity. John's Gospel, written late in the first century, is the most Greek, the least friendly to Judaism, and the most metaphysical [*see*, for example, THE WORD MADE FLESH, p. 253]. The author is almost certainly the John who wrote the three Epistles of John also included in the New Testament, but it is uncertain that he is also the John who wrote Revelation.

It is now clear that the four canonical Gospels were not the only four to be written, and that others—now lost or excluded from the Bible—circulated among the Christian communities of the Roman world. But by the early second century, church leaders had begun to regard Matthew, Mark, Luke, and John as the best and most authoritative records of Jesus' works and teaching. The New Testament canon as we know it took shape as a whole in the fourth century.

The Three Wise Men

Now when Jesus was born in Bethlehem of Judæa in the days of Herod the king, behold, there came wise men from the east to Jerusalem, | Saying, Where is he that is born King of the Jews? for we have seen his star in the east, and are come to worship him.

Matthew 2: 1–2

The birth of Jesus—thanks to Nativity plays, Christmas carols, and crèches—is one of the best-known biblical stories. As a star stood still over Bethlehem, three wise kings and various shepherds gathered around a humble manger to behold in awe the newborn Jesus, the Christian Messiah.

The problem is that this story isn't in the Bible—at least, not in one place. Among authors of the Gospels, Matthew doesn't mention shepherds or a manger; Luke doesn't know about any wise men; and Mark and John ignore the Nativity altogether.

Furthermore, while Matthew's wise men or "magi" (*magoi* in Greek) do hail from the Orient, they're not kings—a misconception bred of Isaiah's prophecy that "the Gentiles shall come to thy [Jerusalem's] light, and kings to the brightness of thy rising" (60: 3). They are rather Gentile astrologers or magicians, whose quest for the "king of the Jews" prefigures the spread of Christianity to pagan nations.

Matthew doesn't even say there are three of these seekers—a popular assumption based only on the fact that they bore three precious gifts (gold, frankincense, and myrrh) to the cradle. Finally, in the Gospel the magi are anonymous; the traditional names Caspar, Balthasar, and Melchior are later inventions.

It turns out that, however learned they might be, these magi aren't all that wise. As they pass through Jerusalem, they unwittingly tip off Herod the Great—named king of the Jews by the Roman senate in 40 B.C.—that a potential competitor has recently been born. Herod doesn't much care if the child is the Messiah or not; he just knows that he'll be in for trouble if people start believing it. So he orders the "massacre of the innocents"—the brutal slaughter of all children two years and under in the neighborhood of Bethlehem, where the wise men had followed a bright star (perhaps the planet Jupiter) to find the infant king.

Matthew obviously has the story of Moses in mind, as Herod's jealousy and crimes directly recall those of Pharaoh in the book of Exodus [see A STRANGER IN A STRANGE LAND, p. 48]. To accentuate the parallel, Matthew has an angel warn Jesus' parents, Joseph and Mary, to flee with the child to Egypt until Herod should die, at which point they may return to Joseph's hometown of Nazareth. (Matthew doesn't explain what Joseph and Mary were doing in Bethlehem, but Jesus had to be born there because the prophets had said so.)

So while many innocent children die, Jesus, like Moses before him, escapes. And soon enough Herod does die—in 4 B.C., to be precise. So if we're to believe Matthew, that's the latest year Jesus could have been born, which means that our calendar is all out of whack.

Locusts and Wild Honey

> In those days came John the Baptist, preaching in the wilderness
> of Judæa, | And saying, Repent ye: for the kingdom of heaven is
> at hand. | For this is he that was spoken of by the prophet Esaias
> [Isaiah], saying, The voice of one crying in the wilderness,
> Prepare ye the way of the Lord, make his paths straight. | And
> the same John had his raiment of camel's hair, and a leathern
> girdle about his loins; and his meat was locusts and wild honey.
>
> Matthew 3: 1–4

According to Matthew, John the Baptist, a Jewish prophet, was no softie. Clad only in a camel hair coat and leather belt, he lived on "locusts and wild honey"—in other words, on whatever he found in the Judaean desert where he made his ministry. (Scholars claim locusts are an excellent source of protein. A peanut butter and locust sandwich is even better.)

If John wasn't much to look at, his preaching wasn't comforting, either. The gist was that God was preparing to establish his kingdom on earth, and it was going to be a dark day for sinful Jews. Among those who repented, though, John practiced "baptism" (thus his nickname), a ritual of purification by water.

John's antisocial life-style and rabble-rousing didn't endear him to Herod Antipas, son of Herod the Great. This Herod had John locked up and finally beheaded, but not before the Baptist had heralded and baptized one "mightier than I" (3: 11). If you believe Luke (1: 36), this mightier personage, namely Jesus, was actually John's relative. Others think Jesus was originally a follower of John, who may have been associated with the Essene sect of Judaism thought to have produced the Dead Sea Scrolls.

"O Generation of Vipers"
AND *The Pharisees*

But when he [John] saw many of the Pharisees and Sadducees come to his baptism, he said unto them, O generation of vipers, who hath warned you to flee from the wrath to come?

Matthew 3: 7

No sinner gets delicate treatment from John the Baptist, but in Matthew's account the prophet holds a particular grudge against two errant Judaic sects: the Pharisees and Sadducees. You wouldn't know that these groups were nothing alike, and in fact hated each other, since John condemns them both as a "generation of vipers."

By "generation" John doesn't mean "age group," as we usually do; he means "brood" or "offspring"—in other words, "sons of vipers." What these people did to offend him is unclear, but obviously John considers them all pernicious hypocrites, pious in word but sinful in deed. (Jesus agreed—he quotes John's curse twice in Matthew's Gospel.)

John might have gone a little lighter on the Pharisees. A predominantly lay group, they promoted within Judaism such avant-garde ideas as resurrection after death, paving the way for Christianity. The Sadducees, on the other hand, were priestly, conservative, and given to strict interpretation of the Torah—so they were naturally opposed to the Pharisees, John himself, and ultimately Jesus, who was no fundamentalist. Whatever each group's sins in Matthew's eyes, it is the Pharisees who have come in for harsher treatment in English literature—their name is now practically synonymous with "hypocrites."

Blessed Are the Poor in Spirit

And seeing the multitudes, he went up into a mountain: and
when he was set, his disciples came unto him: | And he opened
his mouth, and taught them, saying,| Blessed are the poor in
spirit: for theirs is the kingdom of heaven. | Blessed are they that
mourn: for they shall be comforted. | Blessed are the meek, for
they shall inherit the earth. | Blessed are they which do hunger
and thirst after righteousness: for they shall be filled. | Blessed are
the merciful: for they shall obtain mercy. | Blessed are the pure in
heart, for they shall see God. | Blessed are the peacemakers: for
they shall be called the children of God. | Blessed are they which
are persecuted for righteousness' sake: for theirs is the kingdom
of heaven. | Blessed are ye, when men shall revile you, and
persecute you, and shall say all manner of evil against you falsely,
for my sake. | Rejoice, and be exceeding glad: for great is your
reward in heaven: for so persecuted they the prophets which were
before you.

Matthew 5: 1–12

The Sermon on the Mount is Jesus' most famous continuous
speech, and it begins with the first of nine "beatitudes"—statements in the form "Blessed are …": "Blessed are the poor in
spirit."

Unfortunately, it is doubtful Jesus ever gave the speech as
Matthew records it, and if he did we don't know what mount he
did it on—the location is given only as somewhere in Galilee.
Since in the Gospel according to Luke Jesus gives a similar but
much shorter speech on a plain, Matthew's mount is most likely
only a literary device, used to recall other important biblical rev-
elations from mountaintops, particularly those involving Moses
[see THE BURNING BUSH, p. 50; and THE TEN COMMANDMENTS,
p. 64]. It is Matthew's practice to take various sayings of Jesus,

more scattered in the other Gospels, and to gather them into discourses. Mark and Luke probably come closer to historical truth by depicting Jesus as characteristically speaking in brief aphorisms and parables.

Nonetheless, Jesus probably did say something like "Blessed are the poor in spirit," etc., if not in the form or at the venue of Matthew's presentation. Using the beatitude form found in various books of the Hebrew Bible, he sets forth a radical view, namely that God loves the humble and despised, the pure at heart and the truly righteous. Such views irked the religious and secular leaders of Jesus' day, who naturally didn't like to think that the rabble had anything on them.

In Luke's Gospel Jesus goes even further, saying "Blessed be ye poor" (Luke 6: 20), rather than "poor in spirit." And while Luke quotes only four beatitudes (where Matthew has nine), he fills out the passage with four corresponding "woes"—for example, "woe unto you that are rich! for ye have received your consolation" (6: 24). Luke and Matthew probably had the same collection of Jesus' sayings in front of them as they wrote, but each put a different spin on them. Matthew, by adding beatitudes and such qualifiers as "in spirit," probably gives us a more spiritual Jesus than Jesus.

The Salt of the Earth

Ye are the salt of the earth: but if the salt have lost his savour,
wherewith shall it be salted? it is thenceforth good for nothing,
but to be cast out, and to be trodden under foot of men.

Matthew 5: 13

The preservative quality of salt is still one of its chief virtues.
And to those attending Jesus' Sermon on the Mount, who
lacked refrigerators, salt was an even more admired mineral, especially since hypertension seems to have been rare in biblical
times. "Can that which is unsavoury be eaten without salt?"
asks Job (Job 6: 6). Salt was necessary, but also thought quite
tasty; so it was a sad day when one's salt lost its savor, as in its
impure form it was apt to do.

Thus when Jesus calls the poor in spirit, the meek and mild,
the peacemakers and the persecuted the "salt of the earth," this
is high praise indeed: the pure in heart preserve the world. But
no man or woman is so pure that he or she is not, like salt,
touched with impurities and thus subject to the corruptions of
time. So faith and vigilance are still necessary, lest the salt of the
earth lose its worth.

"Salt" in the sense of "flavor" and "vigor" appears in numerous English expressions. Shakespeare's "salt of youth" is self-explanatory, and we still use "salty" to mean "a bit *too* savory" (like
some jokes).

A City on a Hill

Ye are the light of the world. A city that is set on an hill cannot be hid. I Neither do men light a candle, and put it under a bushel, but on a candlestick; and it giveth light unto all that are in the house. I Let your light so shine before men, that they may see your good works, and glorify your Father which is in heaven.

Matthew 5: 14–16

The poor in spirit, says Jesus, aren't just the salt of the earth; they're also like a "city that is set on a hill" and like a great candle visible far and wide. Their righteousness, in other words, is a beacon to the sinful world.

But according to Jesus, a city on a hill "cannot be hid," while a candle can. So can the blessed hide their blessedness from the world, or not? Jesus seems to think so, or that one could try (thus the proverb, "to hide one's candle [*or* light] under a bushel")—but then this makes nonsense of the city metaphor.

Whatever the logic, Jesus likely has no particular city in mind, though those familiar with Isaiah would think of Jerusalem [*see* TO BEAT SWORDS INTO PLOWSHARES, p. 137]. This hasn't prevented Americans from assuming Jesus was speaking prophetically about them. Upon the founding of the Massachusetts Bay Colony in 1630, Governor John Winthrop predicted that his pious community would "be a city upon a hill" and noted that the "eyes of all people are upon us." Winthrop was a theocrat, not a democrat, but when President Ronald Reagan used the phrase, he meant that the United States had a missionary duty to shine its democractic principles far and wide. And to those who refused to see it, the light had to be carried—by men in uniform, if necessary.

Jot or Tittle

> Think not that I am come to destroy the law, or the prophets: I am not come to destroy, but to fulfil. | For verily I say unto you, Till heaven and earth pass, one jot or one tittle shall in no wise pass from the law, till all be fulfilled.
>
> Matthew 5: 17–18

Those who are surprised to find "jot or tittle" in the Bible will be even more surprised to know the Scriptures are full of jots and tittles.

For those who think he's a radical, Jesus wants to make it perfectly clear exactly what kind of radical he is. The self-important Pharisees and Sadducees must have been spreading the word that he had come "to destroy the law, [and] the prophets"—namely, the Hebrew Scriptures on which they based their practices.

Not so, Jesus says. He doesn't want to destroy Scripture but "fulfil" it. He will do this by going beyond the letter of the Law and perfecting a new understanding of Scripture based on the inner principle of love. Thus he preaches a better "righteousness" than that based on slavish obedience to the Torah, which to his mind doesn't go far enough in some respects. Nonetheless, he wouldn't change "one jot or one tittle" of it, at least until "heaven and earth pass"—a day most early Christians, if not Christ himself, thought was soon at hand.

By "jot" and "tittle," Jesus is referring to the literal letters of the Law. "Jot" is an Englishing of the Greek *iota* (ι), which is equivalent to *yodh* (*y* or *i*), the tiniest consonant in late Hebrew script. "Tittle" (Greek *keraia*, "little horn") is more obscure, but it probably refers to the tiny curls added to Hebrew consonants.

Both words effectively mean "the least mark" or "the most precise point."

"Tittle" is actually the older word, dating to Wyclif's 1382 translation, which reads "oon *i* or titil" (*i* representing *iota*). "Jot" first shows up as "iott" in Tyndale's 1526 rendering, and outside such phrases "jot or tittle" and "not a jot" it's obsolete as a noun (even the Greek "iota" is more common than the English "jot"). The noun "jot" did however give way, in the early eighteenth century, to a verb that is very much alive, and which originally meant "to make small marks with a pen or pencil."

To Turn the Other Cheek

Ye have heard that it hath been said, An eye for an eye, and a tooth for a tooth: | But I say unto you, That ye resist not evil: but whosoever shall smite thee on thy right cheek, turn to him the other also.

Matthew 5: 38–39

After protesting otherwise, Jesus proceeds to rearrange lots of jots and tittles in the Hebrew Torah. Here he takes particular issue with a passage found in Exodus (21: 24) and Leviticus (24: 20): "eye for eye, tooth for tooth" [*see* p. 69].

This is where the novelty of Jesus' message is most clear. Where the law mandates retribution in kind for various evils, Jesus urges his audience to "resist not evil" (that is, not to fight back against wrongs). Rather, they should turn their left cheek to he who smites the right, or, as we paraphrase it, "turn the other cheek." Two wrongs don't make a right, and righteousness demands that you "Love your enemies" (Matthew 5: 44).

Though Jesus takes it to a new level, the mandate to "Love thy neighbor" is already found in Leviticus [*see* p. 77]. And in Lamentations, attributed to Jeremiah, we learn that it is "good for a man" to "giveth his cheek to him that smiteth him" (3: 30)—though such humility is good only because some day the LORD will take care of the smiter.

The exact words "turn the other cheek" aren't found anywhere in the Gospels (Luke gives "offer also the other" at 6: 29). That form of Jesus' advice is first found in Oliver Wendell Holmes's poem *Astræa* (1850): "Wisdom has taught us to be calm and meek, / To take one blow, and turn the other cheek." Such wisdom is usually in short supply.

"Let Not Thy Left Hand Know What Thy Right Hand Doeth"

Therefore when thou doest thine alms, do not sound a trumpet before thee, as the hypocrites do in the synagogues and in the streets, that they may have glory of men. Verily I say unto you, They have their reward. | But when thou doest alms, let not thy left hand know what thy right hand doeth: | That thy alms may be in secret: and thy Father which seeth in secret himself shall reward thee openly.

Matthew 6: 2–4

We take "his left hand doesn't know what his right is doing" as a description of confused or hypocritical behavior. But Jesus means nothing of the kind; he advises us to *deliberately* keep our left hand ignorant of our right hand's actions.

This is because by "left hand" he means something like "ego" or "public persona" and by "right hand" "private charitable instincts." Put plainly, you shouldn't advertise your own good deeds, because this shows too much desire for earthly glory. If you give alms only in order to be thought good and holy, then your motives aren't really charitable. God can discern true righteousness, and one day he will reward openly good deeds done quietly today.

Unfortunately, Jesus' true meaning has been largely forgotten. And so the corrupt protagonist in Christopher Isherwood's *Mr. Norris Changes Trains* (1935) introduces Herr Schmidt as "my secretary and my right hand," and then titters nervously that "in this case ... I can assure you that the right hand knows perfectly well what the left hand doeth." Too bad that, for the sake of a pun, he got the phrase backwards.

Daily Bread

After this manner therefore pray ye: Our Father which art in heaven, Hallowed be thy name. | Thy kingdom come. Thy will be done in earth, as it is in heaven. | Give us this day our daily bread. | And forgive us our debts, as we forgive our debtors. | And lead us not into temptation, but deliver us from evil: [For thine is the kingdom, and the power, and the glory, for ever. Amen.]

Matthew 6: 9–13

Every Christian has had the "Lord's Prayer" (or "Our Father") drilled into him or her, to the point that reciting it is only rarely better than rote. (Do you think about what "hallowed" means as you say it?) But Jesus, if anyone, disapproves of rote rituals: a loving heart is worth infinitely more to him than empty recitations or fulfillments of the Law. So it's doubtful he intended his prayer—which he merely offers as a good example—to become the formula it has, its words and ideas taken for granted.

One phrase taken for granted is "our daily bread." It sounds obvious enough, but the phrase translates an obscure bit of Greek that might actually mean "our bread for the morrow." To ask God for such "bread" is perhaps to anticipate that "morrow" when his kingdom will come (verse 10). Since nobody's going to need real bread then, the petition might be an apocalyptic metaphor meaning "care for us at the end of the world."

In either case, the simpler meaning has been preferred in common usage, where "daily bread" has come to mean "a day's basic provision," namely one's paycheck. W. N. P. Barbellion, in a characteristic turn of the phrase, remarks that Samuel Johnson's friend Oliver Goldsmith "might have been a naturalist had the opportunity presented itself. But it was his lot to earn his daily bread by scribbling catchpenny compilations for the book-sellers" (*Enjoying Life,* 1919).

There are a few other ambiguous passages in the Lord's Prayer worthy of remark. Where Matthew gives the phrase "forgive us our debts," Luke gives "forgive us our sins" (Luke 11: 4), and it's unclear which, if either, is more authentic; Luke may use "sins" because it would have made more sense to his Gentile audience. To further complicate the issue, Catholics and many Protestant denominations substitute "trespasses" for Matthew's "debts"; and it was the form "trespasses" that was used in American public schools.

Also obscure is Matthew's last verse (verse 13). Some scholars think "deliver us from evil" really means "save us from the evil one," which might amount to the same thing if "evil one" merely means "bad people." But given the apocalyptic undertones of the prayer as a whole, it might very well mean Satan [*see* p. 112], God's final adversary.

As for the second half of the verse, beginning "For thine is the kingdom," many doubt Matthew actually wrote it, since it doesn't appear in the best manuscripts. Saint Jerome omitted it in his Vulgate Bible, the basis for all Catholic Bibles, but Protestants, including the King James translators, include the tag, which is technically known as a "doxology" and which very likely dates to near the time Matthew's Gospel was written. Even if Jesus had wanted us to repeat his prayer exactly, we can't be sure our translations, let alone the Greek original, are correct.

Mammon

No man can serve two masters: for either he will hate the one,
and love the other; or else he will hold to the one, and despise
the other. Ye cannot serve God and mammon.

Matthew 6: 24

Translator William Tyndale has already demoted an evil demon
(Azazel) to a common noun ("scapegoat"). Here he has decided
to leave well enough alone, leaving the obscure term "mammon" untranslated. (The King James Version follows suit.)

But some imagine that mammon—from the common Aramaic noun *mamona* ("riches")—is actually the name of an evil
demon. Though it's true Jesus' parallelism—"Ye cannot serve
God and mammon"—implies that mammon is some sort of
personage, what Jesus really means is that "God cannot be your
master if you make an idol of money."

Though medieval writers beat him to the punch, John Milton is most responsible for the current notion that mammon is
a devil. His Mammon appears in *Paradise Lost* (1667) as one of
Satan's lackeys, who more admired the "trodd'n Gold" of
Heaven's pavement than anything "divine or holy" (Book I).
Even when mammon isn't personified today, there's always the
suggestion that wealth has become the object of an unseemly,
if not idolatrous, regard. Reporter John Carlin of the *London
Independent*, filing a story in March 1993 on the Miss World
contest in Bophuthatswana, South Africa, noted the ostenta-
tion of the surroundings thus: "The venue is the Superbowl
amphitheatre at Sun City, a casino resort carved out of the
bush, a glittering shrine to Mammon set in a sea of dusty desolation."

"Judge Not, That Ye Be Not Judged"

Judge not, that ye be not judged. | For with what judgment ye judge, ye shall be judged: and with what measure ye mete, it shall be measured to you again.

Matthew 7: 1–2

Jesus' words here are quite familiar, but also ambiguous. Who is going to judge you if you judge others? Is it God who will hold you to the standards you use to "judge" others, or is it other men who will be waiting for you to slip up?

Perhaps Jesus has in mind something less sweeping than either interpretation. Elsewhere he indicates his disapproval of taking private disputes before public courts; if you cannot "turn the other cheek" when someone wrongs you [see p. 176], then at least you should "tell him his fault between thee and him alone" (Matthew 18: 15). The apostle Paul, likewise, wonders if any true Christian would dare take a dispute "to the law before the unjust, and not before the saints" (I Corinthians 6: 1).

In other words, Jesus is probably saying that there is nothing necessarily "just" about the judgment of men, and that God will see to sinners in the end. So it's a mistake to take your case to court, where you will find yourself at the mercy of the same distorted "judgment" to which you hope to subject your adversary.

Nonetheless, Matthew, as is his wont, gives Jesus' words a broader and more spiritual application. The passage does seem to imply that God will take care of *you* if you run around condemning others' behavior, though it unfortunately also implies that God is ready to hold you to the same bad standards you apply to others.

In the same vein, verse 2 continues by promising that "with what measure ye mete, it shall be measured to you again," a biblical way of saying "what goes around comes around." Scholars consider this verse more benign than the first, but it doesn't seem obvious to me, nor did it to Shakespeare. The title of his tragicomedy *Measure for Measure* (1604) is principally targeted at the corrupt official Angelo, whose harsh judgment of others rightly brings the same upon his own head.

Luke's version of verse 1—"Judge not, and ye shall not be judged" (6: 37)—is actually closer to our usual quotation than Matthew's, though we now substitute "you" for "ye." On the other hand, it doesn't provide much more substantiation for modern usage, which is principally as a warning to those who would hold their fellow men to too strict an account.

A Mote in the Eye

And why beholdest thou the mote that is in thy brother's eye,
but considerest not the beam that is in thine own eye? | Or how
wilt thou say to thy brother, Let me pull out the mote out of
thine eye; and, behold, a beam is in thine own eye? | Thou
hypocrite, first cast the beam out of thine own eye; and then
shalt thou see clearly to cast out the mote out of thy brother's
eye.

Matthew 7: 3–5

Despite the strange language and redundant text, Jesus makes a
fairly simple point: stop complaining about other people's problems when your own are worse. This continues the idea of the
previous verses—"Judge not, that ye be not judged"—and it's a
point he drive home again and again.

Jesus' metaphor, though, soon gets out of hand. The "mote
[speck of dust] that is in thy brother's eye" is a figurative way of
saying "your neighbor's small imperfections." But when Jesus
completes the metaphor with the hyperbolic "beam," the mind
begins to boggle. Pulling a beam out of your eye, let alone getting one in, is dubious—the pain would be pretty intense.

That's probably why "a mote in the eye"—meaning "trifling
fault"—is better known than its companion, "a beam in one's
own eye." The former is actually one of the oldest biblical allusions in English, dating to a translation of this passage circa
1000. It is now usually used trivially, to score obvious points, as
in this passage from L. Susan Stebbing's *Thinking to Some Purpose* (1939): "We are all of us prejudiced about something or
other. Whilst we can see the mote in our neighbor's eye it is often difficult to discover the beam in our own."

Pearls before Swine

> Give not that which is holy unto the dogs, neither cast ye pearls before swine, lest they trample them under their feet, and turn again and rend you.
>
> Matthew 7: 6

This verse from the Sermon on the Mount pretty much stands on its own, with no obvious connection to either the preceding or succeeding verses. But the context does matter; otherwise these lines are liable to seem rather elitist.

If you haven't been following the sermon, you might naturally think that by "dogs" and "swine" Jesus means the uncomprehending masses. But such an attitude would align him with the hated Pharisees and Sadducees, who arrogantly thought themselves very holy, so he must mean something else.

Elsewhere Jesus uses "dogs" to refer to the Gentiles (Matthew 15: 26), so perhaps he's counseling his Jewish followers not to cast the "pearls" of his Gospel before swinish pagans, who would only "trample" on them and then attack ("rend") the messengers. More likely is that the "swine" he means are the very scribes and Pharisees who so disdain his own followers. In other words, those who fancy themselves "holy" will trample on that which is truly holy, namely the Gospel of humility and love.

When we use the phrase today, however, the "swine" are more likely lowbrow philistines than self-styled guardians of holiness. It has become the equivalent of another famous phrase, Hamlet's "caviar to the general" (*Hamlet*, 1601), which is full of contempt for the vulgar multitude.

Brush Up Your Bible

Seek, and Ye Shall Find

Ask, and it shall be given you; seek, and ye shall find; knock, and it shall be opened unto you: | For every one that asketh receiveth; and he that seeketh findeth; and to him that knocketh it shall be opened.

Matthew 7: 7–8

As an inspirational verse Jesus' "Seek, and ye shall find" has fared rather well over the centuries. But the phrase is often misapplied to short-term seeking, meaning something like "you'll get what you want if you go for it."

Jesus isn't really talking about what you're going to find in this lifetime. By "seeking," "knocking," and "asking," he's referring to prayer, and its rewards aren't guaranteed until Judgment Day, when God's kingdom has come. According to Jesus' philosophy, it's a sure bet that if you seek earthly profit, you're not likely to find yourself in comfortable circumstances when the End has come.

The point is all the clearer for appearing a mere handful of verses after Jesus' admonition to "Judge not, that ye be not judged." In God's coming kingdom, men and women shall be punished or rewarded both according to their private attitudes and prayers and according to how they have treated others in life. So be sure to "do unto others" [see THE GOLDEN RULE, p. 328].

The Straight and Narrow Path

Enter ye at the strait gate: for wide is the gate, and broad is the way, that leadeth to destruction, and many there be which go in thereat: | Because strait is the gate, and narrow is the way, which leadeth unto life, and few there be that find it.

Matthew 7: 13–14

You may know what a "straight and narrow path" is, but few know that the phrase distorts this passage from the Sermon on the Mount. As you can see from Jesus' comparison of "wide" and "broad" with "strait" and "narrow," each pair of words is a pair of synonyms. "Strait" does not mean "straight" but rather "tight, constricted, narrow." These days, we use "strait" only as a noun—as in the "Bering Strait" or "desperate straits."

The transition from "strait and narrow" to "straight and narrow" seems to have begun earlier in this century but to have proceeded haltingly. Theodore Dreiser, for example, uses "the straight and narrow path" in his 1912 novel *The Financier*, while in a later work on Mark Twain, Van Wyck Brooks speaks ironically of "the strait and narrow path to success."

The confusion of "strait" with "straight," even apart from resemblance in sound, is understandable. We naturally associate moral strength with "straightness," resolve, and an unswerving course through life. The "straight" person navigates a straight path to salvation. But in substituting straightness of course for difficulty of access, we inject more moralism into the phrase than Christ put there. We have also, in turn, rendered the phrase more subject to mockery: someone who steers a straight and narrow course is not, these days, universally admired.

Wolves in Sheep's Clothing

Beware of false prophets, which come to you in sheep's clothing,
but inwardly they are ravening wolves.

Matthew 7: 15

Several of Jesus' most famous sayings are in fact quotations of
Hebrew Scriptures [*see* LOVE THY NEIGHBOR, p. 77]. And he had
other sources, too, including Greek literature, with which he
must have been at least passingly familiar.

While "Beware of false prophets" is entirely his, he borrowed
the rest of this verse from Aesop (sixth century B.C.). In the
fabulist's charming tale, a wolf with designs on a flock dons a
sheepskin in order to fool the watchful shepherd. Unfortunately
for the wolf, when master comes to fetch some mutton for dinner, it's the interloper he puts to the blade.

The surprise ending is largely forgotten today, but Jesus (or at
least Matthew, the only evangelist to report the saying) probably
expected his audience to know it. Whoever the "false prophets"
are—perhaps rabble-rousing rivals in Jesus' time, or charismatic
sectarians in the days of the early church—they may prey for a
while on the gullible, but in the end God will "have them for
dinner," so to speak. Even now their "disguise" as prophets is
ineffectual, for "by their fruits"—their evil deeds, rather than
their "holy" words—"ye shall know them" (verse 16).

This last line is quotable in its own right. Lexicographer and
essayist Logan Pearsall Smith, a Philadelphian, reports in
Unforgotten Years (1938) the claim of an Italian friend that
America was "rapidly becoming ... the [world's] center of scholarship and thought. I should like to believe this," he continues,

"but there is a saying in the Bible, 'By their fruits ye shall know them,' which tends to make me hesitate."

As if in reply, the cousins Frederic Dannay and Manfred B. Lee (a.k.a. Ellery Queen, a.k.a. Barnaby Ross) wrote in *The Tragedy of Z* (1933) of perusing popular American magazines and finding "especially interesting those samples of American enterprise and development which stared at me from the pages of the advertising section. By their ads shall ye know them!" (chapter 4). It would be safe to say that little has changed in 60 years.

Let the Dead Bury Their Dead

And a certain scribe came, and said unto him [Jesus], Master, I
will follow thee whithersoever thou goest. | And Jesus saith unto
him, "The foxes have holes, and the birds of the air have nests;
but the son of man hath not where to lay his head. | And another
of his disciples said unto him, Lord, suffer me first to go and
bury my father. | But Jesus said unto him, Follow me; and let the
dead bury their dead.

Matthew 8: 19–22

Jesus would like prospective disciples to know that the missionary life is no picnic. The lodgings won't be cozy, and the pace is liable to be hectic. To one who would follow him, but who wants to bury his father first, Christ replies: "Follow me; and let the dead bury their dead."

The saying is rather mysterious, but what Jesus must mean is something like, "If you want to follow me, then you must be willing to give up family obligations and conventional practices." By "the dead" Jesus may mean those who refuse his invitation to a new kind of life—however uncomfortable and antisocial, a life that is truly righteous.

Today we frequently substitute "the" for "their" and mean something more like "Let bygones be bygones" or "Let's forget the past and move on." Aldous Huxley applied the phrase in this sense to his own writing: "They're irrelevant, one's old books—irrelevant because they're written by someone who has ceased to exist. Let the dead bury their dead. The only book that counts is the one one's writing at the moment" (*Those Barren Leaves*, 1925). True, but depressing.

O Ye of Little Faith

> And when he [Jesus] was entered into a ship, his disciples
> followed him. | And, behold, there arose a great tempest in the
> sea, insomuch that the ship was covered with the waves: but he
> was asleep. | And his disciples came to him, and awoke him,
> saying, Lord, save us: we perish. | And he said unto them, Why
> are ye fearful, O ye of little faith? Then he arose, and rebuke the
> winds and the sea; and there was a great calm.
>
> Matthew 8: 23–26

There are passages in all the Gospels—especially Mark's—that
make you wonder who Jesus' disciples thought they were dealing with. They do call him "Lord" (*kyrios* in Greek), but they
mean "Sir" or "Master," not "God." By and large they seem to
think Jesus merely a great prophet, and they are amazed anew
each time Jesus performs a miracle. At the end of the passage
cited here, they marvel, "What manner of man is that, that even
the winds and the sea obey him!" (verse 27).

Not that Jesus himself isn't a little coy; after all, he never actually claims to be God, or even the Messiah. Nonetheless, he rou-
tinely performs miracles, and though the Gospels suggest there
were other miracle-workers about, Jesus' work is clearly superior. So when the disciples' ship is threatened by an earthquake
and tempest, they expect him to do something about it.

Which is why the outcome is so confusing. If they expected
him to save them, why are they so surprised when he does? And
why does Jesus famously accuse them—"O ye of little faith"—
when they come running to him?

Maybe he's just angry at losing his beauty rest, but there's a
likelier answer. Matthew borrowed this whole incident from

Mark's Gospel (4: 35–41), where the disciples wake Jesus up only to ask whether he cares if they all die. Matthew generally makes the disciples more savvy than they are in Mark, but not savvy enough to let Jesus sleep.

Jesus doesn't mean that his mere presence on the ship is enough to save it, though that seems the obvious implication. Rather, he rebukes his disciples for worrying at all about when and how they're going to die. The problem isn't their lack of faith in him, but their lack of faith in their creator. This sense is clearer in Mark's version, where Jesus' divinity is more open to question.

In any case, the disciples shouldn't take Jesus' rebuke too personally—"O ye of little faith" is one of his favorite lines (see, for example, Matthew 6: 30 and 14: 31). In each case, however, he speaks solemnly, while modern quotation is often in the vein of mock-bravado.

New Wine in Old Bottles

> No man putteth a piece of new cloth unto an old garment, for that which is put in to fill it up taketh from the garment, and the rent is made worse. | Neither do men put new wine into old bottles: else the bottles break, and the wine runneth out, and the bottles perish: but they put new wine into new bottles, and both are preserved.
>
> Matthew 9: 16–17

"Old wine in new bottles" is now so familiar that many believe that's the line found in the Bible, when Jesus actually says the inverse: "new wine into old bottles." He's responding to a challenge by one of John the Baptist's disciples: "Why do we and the Pharisees fast oft, but thy disciples fast not?" Jesus' answer is that fasting and other traditional rites are like "old bottles" unsuited to the "new wine" of his radical new teaching.

Actually, what Jesus says in Greek is "old wineskins," which would have grown too worn and fragile to hold new wine as it continued to ferment. (By and large, old bottles are equivalent to new ones.) This is a better metaphor than the patch, where the point seems to be that if you sew a piece of new cloth onto an old garment, it will shrink in the washing and thus create new tears along the seam. Surely Jesus expected his teachings to ferment, not to shrink.

Until very recently, the original phrase—"to put new wine into old bottles"—held the day. It meant "to cloak what is new and potentially threatening in the comfortable guise of more of the same." But in this age of style over substance, the misquote is handier; people are now more apt to try serving tired ideas in attractive new packages.

To Shake the Dust Off Your Feet

And when ye come into an house, salute it. | And if the house be
worthy, let your peace come upon it: but if it be not worthy, let
your peace return to you. | And whosoever shall not receive you,
nor hear your words, when ye depart out of that house or city,
shake off the dust of your feet.

Matthew 10: 12–14

If you thought "shaking the dust off your feet" was something
you did on the doormat, think again. As Jesus advises his
apostles, it's what they should do, as they spread the Gospel
among the Jews, if they find an unhospitable welcome. When
they *leave* such a house they should "shake off the dust of your
feet," if just to make the point that they'll have nothing more to
do with it.

What the phrase really means, therefore, is "clear out of a bad
situation, leaving every trace of it behind"—and good riddance.
[*Compare* TO WASH ONE'S HANDS, p. 235.] It's a saying I'd rec-
ommend to anyone deserting an abusive landlord's apartment
or quitting graduate school. Even Hitler found it handy, as if to
prove that quoting the Bible says nothing about your character.
"I found myself," he writes in *Mein Kampf* (1924), "in the same
situation as all those emigrants who shake the dust of Europe
from their feet, with the cast-iron determination to lay the
foundations of a new existence in the New World and acquire
for themselves a new home." If he'd actually done so, things
might have worked out better for all concerned.

Judgment Day

> Verily I say unto you, It shall be more tolerable for the land of
> Sodom and Gomorrah in the day of judgment, than for that city.

Matthew 10: 15

"Day of judgment," from Wyclif's 1382 translation of this verse, is the closest the Bible comes to the now more familiar "Judgment Day." ("The Last Judgment," coined by 1340, is nowhere to be found.) Though Jesus has earlier alluded to such a reckoning [*see* "JUDGE NOT, THAT YE BE NOT JUDGED," p. 181], this is the first time he names a particular day when God shall mete out ultimate justice.

The context is his instructions to the disciples, who are charged with spreading the Gospel among the Jews, and whom, incidentally, he has granted the power to "Heal the sick, cleanse the lepers, raise the dead, cast out devils," etc. (10: 8). For those who refuse to believe, the fate of Sodom and Gomorrah [*see* p. 37] will seem enviable when God's kingdom has come and we are all arraigned in the heavenly court. The angry God has not been left behind in the Old Testament.

"Day of judgment" is synonymous with "day of doom," a phrase Wyclif would use in the next chapter (11: 22). Only in the seventeenth century did "doom," originally meaning "decree" or "judgment," begin taking on the principal meaning "unpleasant end." Wyclif, however, coined neither "day of doom" nor "doomsday," which trace back to the fourteenth and tenth centuries, respectively.

A Sparrow Shall Not Fall ... AND
The Hairs of Your Head Are All Numbered

And fear not them which kill the body, but are not able to kill the soul: but rather fear him which is able to destroy both soul and body in hell. | Are not two sparrows sold for a farthing? and one of them shall not fall on the ground without your Father. | But the very hairs of your head are all numbered. | Fear ye not, therefore, ye are of more value than many sparrows.

Matthew 10: 28–31

After the incident on the boat [*see* O YE OF LITTLE FAITH, p. 190], Jesus can't be all that confident in his disciples' staying power. So here he offers them a little reassurance: though men will scourge you, and interrogate you, and hate you, and persecute you, and even try to kill you, have no fear. It's your soul, and not your body, you should worry about, so if you fear anybody, fear God—"him which is able to destroy both soul and body in hell" (*Gehenna* in Greek).

In case this doesn't make the disciples feel better, Jesus uses an analogy to clarify God's investment. You can buy two sparrows at the local market for a farthing (less than a penny), but not one sparrow dies without God's leave. And since a human life is infinitely more valuable to its creator than a sparrow's, you can be sure that God is that much more concerned—in fact, he knows precisely how many hairs there are on every man's head. So you will only die if God really wants you to.

This is obviously a comforting notion, so comforting that it would finally enable the hero of Shakespeare's *Hamlet* (1601) to act. Preparing to fence with his nemesis Laertes, who might easily resort to foul play, Hamlet shrugs off his friend Horatio's worries by citing Matthew: "There is special providence in the fall of a sparrow. If it be now, 'tis not to come; if it be not to come, it will be now; if it be not now, yet it will come. The readiness is all" (Act 5, scene 2). "It," of course, is his own death, whose time does not matter; what does is being ready for it always. (On this last point, Hamlet alludes to Matthew 24: 44: "Therefore be ye also ready: for in such an hour as ye think not the Son of man cometh.") Shakespeare has helped keep the "sparrow" quote in circulation, but the slightly more ominous "the hairs of your head are all numbered" is less often heard these days.

A House Divided against Itself

> But when the Pharisees heard it [about an exorcism], they said,
> This fellow doth not cast out devils, but by Beelzebub the prince
> of the devils. | And Jesus knew their thoughts, and said unto
> them, Every kingdom divided against iteself is brought to
> desolation; and every city or house divided against itself shall not
> stand: | And if Satan cast out Satan, he is divided against himself;
> how shall then his kingdom stand?
>
> Matthew 12: 24–26

The Pharisees sure are stubborn. First off, they're constantly
grumbling about Jesus' transgressions of the Torah. And even
while Jesus continues performing miracles and "casting out devils" (exorcizing), they continue refusing him credit. "He casteth
out devils through the prince of devils," they cry at Matthew 9:
33. In other words, if Jesus has the power to exorcize, he must
be getting it from Satan—or, as they call him here, Beelzebub.

Jesus has to laugh at the logic of that one. If Satan wants his
"devils" to possess human beings, why in the world would Satan
help cast them out? Again he uses an analogy, comparing the
devils' kingdom to a household that cannot survive if at war
with itself. If Mom keeps writing checks, and Dad keeps cancel-
ing them, then Mom and Dad are ultimately headed for divorce. Just so, if devils possess people and then Satan casts them
out, he won't have much of a kingdom, at least on earth.

The analogy is well known in America because Abraham Lincoln quoted it in a speech in 1858, when he was running for the
U.S. Senate and the nation was on the verge of civil war. As he
correctly predicted, a union of slave states and free states could

not be sustained—the division was too fundamental and too explosive.

Since Lincoln's time, the phrase has shown up repeatedly in literature, most often with reference to real or supposed divisions within a nation. "What ignorance of the French temper it showed," wrote W. Somerset Maugham in *France at War* (1940), "when the Germans thought that in France they were fighting a house divided against itself!" He means that the country stood behind the French Resistance, though perhaps he's too quick to forgive collaboration.

Brush Up Your Bible

He That Is Not with Me Is against Me

But if I cast out devils by the Spirit of God, then the kingdom of God is come unto you. | Or else how can one enter into a strong man's house, and spoil his goods, except he first bind the strong man? and then he will spoil his house. | He that is not with me is against me; and he that gathereth not with me scattereth abroad.

Matthew 12: 28–30

Having rebuked the Pharisees for claiming that he casts out devils only with Satan's help, Jesus proposes the alternative: that he does so "by the Spirit of God." If this is so, the kingdom of God has begun to manifest itself on earth, in which case the Pharisees had better start looking to themselves.

With another "house" metaphor, Jesus insists that he's saving men through his exorcisms, overpowering Satan with the Spirit's help. To this he adds a warning: "He that is not with me is against me; and he that gathereth not with me scattereth abroad." The meaning of the first half is obvious and is reflected in modern citations of the phrase. The neglected second half is a little harder to grasp, but what Jesus may mean is that those who do not join him in "gathering" converts to the true Gospel are effectively "scattering" people from it, luring them to bad old ways. And so, ironically, it is the Pharisees and people like them who are doing Satan's work.

Sackcloth and Ashes

> Then began he to upbraid the cities wherein most of his mighty
> works were done, because they repented not: | Woe unto thee,
> Chorazin! woe unto thee, Bethsaida! for if the mighty works,
> which were done in you, had been done in Tyre and Sidon, they
> would have repented long ago in sackcloth and ashes.
>
> Matthew 11: 20–21

Wall Street helped heap ruin on the U.S. economic system by fostering "speculative mania," wrote Frederick Lewis Allen, even in 1933, after brokers "had supposedly been wearing the sackcloth and ashes of repentance" (*Since Yesterday,* 1940). "Eventually," predicts P. G. Wodehouse in *Uncle Fred in the Springtime* (1939), "after he has been running round in circles for some weeks, dashing into his tailors' from time to time for a new suit of sackcloth and ashes and losing pounds in weight through mental anguish, you will forgive him."

You get the general idea: to "wear" or "sit" in "sackcloth and ashes" is to repent abjectly for all the world to see; occasionally, it also means "to be stricken with grief." The practice of wearing "sackcloth" (coarse material, of goats' or camels' hair, used in making sacks) and having ashes sprinkled on one's head was an old Jewish custom, a sign of penitence or shame.

We hear of this ritual as early as II Samuel 3: 31, but the English phrase "sackcloth and ashes" was first rendered in 1526 as William Tyndale translated Matthew. It has often been quoted in literature, but more popular today is the expression "to put on a hair shirt," which is what sackcloth was; donning such garb became common among religious ascetics who wished to punish themselves in a slightly less public manner.

To Fall by the Wayside

And he [Jesus] spake many things unto them in parables, saying,
Behold, a sower went forth to sow; | And when he sowed, some
seeds fell by the way side, and the fowls came and devoured them
up: | Some fell upon stony places, where they had not much
earth: and forthwith they sprung up, because they had no
deepness of earth: | And when the sun was up, they were
scorched; and because they had no root, they withered away. |
And some fell among thorns; and the thorns sprung up, and
choked them: | But other fell into good ground and brought
forth fruit, some an hundredfold, some sixtyfold, some
thirtyfold. | Who hath ears to hear, let him hear.

Matthew 13: 3–9

The word "wayside"—meaning "the side of the way or road"—
dates in English to the fifteenth century, but Jesus coined the
familiar phrase "to fall by the wayside," first translated as such
by William Tyndale in 1526 (compare Luke 8: 5).

The phrase crops up in one of Jesus' parables about sowing,
which is actually a parable about parables. As a sower scatters his
seeds almost at random, so Jesus addresses parables to the
crowd. He compares each sort of listener to a type of ground—
hard and exposed like a "way side" (footpath); shallow like stony
ground; thorny like thistles; or fertile like good soil. His
parables are like seeds that grow according to the soil; that is, his
Gospel will profit only those who "have ears to hear."

Thus Jesus justifies speaking in riddles: it is not for the shallow masses that his message is intended; he will not reveal to just
anyone "the mysteries of the kingdom of heaven" (verse 11).
Only those already disposed to understand and accept those
mysteries are worthy to be healed and saved; it is they who will

grasp the true meaning of the parables and embrace the life they prescribe. Others are like the wayside upon which parables fall fruitlessly, only to be snatched up by "fowls" ("the wicked one," verse 19)—and they, too, will fall by the wayside in the final reckoning.

Today we use the phrase in the sense "to be left aside" or "to be ignored or forgotten," which isn't exactly what Jesus means. His "wayside" is a hard patch of ground that doesn't take up the seed, but leaves it exposed to predators: the seed may be ignored, but it isn't forgotten—his parables are turned into food for evil thought rather than good. But, as usual, the biblical context has fallen by the wayside in modern quotation.

Loaves and Fishes

And when it was evening, his disciples came to him [Jesus], saying, This is a desert place, and the time is now past; send the multitude away, that they may go into the villages, and buy themselves victuals. | But Jesus said unto them, They need not depart; give ye them to eat. | And they said unto him, we have here but five loaves, and two fishes. | He said, bring them hither to me.

Matthew 14: 15–18

This is one of Jesus' neatest and most famous tricks. Thinking the natives might be restless after sitting through a series of healings on an empty stomach, the disciples urge Jesus to send the crowd into town for dinner.

Jesus, more hospitably, suggests whipping up a little something for them on the spot. But the disciples have but five loaves of bread and two medium-size fishes, hardly a feast for a "multitude." (The crowd included some 5,000 men, plus women and children.)

Time for another miracle. Jesus takes the loaves and fishes

from his puzzled helpers and—anticipating the Last Supper [*see* TO BREAK BREAD, p. 230]—casts his eyes heavenward, blesses the food, and breaks the bread. Somehow, when the disciples distribute the charmed victuals, not only do they feed the entire assembly, but there are twelve baskets of leftover breadcrumbs.

Oddly, the phrase "loaves and fishes" has not had a happy career in quotation, as it often stands for "mere material gain or comfort," as opposed to spiritual reward. Sir John Arthur Thomson, for example, laments most people's attitude that science should serve above all to make life more comfortable: "When things [that is, practical considerations] get into the saddle and override ideas and ideals and all good feeling, when the multiplication of loaves and fishes becomes the only problem in the world, we know the results to be vicious" (*Introduction to Science,* 1911). On the other hand, starvation isn't much of an alternative.

To Walk on Water

And straightaway Jesus constrained his disciples to get into a ship, and to go before him unto the other side, while he sent the multitudes away. | And when he had sent the multitudes away, he went up into a mountain apart to pray: and when the evening was come, he was there alone. | But the ship was now in the midst of the sea, tossed with waves: for the wind was contrary. | And in the fourth watch of the night Jesus went unto them, walking on the sea. | And when the disciples saw him walking on the sea, they were troubled, saying, It is a spirit; and they cried out for fear.

Matthew 14: 22–26

When we say someone "can't walk on water," our implicit meaning is always, "after all, she (or he) isn't God," a reference to an incident that would seem to prove Jesus is.

Even after the sinking-ship episode [*see* O YE OF LITTLE FAITH, p. 190], and after Jesus has granted his disciples power to perform miracles, they don't seem to have any real idea who they're dealing with. So Jesus has to keep producing amazing feats to put the point across. In this case, he sends his disciples ahead to cross the Sea of Galilee in the traditional method—by boat. When Jesus joins them later after some solitary prayer, he reaches the boat by his own special method—walking on the water.

In the dark the disciples can't see who's coming, and they fear it's some evil spirit. Even when Jesus calls out to comfort them, they remain suspicious, so Peter answers back: "Lord, if it be thou, bid me come unto thee on the water" (verse 28). Jesus bids, and Peter hops in, but within a few minutes he begins to doubt he'll make it and so he begins sinking. Jesus has to pull

Peter's fat out of the water, so to speak, if only so he can lecture him: "O thou of little faith, wherefore didst thou doubt?" (verse 31).

But now the disciples doubt no more: "Of a truth," they proclaim, "thou art the Son of God" (verse 33). Notice that they don't actually call Jesus "God," and they never will, which has given rise to serious theological disputes. At the least they're ready to admit that Jesus is somebody pretty special, namely the Messiah.

Such is not the case in the oldest form of the tale, found in Mark's Gospel, where the disciples are more thickheaded and their "heart was hardened" (Mark 6: 52). John is entirely silent on the issue. These differences between the Gospels probably reflect disputes in the early church, in which Jesus may first have been seen only as a great prophet, then later as the Messiah, and finally as God. It is now believed, to take another example, that the resurrection story in Mark's Gospel was added later by another hand. Mark seems to have believed Jesus was the Messiah, but he certainly doesn't go as far as Matthew.

The Blind Leading the Blind

Then came his disciples, and said unto him, Knowest thou that the Pharisees were offended, after they heard this saying? | But he answered and said, Every plant, which my heavenly Father hath not planted, shall be rooted up. | Let them alone: they be blind leaders of the blind. And if the blind lead the blind, both shall fall into the ditch.

Matthew 15: 12–14

The Gospels would be a lot shorter if it weren't for people like the scribes and Pharisees. By constantly accusing Jesus of heresy, these self-important upholders of traditional Judaism provide continued opportunities for him to engage in lengthy discourses.

In this case, Jesus rebukes the Pharisees for insisting on various purity regulations while ignoring more essential laws, such as "Honour thy father and mother" (15: 4). The Pharisees take offense, but Jesus couldn't care less. As he tells his disciples, God will take care of them in the end, and for now you should ignore them: for they are "blind leaders of the blind," who lead themselves and their followers into moral ditches.

Ever since, "the blind leading the blind" has been used to scorn leaders as unenlightened as their followers, but who pretend to be smarter. In an unkind essay from early in this century, for example, J. C. Squire laments philistinism in the book trade thus: "If only … books were sold by men of taste, familiar with their contents, the public would buy more good literature: as things are, the blind bookseller leads the blind customer" ("A Horrible Bookseller").

Signs of the Times

The Pharisees also with the Sadducees came [to Magdala], and tempting desired him that he would shew them a sign from heaven. | He answered and said unto them, When it is evening, ye say, It will be fair weather: for the sky is red. | And in the morning, It will be foul weather to day: for the sky is red and lowring. O ye hypocrites, ye can discern the face of the sky; but can ye not discern the signs of the times?

Matthew 16: 1–3

Jesus' critics think they're pretty hot at reading some signs from heaven—those foretelling the weather. But they're awfully slow when it comes to the signs Jesus shows, day in and day out, that God's kingdom is at hand.

"Signs of the times" here means "indications that the Messiah has arrived and the End is near." The phrase is hardly so apocalyptic in modern quotation, since the issue is usually social progress or decline rather than articles of faith. Jesus looked ahead to a better future under God, but the signs we read as often as not bode ill. "One of the most disturbing signs of the times," observed the London *Spectator* (a bit belatedly) in February 1939, "is that the centre of Europe is now dominated by a powerful and highly intelligent Government." And that happened because most people ignored some evident early signs.

Younger readers are less apt to think of World War II than of Prince, the strange pop genius who has often turned to the Bible for inspiration—in this case for his album *Sign o' the Times* (1987) and the hit song of the same name. Among his other biblical titles are "The Cross," "Thieves in the Temple," "And God Created Woman," and "7," the last of which is based on Revelation.

The Keys of the Kingdom

He [Jesus] saith unto them, But whom say ye that I am? | And
Simon Peter answered and said, Thou art the Christ, the Son of
the living God. | And Jesus answered and said unto him, Blessed
art thou, Simon Bar-jona: for flesh and blood hath not revealed
it unto thee, but my Father which is in heaven. | And I say unto
thee, That thou art Peter, and upon this rock I will build my
church; and the gates of hell shall not prevail against it. | And I
will give unto thee the keys of the kingdom of heaven: and
whatsoever thou shalt bind on earth shall be bound in heaven:
and whatsoever thou shalt loose on earth shall be loosed in
heaven.

Matthew 16: 15–19

As far as the Catholic Church is concerned, this is perhaps the
most important passage in the entire New Testament. Not only
does Jesus finally acknowledge his true identity as "the Christ"
("the Annointed One" in Greek, meaning "the Messiah"); he
also renames the disciple Simon bar-Jona "Peter" (from the
Greek for "rock") and grants him the metaphorical "keys to the
kingdom of heaven." This is taken to mean that Peter will found
the true Church, and that his successors, the Catholic popes,
will have unique access to God in heaven.

This passage, however, is unique to Matthew, as is the only
other reference in the Gospels to a "church" (18: 17)—by which
Jesus seems to mean "community of the faithful." All the Evangelists assume Jesus is "the Christ," but nowhere else does he
himself sanction a church, let alone appoint Peter as its head,
with ultimate say over who would be admitted or expelled.
(Jesus will later, in chapter 18, transfer Peter's special powers to
all the disciples.)

In truth, it is more likely Matthew rather than Jesus who came up with the language of this passage; Matthew's gospel often takes pains to locate in Jesus' teaching the origins of the Christian community he was addressing. Ironically, this community or "church" was primarily Jewish, not Gentile.

As for the "keys to the kingdom of heaven," Jesus is perhaps alluding to the book of Isaiah: the prophet foresees that a certain Eliakim will receive the "key of the house of David" (22: 22), meaning the keys of the royal palace. Jesus grants Peter ultimate authority over the metaphorical palace of his church, which is what he means here by "the kingdom of heaven." Though God is king, Peter is his most trusted and most important servant, and God will respect Peter's decisions.

Since Peter's time, "the keys to the kingdom" has come to refer particularly to the power of the pope but also more generally to open access to any sort of privilege or treasure. In this latter sense the phrase often lends itself to ironic hyperbole. Of a character's inheritance and engagement, W. Somerset Maugham wrote: "Bertha had some sense of dramatic effect and looked forward a little to the scene when, the keys of her kingdom being handed to her, she had made the announcement that she had already chosen a king to rule by her side" (*Mrs. Craddock,* 1902).

To Take Up a Cross AND To Gain the Whole World but Lose Your Own Soul

Then Jesus said unto his disciples, If any man will come after me, let him deny himself, and take up his cross, and follow me. | For whosoever will save his life shall lose it: and whosoever will lose his life for my sake shall find it. | For what is a man profited, if he shall gain the whole world, and lose his own soul? or what shall a man give in exchange for his soul?

Matthew 16: 24–26

With a dramatic irony that would have been apparent to all Matthew's readers, Jesus tells his disciples that if they continue to follow him, they must be willing to deny themselves comfort and safety and to take up their crosses. He refers by metaphor to a common practice of the day, whereby criminals condemned to be crucified were also forced to carry their own crosses to the place of execution.

Today, "to take up one's cross" means only "to bear one's burden," a bizarre and watered-down version, since everyone knows what "cross" means in the New Testament. As John Ruskin noted in "The Mystery of Life and Its Arts," "we continually talk of taking up our cross, as if the only harm in a cross was the weight of it." Jesus goes out of his way to let the disciples know they might literally die like criminals. They must be willing to lose their lives, to risk persecution and even crucifixion in order to follow him on the path of righteousness. But if they are concerned with saving their own hides, then they are too timid to follow, lacking a deep enough belief in his identity and his message.

This is the meaning of Jesus' quotable paradox: "Whosoever will save his life shall lose it: and whosoever will lose his life for my sake shall find it" (an echo of Matthew 10: 39). On one level, "life" means mortal existence; but on a deeper level, "life" means salvation in the End when God's kingdom has come. This profound statement has served many purposes over the centuries, including a psychological one: only if you're willing to risk the comfort of a familiar old life can you discover a potentially richer new self.

And Jesus continues in this powerful vein, coming to perhaps the most famous line in the speech: "For what is a man profited, if he shall gain the whole world, and lose his own soul?" The message is essentially the same: concern with one's mortal comfort or material gain prevents accepting the Gospel's truth—that you must sacrifice everything to the will of God in order to be saved when "the Son of man shall come in the glory of his Father with his angels" and every man shall be rewarded "according to his works" (verse 27).

Jesus might have stopped there, but he goes on in the last verse of the chapter to make a rash prediction: that among his disciples, some "shall not taste of death, till they see the Son of man coming into his kingdom" (verse 28). This is clearly an apocalyptic prophesy, and one he will repeat later (23: 36 and 24: 34). The world did not, of course, come to an end within a generation, and later interpreters struggled to make this verse still somehow true—suggesting, for example, that Jesus is predicting the fall of Jerusalem in A.D. 70 rather than the End itself. Such arguments aren't very convincing.

A Millstone around Your Neck

> Whosoever therefore shall humble himself as this little child, the same is greatest in the kingdom of heaven. | And whoso shall receive one such little child in my name receiveth me. | But whoso shall offend one of these little ones which believe in me, it were better for him that a millstone were hanged about his neck, and that he were drowned in the depth of the sea.
>
> Matthew 18: 4–6

In answer to one of the disciples' queries—"Who is the greatest in the kindgom of heaven?"—Jesus presents a small child as your typical case. (Presumably they had meant "besides God," or else by "kingdom of heaven" they mean the Christian community.)

By doing so, Jesus is simply following up on his Sermon on the Mount [*see* BLESSED ARE THE POOR IN SPIRIT, p. 170], the gist of which his disciples seem to have forgotten. He who is least on earth shall be greatest in heaven, and they must "become as little children"—innocent, humble, and faithful—to "enter into the kingdom of heaven" at all (verse 3).

But he takes this point one step further. Each childlike believer is a representative of Jesus himself: accept him, and you accept Christ; reject him, and you're in for a heap of trouble on Judgment Day. In fact, it would be better for you to have a millstone tied around your neck and be tossed into the sea.

Matthew picks up this saying from Mark's Gospel (Mark 9: 42). By "millstone" Mark was referring to a large disk of basalt or some other heavy mineral. Such stones, used to grind or "mill" grains into meal, would have had the same effect as concrete boots.

Somehow this grim image has come to refer not to righteous punishment but to undeserved or excessive affliction. The phrase is virtually synonymous these days with "an albatross around the neck," that is, a burden you can't shake. The change seems to date to the nineteenth century, and a typical example of the new usage may be found in Rudyard Kipling's story "Kidnapped" (in *Plain Tales from the Hills,* 1888): "Peythroppe

was burningly anxious to put a millstone round his neck at the outset of his career; and argument had not the least effect on him. He was going to marry Miss Castries, and the business was his own business." Later, D. H. Lawrence would attempt to put the phrase to humorous use with reference to the Ten Commandments: "I believe the old Moses wouldn't have valued the famous tablets if they hadn't been ponderous, and millstones round everybody's neck" (*Letters,* 1932, reprinted in 1939 by the Albatross Press).

What God Hath Joined Together ...

The Pharisees also came unto him [Jesus], tempting him, and
saying unto him, Is it lawful for a man to put away his wife for
every cause? | And he answered and said unto them, Have ye not
read, that he which made them at the beginning made them
male and female, | And said, For this cause shall a man leave
father and mother, and shall cleave to his wife: and they twain
shall be one flesh? | Wherefore they are no more twain, but one
flesh. What therefore God hath joined together, let not man put
asunder.

Matthew 19: 3–6

Our friends the Pharisees are at it again—trying to trip Jesus up
with queries about the Law. ("Tempt" in the King James Version often means "test" or "challenge.") Having failed with a
variety of other questions, this time they ask about marriage: on
what grounds is divorce lawful?

The Pharisees aren't concerned with civil law—which at the
time was quite permissive on divorce—but with the Torah,
which is ambiguous. The only direct statement, which is hardly
helpful, is found in Deuteronomy (24: 1–4), where it says that a
man cannot remarry a woman he has divorced and who has
subsequently remarried. The Torah thus implies that divorce is
lawful under some circumstances, but it doesn't specify which.

Jesus has already taken a hard line on the issue. In the Sermon
on the Mount, he said that "whosoever shall put away his wife,
saving for the cause of fornication, causeth her to commit
adultery: and whosoever shall marry her that is divorced com-
mitteth adultery" (Matthew 5: 32). (He is less strict in the other
Gospels.)

Here he repeats the point, but in stronger terms. Citing both creation accounts from Genesis, Jesus argues that a man's wife is, like Eve to Adam, the bone of his bones and the flesh of his flesh [*see* p. 19]. As Adam said, "Therefore shall a man leave his father and his mother, and shall cleave unto his wife: and they shall be one flesh" (Genesis 2: 24). In Jesus' view, what went for Adam and Eve goes for everybody: God joins each married couple together and intends the arrangement to be permanent—"let no man put [it] asunder."

These sentiments and the quotation itself are so familiar today mostly because they were adapted for the Betrothal and Wedding sections of the English Prayer Book, used since the seventeenth century as the text of wedding ceremonies. Matthew is quoted almost word for word: "Those whom God hath joined together let no man put asunder." (The phrasing has been modernized since then, mainly by substituting "apart" for "asunder.") Unfortunately, even among Catholics few people mean it anymore.

A Camel through the Eye of a Needle

Then Jesus said unto his disciples, Verily I say unto you, That a rich man shall hardly enter into the kingdom of heaven. | And again I say unto you, It is easier for a camel to go through the eye of a needle, than for a rich man to enter into the kingdom of God. | When his disciples heard it, they were exceedingly amazed, saying, Who then can be saved?

Matthew 19: 23–25

Virtually every Christian picks and chooses among Jesus' teachings, and this passage (along with those on divorce) is often passed over, or explained away as instructions only to the clergy.

Here Jesus instructs a man who seeks eternal life. First he recites five of the Ten Commandments (plus "love thy neighbour"). When the man says he's observed them all, and asks what he still lacks, Jesus attaches a new string: "If thou wilt be perfect, go and sell [what] thou hast, and give to the poor, and thou shalt have treasure in heaven: and come and follow me" (Matthew 19: 21).

The man has refrained from murder, adultery, theft, and false witness; he has honored his father and mother and has loved his neighbor; but this is too much. As he skulks off, Jesus explains to his incredulous disciples that few among the wealthy will ever see heaven. "It is easier for a camel to go through the eye of a needle," in fact, "than for a rich man to enter into the kingdom of God." Which does narrow the possiblities.

Mark Twain had a bit of fun with Jesus' hyperbole when he wrote in his notebook that "It is easier for a cannibal to enter the Kingdom of Heaven through the eye of a rich man's needle than it is for any other foreigner to read the terrible German script."

The Last Shall Be First, and the First Last AND *Many Are Called, but Few Are Chosen*

> So the last shall be first, and the first last; for many be called, but few chosen.
>
> Matthew 20: 16

In this verse Jesus combines two sayings found elsewhere—at Matthew 19: 30 and 22: 14, respectively. Whether they belonged together in original manuscripts is doubtful, and the relation between them is unclear.

With "the last shall be first, and the first last," Jesus restates a point he's made before: those who seem least on earth will be greatest in heaven, and vice versa. Here he uses the line to sum up a peculiar parable about laborers in a vineyard and, come to think of it, it makes as little sense in this context as "may be called, but few chosen."

Modern editors now leave this second phrase in what must have been its only original place: Matthew 22: 14. There it is the punchline of another parable, this one about a king's wedding banquet for his son. The king "calls" everyone in the neighborhood to the banquet, but many refuse, some even killing his servants. (This is quite plainly an allegory: the king is God, and his servants Jesus and the disciples.) In the end, though, a sufficient crowd is pulled in off the streets, at which point the king begins haranguing one man who apparently isn't properly dressed for the festivities. The king has the man bound hand and foot and cast out into the darkness, where, he says, "There shall be weeping and gnashing of teeth" (22: 13).

It is here that Jesus adds the gloss: "For many are called, but few are chosen." By "called" he means merely "invited"; the phrase shouldn't be confused as a reference to some sort of religious "calling," in the sense of an interior and irresistible impulse. And by "chosen" he means "accepted," and those who are accepted by the king/God are those who accept his invitation fully, not just partly. God offers everyone a chance to attain the kingdom of heaven, but he will welcome only those who are really willing to make the effort.

It is only slightly less difficult to break into society in New York's Upper East Side, which gossip columnist Suzy recently referred to as the ultimate "location," where attitude and pose are everything. "He/she's so uptown, someone says, and immediately a picture forms. Smart, sophisticated, and rich enough to carry it off. Everyone wants to be—and look—uptown. Few are called. Fewer are chosen."

A Den of Thieves

And Jesus went into the temple of God, and cast out all them
that sold and bought in the temple, and overthrew the tables of
the moneychangers, and the seats of them that sold doves, | And
said unto them, It is written, My house shall be called the house
of prayer; but ye have made it a den of thieves.

Matthew 21: 12–13

If there's one phrase in the Bible tailor-made for the institutions
of modern finance, this is it, as the author of a recent Wall Street
exposé well knew. But at least today's white-collar criminals op-
erate in the temples of Mammon [*see* p. 180], unlike the money
changers in Matthew, who have set up shop in the House of
God.

Casting these money changers out of the Jerusalem temple is
Jesus' first act upon entering that city at what will prove the end
of his career. (In Mark's older Gospel, Jesus gets around to
cleansing the temple slightly later.) Jesus is upset that men are
enriching themselves in a place that should be reserved for
prayer, but it isn't really their fault.

It was the temple's own regulations, after all, that called for
animal sacrifices (see Leviticus 1: 14), and the temple allowed
animals to be sold in its outer court. Furthermore, all exchanges
had to be in coins from Tyre, which few arriving at the temple
would have in their wallets. At worst, the money changers were
a necessary evil, like currency exchanges at airports. And the
men selling pigeons were only trying to help; people who
couldn't afford to sacrifice lambs had to sacrifice something.

But Jesus doesn't care for the laws of supply and demand, and
he condemns the whole system by overthrowing the tables and

chairs in this "den of thieves," a phrase he borrows from Jeremiah, chapter 7. There the prophet, quoting the LORD, maligns a whole series of abominations apparently common in the temple, including theft, murder, adultery, swearing, and the worship of Baal. "Is this house," God demands to know, "which is called by my name, become a den of robbers in your eyes?" (verse 11, King James translation).

"Den of thieves" has always borne the contempt of the original, though in quotation it rarely refers to a place quite so sacred. "There are countries"—like the United States, perhaps?—"where broadcasting is prostituted to advertisement," wrote G. Lowes Dickinson in his introduction to a collection of broadcast addresses, *Points of View* (1930). "That is to make the temple a den of thieves." As I write this book, when the high priests of that temple are Howard Stern and Rush Limbaugh, there wouldn't seem to be much left to prostitute.

Render unto Caesar ...

Then went the Pharisees, and took counsel how they might
entangle him [Jesus] in his talk. | And they sent out unto him
their disciples with the Herodians, saying, Master, we know that
thou art true, and teachest the way of God in truth, neither
carest thou for any man: for thou regardest not the person of
men. | Tell us therefore, What thinkest thou? Is it lawful to give
tribute unto Cæsar, or not? | But Jesus perceived their wicked-
ness, and said, Why tempt ye me, ye hypocrites? | Shew me the
tribute money. And they brought unto him a penny. | And he
saith unto them, Whose is this image and superscription? | They
say unto him, Cæsar's. Then saith he unto them, Render
therefore unto Cæsar the things which are Cæsar's; and unto
God the things that are God's.

Matthew 22: 15–21

In the recently revised edition of the Catholic catechism, tax
evasion is added to the list of sins. I don't know why it took so
long, since Jesus' position has been clear for nineteen centuries.

Matthew has already noted (17: 24–27) that Jesus approves of
paying the taxes ("tribute") demanded by the Roman rulers of
Palestine. The Pharisees don't seem to know this, for here they
try to trip him up. The Pharisees themselves are nominally opposed to the tax, unlike the Herodians, Jewish supporters of
Herod Antipas, Rome's appointed governor.

Each group has its own reasons to cause Jesus trouble, so they
collaborate in testing ("tempting") him with the tax question. If
he approves the tax, he would seem to contradict his position
against temporal authority in general and would alienate a large
portion of the Jewish community. If Jesus rejects the tax, the
Herodians would tattle, and he would likely be arrested.

Of course, Jesus sees through the ruse, and he artfully dodges it. Demanding to see a coin (a denarius) with which such a tax would be paid, he asks of the Pharisees' disciples whose "image and superscription" appears on it. They admit that the image on the coin is Caesar Tiberius's, whose name would also have been inscribed on it. The coin, Jesus implies, therefore belongs to Caesar—that is, it was issued by Rome—and so there is no reason not to return it to Caesar. "Render therefore unto Caesar," he concludes, "the things which are Caesar's."

In effect, Jesus nullifies the challenge. Without saying whether he likes it or not, he simply acknowledges Rome's hegemony in Palestine. So long as Jews accept Roman coins, they accept Roman rule and Caesar's authority to demand the coins back. Jesus himself has no coins, or else he wouldn't ask to see one; therefore, by accepting a life of poverty, he avoids the conflicts faced by the obsequious Pharisees, who like the coins but hate the tax.

But there is another part to Jesus' reply: "and [render] unto God the things that are God's." He implicitly rebukes both the Pharisees and the Herodians for confusing Caesar's temporal authority with God's divine authority and for letting material concerns cloud their spiritual obligations. If they would embrace his Gospel, they would see things clearly and understand that true piety requires freeing oneself from concerns of security and position.

To Strain at a Gnat
AND *Whited Sepulchres*

> Woe unto you, scribes and Pharisees, hypocrites! for ye pay tithe
> of mint and anise and cummin, and have omitted the weightier
> matters of the law, judgment, mercy, and faith: these ought ye to
> have done, and not to leave the other undone. | Ye blind guides,
> which strain at a gnat, and swallow a camel. | Woe unto you,
> scribes and Pharisees, hypocrites! for ye make clean the outside of
> the cup and of the platter, but within they are full of extortion
> and excess. | … Woe unto you, scribes and Pharisees, hypocrites!
> for ye are like unto whited sepulchres, which indeed appear
> beautiful outward, but are within full of dead men's bones, and
> of all uncleanness.
>
> Matthew 23: 23–27

Jesus, recently arrived in Jerusalem, isn't going out of his way to make new friends. In fact, he spends thirty-eight verses condemning the local chapters of scribes and Pharisees for being more attentive to their impressive outfits than to their inner purity.

These blind leaders of the blind, Jesus cries, are the sort of people who "strain at a gnat, and swallow a camel"—a grotesque analogy, typical of Jesus, expressing both contempt and ridicule. What he means, though, is difficult to discern in the King James translation. "Strain at a gnat" seems to refer to making a huge effort in pursuing a trivial goal. This reading is certainly in keeping with Jesus' criticism that the scribes and Pharisees are so obsessed with precisely observing the most minute regulations in the Torah that they neglect more important laws.

But what the Greek actually says is "strain *out* a gnat." This is what most Jews did with their wine, observing the injunction in Leviticus: "And every creeping thing that creepeth upon the earth shall be an abomination; it shall not be eaten" (Leviticus 11: 41). Apparently, creeping things were fond of casks, wineskins, and decanters.

This law is typical of what Jesus finds trivial in the Torah, and he accuses his enemies of literally straining out gnats while figuratively swallowing camels, the largest animals native to Palestine. In other words, the scribes and Pharisees can "swallow" the grossest unrighteousness even as they make such a show of being righteous; they are penny wise and pound foolish; they miss the forest for the trees.

Taking this criticism to an even more repulsive level, Jesus compares the hypocrites to pristine dishware full of filthy food and drink. Stinting no effort to appear pure, they are corrupt inside, "full of extortion and excess." They are, Jesus asserts, "like unto whited sepulchres," that is, whitewashed tombs, beautiful without but full of death and "uncleanness" within. Tombs were in fact whitewashed to identify them as tombs, thus preventing inadvertent contact, which was thought to make one "unclean."

The point of "whited sepulchres" is hard to mistake, and literary citation has usually been faithful to Jesus' meaning. The phrase was virtually tailor-made for such masters of invective as H. L. Mencken, who once direly observed on the American scene "a steady increase of scandals, a constant collapse of moral organizations, a frequent unveiling of whited supulchres" (*A Book of Prefaces*, 1917, chapter 4). *Plus ça change....*

To Separate Sheep from Goats

When the Son of man shall come in his glory, and all the holy
angels with him, then shall he sit upon the throne of his glory: |
And before him shall be gathered all nations: and he shall
separate them one from another, as a shepherd divideth his sheep
from the goats: | And he shall set the sheep on his right hand,
but the goats on the left.

Matthew 25: 31–33

Jesus knows that his time is nearly come, so he has begun to step
up the rhetoric. He launches into a long apocalyptic discourse
(chapter 24) in which he announces the so-called "Second
Coming." Though he will soon die, it won't be long before he
reappears on earth to herald the universal Kingdom of God.
And then the righteous shall be amply rewarded, while the evil
are cast "into outer darkness: there shall be weeping and gnashing of teeth" (25: 30).

First, Jesus shall sit in judgment over "all nations," and he
shall divide them into good and evil as "a shepherd divideth his
sheep from his goats." Jesus refers here to a practice that survives
today in Palestine: though sheep and goats pasture together,
whenever a shepherd moves them to a new locale he first divides
them by kind. Apparently sheep don't like having goats on the
bus.

In a further bit of discrimination, this time against the left-
handed, Jesus claims he shall set the "sheep" on his right hand
and the "goats" on his left, to prepare for God's arrival. Then
God will congratulate the sheep and banish the goats "into everlasting fire, prepared for the devil and his angels" (25: 41).

Today, though, the fire into which metaphorical "goats" are separated is somewhat more ephemeral—like the perdition of critical disfavor. Thomas Carlyle may have been the first to make critical capital out of the biblical allusion when he wrote, in *Inaugural Address at Edinburgh* (1866), that "Books are like men's souls—divided into sheep and goats." "To separate the sheep from the goats" now means "to divide winners from losers," which is admittedly not that far these days from discriminating good and evil. This biblically inspired prejudice against goats is hard to understand; maybe the Gauls of Jesus' time hadn't perfected the making of chèvre.

Thirty Pieces of Silver

> Then one of the twelve, called Judas Iscariot, went unto the chief
> priests, | And said unto them, What will ye give me, and I will
> deliver him [Jesus] unto you? And they covenanted with him for
> thirty pieces of silver. | And from that time he sought opportu-
> nity to betray him.
>
> Matthew 26: 14–16

If there's a more infamous sum in literature, I don't know of
it. The $24 paid for Manhattan and Michael Milken's $550
million income don't even come close.

At this point in the story, Matthew reintroduces a figure we
haven't heard from since chapter 10, where he's mentioned
among the apostles as "Judas Iscariot, who also betrayed
[Jesus]." Matthew clearly expects his readers to understand
what he means by "betrayed," but the issue isn't that simple.

What is clear is that the high priests and elders of Jerusalem
would like nothing better than to see Jesus, whom they view as
a threat, arrested and executed. So they seek out the insider
Judas, who agrees to "deliver" Jesus for "thirty pieces of silver"
(that is, thirty silver shekels). Telling the same story, neither
Mark nor Luke mentions the exact sum; Matthew certainly invented it so as to create another "fulfillment" of Hebrew
prophecy (Zechariah 11: 12, referring back to Exodus 21: 32).

However much Judas got for selling his trust, it was a bad
deal. Repenting later, Judas returns the silver and commits
suicide. Even that didn't put an end to his troubles: he's since
been cast into one of the darkest corners of the Christian Hell
(as in Dante's *Inferno*), and his name is now synonymous with
"traitor."

process be repeated sacramen
your interpretation of variou:
which are by no means unequ
in the fifteenth and sixteentl
would be one root of the Pro
Church.

Popular usage tends to tak
bread" really has nothing sac
"to sit down and begin a mea
ally implies in Matthew.

On the other hand, Judas doesn't have much to do to earn his fee. His task is merely to lead a crowd to Jesus and identify him (by kissing him on the cheek). But virtually everyone already knows who Jesus is; maybe the party sent by the priests had never seen him, or maybe it was just too dark.

If we read between the lines, though, a rationale emerges. Jesus has been a thorn in the authorities' sides since his arrival in Jerusalem. But when they tried to arrest him in broad daylight, they failed, because "they feared the multitude" who "took him [Jesus] for a prophet" (Matthew 21: 46). They decide, therefore, to arrest him at night and in private, choosing a particular night during Passover to execute their plan. To find Jesus when they want him, they need inside information: thus Judas's role as the instrument for a precise and discreet arrest.

The Spirit Is Willing, but the Flesh Is Weak

And he [Jesus] cometh unto the disciples, and findeth them
asleep, and saith unto Peter, What, could ye not watch with me
one hour? | Watch and pray, that ye enter not into temptation:
the spirit indeed is willing, but the flesh is weak.

Matthew 26: 40–41

And as they were eating, Je
brake it, and gave it to the
my body. | And he took th
them, saying, Drink ye all
testament, which is shed fc
I say unto you, I will not d
vine, until that day when I
kingdom.

Everything in Matthew's (
the "Last Supper"—as its
gathering of Jesus with all
sion of his instructions to
   What Jesus means in (
here is uncontroversial: he
yet to be written but to a r
of which our New Testam(
is based on a different unc
current in the Jewish cor
righteousness, which is p
presents his own impendir
as a means of sealing the
mitting" (winning forgive
slate clean for the new reg
   It's the rest of the passag
mean by calling the bread
offers "my blood"? Is he
some combination of bo
("transubstantiating") the

Despite our best New Year's resolutions, it's notoriously difficult to get the body and its various appetites to obey the mind.
"I can say without truth that I have a soul above food," says one
of W. Somerset Maugham's characters (*Don Fernando,* 1935,
chapter 5), "but alas, though my spirit is strong my flesh is
weak, and a poor meal, which I have devoured without complaint, will make me sick as a dog for a week."

   Jesus, however, is talking about another weakness of the flesh.
After the Last Supper, he leads his disciples to Gethsemane (an
olive grove), where he intends to pray before his final ordeal.
Jesus instructs eight of them to sit and watch while he goes
"yonder" with Peter, James, and John (Judas has already snuck
away). Though Jesus' prayer is relatively short (only an hour),
his three companions doze off. Peter, as usual, bears the brunt of
Jesus' lecture: if you aren't more watchful in the future, temptation will get you, because no matter how willing your spirit (in-
tention, psyche), the flesh (body) is weak.

   It's unclear why Jesus would make staying awake a test of
faith, but in any case their flesh remains weak—the three fall
asleep two more times before Jesus is through. He would have
let them sleep on the third time, but their bliss is interrupted by
a commotion, as Judas arrives with "a great multitude with
swords and staves" (26: 47). Jesus' time is at hand.

Who Lives by the Sword
Shall Die by the Sword

And forthwith he [Judas] came to Jesus, and said, Hail, master;
and kissed him. | And Jesus said unto him, Friend, wherefore art
thou come? Then came they, and laid hands on Jesus, and took
him. | And, behold, one of them which were with Jesus stretched
out his hand, and drew his sword, and struck a servant of the
high priest's, and smote off his ear. | Then Jesus said unto him,
Put up again thy sword into his place: for all they that take the
sword shall perish with the sword. | Thinkest thou that I cannot
now pray to my Father, and he shall presently give me more than
twelve legions of angels? | But how then shall the scriptures be
fulfilled, that thus it must be?

Matthew 26: 49–54

Jesus rarely misses the opportunity to make a general statement
where a particular one would do. In this case, as a hostile posse
makes to arrest him and one of the disciples cuts off a priestly
servant's ear, Jesus stays his hand: "Put up again thy sword into
his [its] place." Rather than just saying, "I *want* to be arrested,"
Jesus produces this aphorism: "For all they that take the sword
shall perish with the sword."

At one level all Jesus is saying is that a life of violence will
only lead to a violent death. (Compare Revelation 13: 10: "He
that killeth with the sword must be killed with the sword.")
But he must mean more than than. After all, he has said that no
man dies without God's permission [*see* A SPARROW SHALL NOT
FALL ..., p. 195], so taking up a sword can't simply *cause* dying
by another. The best parallel is probably a line from the Sermon on the Mount: "But I say unto you, That ye resist not evil:

but whosoever shall smite thee on thy right cheek, turn to him the other also" [*see* p. 176].

Jesus' arrest is just one of those evils the disciples shouldn't resist. One should let God ("my Father") take care of evildoers, especially since one never knows when evil is actually part of God's plan. In fact, Jesus is a little contemptuous of his disciple's attempts to save him: if he really wanted to be saved, he could easily pray for a dozen legions of angels to smite the mob. (At least he doesn't say "O ye of little faith" again.)

Furthermore, there's a prophecy to be fulfilled—namely this one from the book of Isaiah: "He was oppressed, and he was afflicted, yet he opened not his mouth: he is brought as a lamb to the slaughter" (Isaiah 53: 7). And a little later: "Yet it pleased the LORD to bruise him; he hath put him to grief: when thou shalt make his soul an offering for sin, he shall see his seed, he shall prolong his days, and the pleasure of the LORD shall prosper in his hand" (verse 10). This is all the argument Matthew needs, though Isaiah wasn't necessarily talking about Christ.

You will have noticed that Jesus' actual words don't match the phrase as we know it today—"[He] who lives by the sword shall die by the sword." The phrase has, over the centuries, rarely been quoted exactly, and in any case it's almost always used metaphorically. What we usually mean is that if you treat others badly you can expect bad treatment yourself in the end (so you should "do unto others," etc.). As an associate said of Michael Gartner, erstwhile president of NBC News, "Michael has an unpleasant personality. And when an unpleasant personality makes mistakes, more people want to shoot at him. Michael's a real live-by-the-sword kind of guy." Gartner, after various missteps, was forced to resign early in 1993.

To Wash Your Hands

The governor [Pilate] answered and said unto them [the crowd],
Whether of the twain will ye that I release unto you? They said,
Barabbas. | Pilate saith unto them, What shall I do then with
Jesus which is called Christ? They all said unto him, Let him be
crucified. | And the governor said, Why, what evil hath he done?
But they cried out the more, saying, Let him be crucified. |
When Pilate saw that he could prevail nothing, but that rather a
tumult was made, he took water, and washed his hands before
the multitude, saying, I am innocent of the blood of this just
person: see ye to it. | Then answered all the people, and said, His
blood be on us, and on our children.

Matthew 27: 21–25

Of all the Gospels, Matthew's is not the clearest on what happens to Jesus after his arrest. The workings of Roman law are
murky, although we may take it that nobody read a prisoner his
rights. It also appears that one was guilty until proven innocent.

The Roman prefect Pontius Pilate has gotten a bad rap in this
whole business; it is not he but the chief priests and elders of
Jerusalem who want Jesus executed. To this end they have
hauled him before a high Jewish council called the "Sanhedrin,"
which condemns Jesus to die for miscellaneous blasphemies,
such as claiming to be the Messiah (which he has been careful
not to do in so many words).

The Sanhedrin need Pilate's acquiescence to carry out the
sentence. But they change their tune for the purposes of Pilate's
hearing, now accusing Jesus of having claimed to be "King of
the Jews," a political offense (treason, in fact) rather than religious one. But Jesus has never made such a claim, though others
(like the Magi) have [see p. 166].

Nonetheless, when Pilate queries Jesus on the subject, the prisoner only replies, "Thou sayest"; in other words, "You said it, not me." To Pilate's other questions, Jesus returns only silence. Rather than defend himself, he allows the charges to stand, because he has to fulfill Isaiah's prophecy that like a sheep to the slaughter he would not open his mouth [*see* p. 143]. Besides, God *wants* him to die.

It was a Passover tradition for the prefect to release one condemned prisoner of the people's choosing (Matthew 27: 15); the

Brush Up Your Bible

priests persuade the crowd not only to ask for the guilty Barabbas, rather than the innocent Jesus, but also to demand that Jesus be crucified. Pilate isn't stupid; he knows Jesus is a "just person" and a political victim. But Pilate is also a coward, afraid of the angry mob. Rather than resist, he symbolically washes his hands, as if he could thus wash himself of Jesus' blood. In effect, he tells the crowd that the crucifixion is their doing, not his; they gladly accept the responsibility.

Matthew's point, of course, is that Pilate can't get off so easily—he could have stopped the crucifixion, but he didn't. On the other hand, prophecy and God's will had to be fulfilled, so from a higher perspective there's really nothing Pilate could have done. It's one of those paradoxes Christians have to live with: even if God makes use of your evildoing, you're still doing evil, and you'll eventually have to pay. And Pilate has paid dearly in Christian opinion, though not as dearly as Judas.

This is the context some forget when they quote "to wash one's hands." The phrase may still be used more or less accurately, to describe a cowardly attempt to evade responsibility, as in D. H. Lawrence's story "The Princess": "They debated having him certified unsuitable to be guardian of his own child. But that would have created a scandal. So they did the simplest thing, after all—washed their hands of him." But just as often, the phrase serves as a verbal gesture of contempt: "I wash my hands of you and this whole business." To translate: "I'll have nothing more to do with you."

A Crown of Thorns

> Then the soldiers of the governor took Jesus into the common hall, and gathered unto him the whole band of soldiers. | And they stripped him, and put on him a scarlet robe. | And when they had platted [woven] a crown of thorns, they put it upon his head, and a reed in his right hand: and they bowed the knee before him, and mocked him, saying, Hail, King of the Jews!
>
> Matthew 27: 27–29

Whether or not you accept the Gospels as literally true, there are some passages that demand respectful treatment. But some have felt no shame in appropriating Christ's "crown of thorns" for their own purposes—mostly as a metaphor for a somewhat less drastic affliction. "This loss of the nine hundred pounds," wrote Thomas Hardy in "A Tragedy of Two Ambitions," "was the sharp thorn of their crown."

Hardy's evident irony doesn't come close to the mockery of the Roman soldiers who take Jesus after Pilate has had him whipped. They strip him and then dress him in a scarlet cloak, as if it were a royal robe; they thrust a plaited crown of thorns on his head and hand him a reed for a scepter; they sneer, "Hail, King of the Jews!" (The dramatic irony is intense.) Jesus is silent throughout; he is ready to take up his cross.

"Crown of thorns" entered the language by way of an early reference (ca. A.D. 950) to a parallel passage in John's Gospel (19: 2). Until recently the phrase always alluded to Christ's suffering, but in the April 18, 1964 issue of *The Medical Journal of Australia* it was also bestowed on a variety of spiny, poisonous starfish that entwines itself in coral reefs.

"My God, My God, Why Hast Thou Forsaken Me?"

Now from the sixth hour there was darkness over all the land unto the ninth hour. | And about the ninth hour Jesus cried with a loud voice, saying, Eli, Eli, lama sabachthani? that is to say, My God, my God, why hast thou forsaken me?

Matthew 27: 45–46

Even at the hour of his death (the "ninth hour," or 3:00 P.M.), Jesus cites scripture. To be precise, he quotes from Psalm 22, which begins, "My God, my God, why has thou forsaken me? why art thou so far from helping me, and from the words of my roaring?" (verse 1).

But Jesus doesn't cry out in English, or even Greek (Matthew's original language). He rather mixes Hebrew (*Eli, Eli*) with his mother tongue Aramaic (*lama sabach-thani*), which confuses the onlookers. They think he's calling, not upon God (*Eli*), but upon "Elias," that is, the prophet Elijah. Some Jews had indeed been predicting Elijah's return—in fact, they thought John the Baptist was he. But John the Baptist is dead, and the crowd is not impressed: "Let us see whether Elias will come to save him" (Matthew 27: 49).

Nobody does save him, but Matthew doesn't end the story with Jesus' very human cry of despair. To everyone's surprise, Jesus will disappear within three days from the tomb in which he is buried—but that's another story.

My Name Is Legion

And always, night and day, he was in the mountains, and in the tombs, crying, and cutting himself with stones. | But when he saw Jesus afar off, he ran and worshipped him, | And cried with a loud voice, and said, What have I to do with thee, Jesus, thou Son of the most high God? I adjure thee by God, that thou torment me not. | For he [Jesus] said unto him, Come out of the man, thou unclean spirit. | And he asked him, What is thy name? And he answered, saying, My name is Legion: for we are many.

Mark 5: 5–9

In Gadara, on the Sea of Galilee, Jesus encounters a "man with an unclean spirit"—in fact, with untold numbers of unclean spirits. Jesus, seeing that a demon speaks through the man, asks its name. The demonic spokesman, a shy type, will say only "My name is Legion." (A "legion" in biblical times was an army division of six thousand men.) For some reason, this legion of devils petition Jesus to send them out of the demoniac and into a herd of two thousand swine, whereupon "the herd ran violently down a steep place into the sea … and were choked in the sea." Never trust a pig to harbor a demon hospitably.

The phrase "My name is legion" is not widely used but does turn up now and again, sometimes in third-person form: "Their name is legion." In this latter usage, the phrase merely serves as the equivalent of "there's a whole mess of them." (Speaking of the worthwhile American journals, Charles Dickens quipped that "The name of these is few, and of the others legion.") "My name is legion," however, can also be a boast: "I command untold numbers of followers" or "I personify a very mighty force."

Swaddling Clothes AND
Tidings of Great Joy

And she [Mary] brought forth her firstborn son, and wrapped
him in swaddling clothes, and laid him in a manger; because
there was no room in the inn. | And there were in the same
country shepherds abiding in the field, keeping watch over their
flock by night. | And, lo, the angel of the Lord came upon them,
and the glory of the Lord shone round about them: and they
were sore afraid. | And the angel said unto them, Fear not: for,
behold, I bring you tidings of great joy, which shall be to all
people. | For unto you is born this day in the city of David
[Bethlehem] a Saviour, which is Christ, the Lord.

Luke 2: 7–11

As we have seen [*see* THE THREE WISE MEN, p. 166], each Gospel
deals differently with the birth of Jesus—Mark and John ignore
it, and Matthew and Luke tell contradictory tales. Most Christians favor a hybrid of the latter two, but all their favorite details
(saving the Magi themselves) come from Luke.

As Luke would have it, Jesus' "parents" Joseph and Mary
travel (while Mary is very pregnant) to Bethlehem, the home of
Joseph's Davidic ancestors, where they are to be registered and
taxed. (Joseph is the father only in name, for Mary is pregnant
by the "Holy Ghost," namely the will of God.) Unfortunately,
all the hotels are booked. Apparently the couple has to lodge in
a stable, though Luke isn't very specific on that point.

Very soon after, Mary gives birth to a son—her first, but not
only, child—whom she wraps in "swaddling clothes" and lays in
a "manger." Every Christian knows these terms, but few could
tell you what they mean. "Swaddling clothes" was coined by

Miles Coverdale as he translated Luke in 1535; it means "strips of cloth wrapped around an infant to prevent free movement of the limbs"—which was once thought desirable, I guess. The phrase derives from the verb "swaddle," a fourteenth-century term for binding infants. Before Coverdale used "clothes," others spoke of "swaddling bands" and "swaddling clouts"—not clumps of dirt but shreds of cloth.

"Manger" also goes back to the fourteenth century; it means "a feeding trough for horses or cattle." This is what Jesus had to use for a crib, and I'm sure it was terribly uncomfortable, though we tend to think of it as hay-stuffed and quite cozy.

Meanwhile, as the baby Jesus lies bound in his trough, an angel of the Lord announces the good news to the neighborhood. By the sixteenth century, "tidings"—which originally meant "events"—had come to mean "news, announcement," though usually of a more conventional sort than this. Of all the Gospels, Luke's makes plainest from the start that Jesus is "a Saviour, which is Christ, the Lord"—by which he may or may not mean "God," but by which he certainly means "the Messiah." Here an angel announces that fact, where in Matthew it's merely a bunch of astrologers who do so.

Note, by the way, that contrary to the Christmas carol, Luke doesn't say "tidings of comfort and joy," though he does attempt to soothe the terrified shepherds by proclaiming the Messiah's arrival. I'm not sure that, if I were in their shoes, I'd be comforted, exactly.

It Came to Pass ...

And it came to pass, that, as the people pressed upon him [Jesus] to hear the word of God, he stood by the lake of Gennesaret, | And saw two ships standing by the lake: but the fishermen were gone out of them, and were washing their nets.

Luke 5: 1–2

You might think that "it came to pass ..." is classic biblical phrasing—indeed, it and its variants appear thousands of times in the King James translation. But that has less to do with the original Hebrew and Greek texts than with the history of English.

Probably under the influence of French, which was the official court language in England until the days of Henry the Fifth, Englishmen began to use "come" in the sense of "happen"—as *arriver* is used in French. The first recorded use is from circa 1300, when we find written, "Til it com on a fest dai," meaning, "On a certain feast day it happened [that ...]." Shakespeare also uses "come" this way in *Coriolanus* (1608): "How com'st," asks the tribune Sicinius, "that you/ Have holp [helped] to make this rescue?" (Act 3, scene 1).

By the late fifteenth century we find the expanded phrase "to come to pass," also meaning "to happen," but with an emphasis on the passage of time. The only recorded usage before the 1520s (from 1481) is feeble: "The wolf ... threw the fox all plat [flat] under him, which came him evil to pass." It was William Tyndale who carved out the phrase as we know it, and by doing so in his 1526 translation of the New Testament he endowed it with biblical prestige forever after.

Tyndale used "to come to pass" not because those are the equivalent Greek words, but because the phrase was just coming into vogue. Later translators were impressed; they picked up the phrase and sowed it liberally in both Testaments. In 1535, for example, Miles Coverdale translated a passage from the apocryphal Hebrew book of Tobit this way: "So shall it come to pass, that the face of the Lord shall not be turned away from thee" (4: 7). The phrase was in more general use by the end of the century.

Maudlin

And behold, a woman in the city, which was a sinner, when she
knew that Jesus sat at meat in the Pharisee's house, brought an
alabaster box of ointment, | And stood at his feet behind him
weeping, and began to wash his feet with tears, and did wipe
them with the hairs of her head, and kissed his feet, and anointed
them with the ointment.

Luke 7: 37–38

Although this weeping woman is never named, she has traditionally been associated with Mary Magdalene, who shows up
in the next chapter of Luke (when Jesus casts seven devils out of
her). "Maudlin," the French form of her name, is also how her
name was once pronounced in England—as it still is at
Magdalene College, Cambridge, and at Magdalen College,
Oxford.

Anyway, "maudlin" was used in the seventeenth century to
mean "weepy," in accordance with popular images and stories of
Mary Magdalene. Very quickly, though, "maudlin" came to
mean not just "tearful" but also "sentimental" and "gushy." This
is just before the name "Maudlin" was given to certain varieties
of peaches and pears.

The Good Samaritan

... A certain man went down from Jerusalem to Jericho, and fell
among thieves, which stripped him of his raiment, and wounded
him, and departed, leaving him half dead. I And by chance there
came down a certain priest that way: and when he saw him, he
passed by on the other side. I And likewise a Levite, when he was
at the place, came and looked on him, and passed by on the
other side. I But a certain Samaritan, as he journeyed, came
where he was: and when he saw him, he had compassion on him,
I And went to him, and bound up his wounds, pouring oil and
wine, and set him on his own beast, and brought him to an inn,
and took care of him.

Luke 10: 30–34

Long before Good Samaritans there were just plain Samaritans.
A Jewish sect living in Samaria, they were by and large shunned
by other Jews, who regarded them as little better than Gentiles.
As a Samaritan woman says to Jesus in John's Gospel (4: 9),
"The Jews have no dealings with the Samaritans." But it is precisely a despised Samaritan who comes to a Jew's rescue in this
parable.

When a certain lawyer asks Jesus who the "neighbor" is that
the Law tells him to love [see LOVE THY NEIGHBOR, p. 77], Jesus
takes the opportunity to reinterpret Scripture. As we have seen,
the Israelites took "neighbor" to mean "kinsman," or at least
"another Israelite." But Jesus points out that there are certain
Jews nowadays who don't even take care of other Jews—in this
case a man robbed, stripped, and beaten by thieves on the road
to Jericho.

Jesus doesn't choose a priest and a Levite as his bad guys by
accident: they represent Jews who consider themselves espe-

cially holy. Nonetheless, they treat the dying man the way most people treat homeless people on the street today—by crossing to the other side. Nor does Jesus accidentally pick a Samaritan as his good guy. His point is that *everyone* is your neighbor—at least if you accept Christ's new righteousness. The new Law is a law of unlimited love.

Based on this parable, our phrase "good Samaritan" (which dates to 1640) means "a person who performs good deeds selflessly," even for someone nasty. There is no longer a racial or religious overtone to "Samaritan," though such is important in the original context. Thackeray, for example, puts the phrase into the mouth of a colonel in *The Newcomes* (1855), who hears the tale of two young men. One falls sick, and the other supports him with five of the sixpence at his daily disposal. "I should like to have known that good Samaritan," the colonel cries—but both young men are Americans.

Of course, to be a good Samaritan, one has to have the means, or, as Margaret Thatcher once cynically put it, "No one would remember the Good Samaritan if he'd only had good intentions. He had money as well." Take doctors, for example, who according to "Good Samaritan laws" in some states are now exempt from malpractice suits if they come to the aid of someone in an emergency.

The Prodigal Son

... A certain man had two sons: | And the younger of them said to his father, Father, give me the portion of goods that falleth to me. And he [the father] divided unto them [his sons] his living. | And not many days after the younger son gathered all together, and took his journey into a far country, and there wasted his substance with riotous living. | And when he had spent all, there arose a mighty famine in that land; and he began to be in want.

Luke 15: 11–14

Many people know this story better than they know the word "prodigal," which from this context they figure means "estranged." Actually, though, "prodigal" is defined by verse 13: "wasteful, spendthrift, living beyond one's means." The term seems to date to the mid-fifteenth century, but this tale put it on the English map.

In a Bible published in 1551, this chapter of Luke was given the heading, "The parables of the lost sheep, of the groat [coin] that was lost, and of the prodigal son"—the last of these coining the phrase. (It never appears in the actual text.) All these parables make the same point: no matter how happy we are with what we have, we are rightly happier when we regain something we've lost. A man with a hundred sheep will leave ninety-nine of them to search for one that is lost and rejoice when he finds it. A woman with ten silver pieces will still "sweep the house and seek diligently" when she loses only one and celebrate with the neighbors after plucking it from the dust.

The best example, though, is that of the "prodigal son," who ran off with his early inheritance to blow it on "riotous living" in some dissolute country. When the well has run dry and he's fit

to starve, the son overcomes his shame at having wasted the money his father intended as security. Returning home, he confesses to his father that he has sinned and is "no more worthy to be called thy son" (verse 21). But Dad is much happier to see him than sad at his sinning. He orders up some fine robes for his son, and the best fatted calf for dinner: "For this my son was dead, and is alive again; he was lost, and is found" (verse 24).

All this celebrating, however, angers the prodigal son's elder brother, who after all has husbanded his inheritance and served his father faithfully. "And yet," he complains, "thou never gavest me a kid, that I might make merry with my friends," even while his sibling, "which hath devoured thy living with harlots," gets the fatted calf (verse 29).

Jesus aims this line at the Pharisees and scribes who have been complaining that he "receiveth sinners, and eateth with them" (verse 2). Each of the three parables rebukes these hypocrites, who think themselves too holy to consort with tax collectors and their ilk. But Jesus sees sinners as lost sheep and prodigal sons who ought to be sought out and saved; for "joy shall be in heaven over one sinner that repenteth, more than over ninety-nine just persons, which need no repentance" (verse 7).

Shakespeare is as responsible as anyone for giving "prodigal" broader currency—he was, for example, the first to use it as a noun, meaning "a spendthrift." "There I have another bad match," Shylock says of his debtor Antonio in *The Merchant of Venice* (ca. 1597): "a bankrupt, a prodigal, ... a beggar that was us'd to come so smug upon the mart" (Act 3, scene 1). As an adjective the word plays various roles in *Merchant* and five other plays—sometimes, Shakespeare actually uses it as a compliment (meaning "generous").

Such is rarely the case today, at least when prodigal is used in its proper sense. But the very point of the parable has helped distort the word's meaning: because it's really about losing and finding, prodigal is now used more in the sense of "missing" than of "wasteful"—though bad behavior is also implied.

"Father, Forgive Them; for They Know Not What They Do"

And when they were come to the place, which is called Calvary, there they crucified him [Jesus], and the malefactors, one on the right hand, the other on the left. | Then said Jesus, Father, forgive them; for they know not what they do. And they parted his raiment, and cast lots. | And the people stood beholding. And the rulers also with them derided him, saying, He saved others; let him save himself, if he be Christ, the chosen of God.

Luke 23: 33–35

Jesus preached "Love your enemies" (Matthew 5: 44), and here he practices it. Condemned and sentenced, Jesus is brought to Calvary ("The Place of the Skull") to be crucified, along with two other "malefactors." But rather than rebuking his enemies, Jesus prays for God to forgive them, "for they know not what they do."

This plea for mercy contrasts sharply with Jesus' earlier diatribes against the establishment. Either he's calling for his own prophecies to be softened—which would be a truly superhuman gesture—or by "forgive them" he means "forgive the ignorant crowd," whom the chief priests had manipulated. In either case, only Luke reports this last-minute absolution, which has become an essential element of the crucifixion narrative.

The line has been put to many uses over the years, not all of them as dramatic. Charlotte Brontë is melodramatic, though, in *Jane Eyre* (1847), in which Jane rebukes a wicked aunt: "Yes, Mrs. Reed, to you I owe some fearful pangs of mental suffering. But I ought to forgive you, for you knew not what you did: while rending my heart-strings, you thought you were only uprooting my bad propensities" (chapter 3).

Aldous Huxley waxes more philosophical in *Ends and Means* (1937), where he points out that "Those who know not what they do are indeed in need of forgiveness; for they are responsible for an immense amount of suffering. Yet more urgent than their need to be forgiven is their need to know" (chapter 12).

The Word Made Flesh

In the beginning was the Word, and the Word was with God,
and the Word was God. I ... And the Word was made flesh, and
dwelt among us, (and we beheld his glory, the glory as of the
only begotten of the Father,) full of grace and truth. I John [the
Baptist] bare witness of him, and cried, saying, This was he of
whom I spake, He that cometh after me is preferred before me:
for he was before me.

John 1: 1, 14–15

We use "the word was made flesh" to mean "what was said has
been done"—where "word" stands for "conception" and "flesh"
for "reality." But the author of John has something more precise
and singular in mind, and he really does mean "flesh."

Of all the evangelists, John is the most intent on writing a
book people will take for Holy Scripture. Thus he begins by in-
voking the first verse of the Hebrew Bible [*see* p. 7]. But where
Genesis claims that "in the beginning" were God and chaos,
John omits chaos and adds "the Word" (*logos* in Greek). As verse
14 reveals, by "Word" he means "Jesus," who was made flesh by
being born a man.

Without this Gospel, Christianity might look very different
today. It is John, and John only, who suggests that Jesus incar-
nated a divine power present with God at the Creation. John
doesn't exactly say, however, that Jesus was the same as God, but
rather that Jesus was the "Word" that was "with God." In Hebrew Scripture, God himself speaks his Creation ("Let there be
light: and there was light," Genesis 1: 3). In John, God's "Word"
has an independent existence, though it is not yet a person. It is

more like God's will in abstract form, which will only become concrete—become flesh—when Jesus is born.

John borrowed the term *logos* from the Greek philosophy of his day, in which it stood for the principle of Reason. There are many ways one might render it besides "Word"—in fact, Goethe depicts his antihero Faust struggling to translate the phrase, rejecting in turn "Word," "Thought," and "Power," and finally settling on "Act" (*Faust,* Part 1, 1808). But as early as A.D. 950, English commentators referred to John's *logos* as "word," and the term stuck. It just goes to show that writers look out for their own.

Water into Wine

Jesus saith unto them [the servants], Fill the waterpots with water. And they filled them up to the brim. | And he saith unto them, Draw out now, and bear unto the governor of the feast. And they bare it. | When the ruler of the feast had tasted the water that was made wine, and knew not whence it was ... [he] called the bridegroom, | And saith unto him, Every man at the beginning doth set forth good wine; and when men have well drunk, then that which is worse: but thou hast kept the good wine until now.

John 2: 7–10

If Jesus were reborn today in Bordeaux or Napa County, he would have another brilliant career. That is, if he could be persuaded to show off his talents.

Soon after John the Baptist proclaims him "the Son of God" (John 1: 34), Jesus appears at a marriage banquet in Cana, a town in Galilee. Apparently the bridegroom has underestimated the crowd, or its capacity to party, for in the middle of the proceedings the wine runs out. Jesus' mother—a bit player in this Gospel—wants her son to do something about it, but he doesn't think it's yet time to openly perform miracles (2: 4).

In a compromise, Jesus supplies plenty of wine, but does so secretly. He has some servants fill up huge stone pots with water and then orders them to take a glass to the "governor" (steward) for tasting. Sure enough, the water has been turned to wine, and very fine wine, too. Though the servants know who pulled this trick off, everyone else is ignorant; the steward even rebukes the bridegroom for hiding the good stuff. The groom is left speechless.

Born Again

There was a man of the Pharisees, named Nicodemus, a ruler of the Jews: | The same came to Jesus by night, and said unto him, Rabbi, we know that thou art a teacher come from God: for no man can do these miracles that thou doest, except God be with him. | Jesus answered and said unto him, Verily, verily, I say unto thee, except a man be born again, he cannot see the kingdom of God. | Nicodemus saith unto him, How can a man be born when he is old? can he enter the second time into his mother's womb, and be born? | Jesus answered, Verily, verily, I say unto thee, Except a man be born of water and of the Spirit, he cannot enter into the kingdom of God. | That which is born of the flesh is flesh; and that which is born of the Spirit is spirit. | Marvel not that I said unto thee, Ye must be born again.

John 3: 1–7

This is today perhaps the most famous non sequitur in the Bible. The Pharisee Nicodemus has decided, based on various miracles, that God must be "with" Jesus. Jesus replies off the subject that a man must be "born again" to "see the kingdom of God."

Jesus may be hard of hearing, but Nicodemus is positively dense. Taking Jesus literally, he wonders how in the world he's ever going to get back into the womb; Jesus impatiently explains that he was speaking poetically. One is literally born in the flesh but also figuratively "born of the Spirit"—in other words, one's spirit is born of the Spirit of God. Jesus seems to be saying that in addition to being literally born, one must be "born again" in the second sense: one must receive the Spirit of God through baptism to prepare for the Last Judgment and the "kingdom of God."

This translation, based on the Geneva Bible of 1560, has of course lent us the term "born again" for a movement among Christians (mostly Baptists) who believe that one's first direct experience of God usually happens in adulthood. (Some of these are regularly found at baseball games holding up signs reading "John 3: 3.") But the phrase is not necessarily gospel; the Greek might mean "born from above" rather than "born again," which is Nicodemus's interpretation. And even if Jesus means "again," the term is ambiguous: does he mean "born of the Spirit" in *addition* to being born of the flesh, or does he mean "born of the Spirit" a *second* time? The latter might imply that things went awry the first time, which would be hard to explain. In either case, Nicodemus has no right to be confused, since Jews also used the term "rebirth" for conversion to their faith.

To Cast the First Stone

> They [the scribes and Pharisees] say unto him [Jesus], Master,
> this woman was taken in adultery, in the very act. | Now Moses
> in the law commanded us, that such should be stoned: but what
> sayest thou? | This they said, tempting him, that they might have
> to accuse him. But Jesus stooped down, and with his finger
> wrote on the ground, as though he had heard them not. | So
> when they continued asking him, he lifted up himself, and said
> unto them, He that is without sin among you, let him first cast a
> stone at her.
>
> John 8: 4–7

It's those devils the scribes and Pharisees again, up to their usual
tricks. This time, they'd like Jesus to reconcile his own Gospel of
Love with Scripture, which says that an adulterer or adulteress
"shall surely be put to death" (Leviticus 20: 10).

Does "put to death" really mean "stoning," they ask, and does
the penalty apply in all cases? Jesus knows they're playing games,
so he pretends not to hear, doodling in the dust instead. But
when they insist, he shoots back a cutting reply: let he who is
without sin "first cast a stone" at the adulteress. Shamed, the
scribes and Pharisees slink away without further instruction.

Some have seen the need to "improve" Jesus' line by moving
"first" (in the original an adverb) before "stone" (thus making it
an adjective). In this form, the phrase has been used both as a
warning and as an apology. A good example of the latter may be
found in P. G. Wodehouse's *Indiscretions of Archie* (1921), in
which a transplanted Brit remarks on a curiously named mid-
western town. "Snake Bite? What rummy names you have in
America! Still, I'll admit there's a village in England called
Nether Wallop, so who am I to cast the first stone?"

The Truth Shall Make You Free

Then said Jesus to those Jews which believed on him, If ye continue in my word, then are ye my disciples indeed; | And ye shall know the truth, and the truth shall make you free.

John 8: 31–32

"For the law was given by Moses," writes John toward the beginning of his Gospel (1: 17), "but grace and truth came by Jesus Christ." Jesus himself is of the same opinion, though there remain doubters among the Jews regarding the untruth of Moses.

Saint Paul will emphasize several times that the Gospel has freed him, and every Christian, from rote observance of Moses' Law [*see* THE WAGES OF SIN, p. 275]. But many in Jesus' audience feel no need to be freed from anything; when he tells them his truth shall set them free, they answer, "We be Abraham's seed, and were never in bondage to any man: how sayest thou, Ye shall be made free?" (John 8: 33).

Jesus once again has to explain his poetry: if a man sins, that man is the servant of sin; I have come to show you your sin, and to teach you to avoid it; thus I shall set you free. The odd thing is that Jesus doesn't really believe this is going to work; in fact, he predicts his audience will ignore him, and that they will "seek to kill me, because my word hath no place in you" (verse 37). These nay-sayers aren't sons of Abraham, but sons of the devil, a "murderer from the beginning," in whom "there is no truth" (verse 44). The lecture has, to say the least, gone downhill.

In modern quotation, "The truth shall make [*or* set] you free" rarely refers to the new Gospel of righteousness; more often it expresses a personal "righteousness" about one's own notions of truth.

I Was Blind, but Now I See

Then again called they [some Pharisees] the man that was blind, and said unto him, Give God the praise: we know that this man [Jesus] is a sinner. | He answered and said, Whether he be a sinner or no, I know not: one thing I know, that, whereas I was blind, now I see.

John 9: 24–25

That Jesus restores a blind man's sight isn't good enough for the Pharisees; they're mad because he does it on the Sabbath! In the spirit of such arguments as "I didn't do it, and anyway I didn't do it on purpose, and furthermore if I did it on purpose it wasn't a crime," the Pharisees first try to prove that the man was never blind to begin with. When that fails, they resort to higher logic. Yes, Jesus cured the man, but he did it on the holy day; thus he is a sinner. And if he's a sinner, he can't perform miracles, so it was really God, not Jesus, who restored the man's sight.

The blind man couldn't care less if Jesus is a sinner; "One thing I know," he replies, is that "whereas I was blind, now I see." The man is only speaking literally, but nobody takes him that way anymore. We quote his line exclusively as a metaphor: "I now see the truth I didn't recognize before."

In this we do get some help from Jesus, who tells the healed man a little later in the chapter that "For judgment I am come into this world, that they which see not might see, and that they which see might be made blind" (verse 39). In other words, he has come to "open the eyes" of the spiritually blind to the truth of his revelation. Those who already think they see fine—smug unbelievers—will remain figuratively blind to his message, unable to accept its truth.

"In My Father's House
Are Many Mansions ..."

Let not your heart be troubled: ye believe in God, believe also in me. | In my Father's house are many mansions: if it were not so, I would have told you. I go to prepare a place for you. | And if I go and prepare a place for you, I will come again, and receive you unto myself; that where I am, there ye may be also. | And whither I go ye know, and the way ye know.

John 14: 1–4

Chances are good that at least once someone on the street has offered you a pamphlet bearing a smiley face and the inscription, "Let Not Your Heart Be Troubled." But I doubt it completed the quotation, let alone explained the context. That's what I'm here for.

It is the Last Supper, and Jesus has just given his disciples some good news and some bad news. He's going to die, yet he shall be glorified in heaven. Unfortunately, they will be unable to follow him immediately, because it is his role to die for their sakes, and they lack the courage to "lay down their lives" for his sake (John 13: 38). Nonetheless, someday they will all be reunited in heaven.

Thus he tells them not to be upset but rather to continue believing in him as they believe in God. After all, he continues a little enigmatically, "In my Father's house are many mansions"—which is a little easier to envision once you know that "mansions" is a figure for "dwelling places" or "rooms." What Jesus seems to mean is that there's plenty of room in heaven for true believers—like the Republican party, the kingdom of God is a "big tent."

In fact, as soon as he dies he'll prepare their rooms and at the right time come fetch them. "Where I am," he concludes, "there ye may be also." This line raises another possibility: that his Father's house is wherever Jesus is, for wherever Jesus is, God is. And Jesus is "with" whoever believes in him; so his Father's house has as many "mansions" as there are believers. This, at least, is the view of many Christians.

"In my Father's house are many mansions" may be less familiar today than "Let not your heart be troubled"—thanks to street-corner missionaries. But the former line has been much quoted in literature; it is often a poetic way of saying "there's room for everybody or everything." "My desk was of the first magnitude," writes A. G. Gardiner in his essay "On Being Tidy" (*Windfalls*, 1920). "It had an inconceivable wealth of drawers and pigeon-holes. It was a desk of many mansions."

Still others know that not all houses have more than a few mansions. "Not that I affect ignorance," writes Charles Lamb in "The Old and New Schoolmaster"—"but my head has not many mansions, nor spacious; and I have been obliged to fill it with such cabinet curiosities as it can hold without aching." Having written several books of cultural literacy, I can sympathize; but I can also take comfort in E. M. Forster's assertion, in *Anonymity* (1925), that "If there is on earth a house with many mansions, it is the house of words."

Greater Love Hath No Man ...

This is my commandment, That ye love one another, as I have loved you. | Greater love hath no man than this, that a man lay down his life for his friends. | Ye are my friends, if ye do whatsoever I command you.

John 15: 12–14

This is one biblical quotation that could use retiring. It's easily said but rarely observed, and Jesus, after all, was serious.

"I am the good shepherd," he had said (John 10: 11); "the good shepherd giveth his life for the sheep." As the Last Supper winds down, he looks forward to his own death as an act of love for his friends; he will willingly sacrifice himself to God in atonement for their sins. Not everyone, of course, is Jesus' friend, just true believers—those who "do whatsoever I command." And his best friends, the disciples, can look forward to being good shepherds themselves: "If they [the unbelievers] have persecuted me, they will also persecute you" (15: 20).

Most commonly quoted today is the shorthand expression "to lay down one's life," which always implies a sacrifice, if not love. There is honor among thieves, but John Ruskin was exaggerating when he wrote, in *Unto This Last* (1862) that "a body of men associated for purposes of robbery ... shall be animated by perfect affection, and every member of it be ready to lay down his life for the life of his chief."

The "greater love hath no man" business is probably best reserved for ironic situations, as in Ruth McKenney's story "Chickie Has a Baby" (*My Sister Eileen,* 1938). "The story had a rather novel end," she writes, hastening to the end of an improbable tale. "The hero reproaches the rich man for his evil intentions, and the plutocrat repents, proving there is some good in bankers. However, the plutocrat is still in love with his secretary, and since he has promised not to seduce her, he marries her. The hero is best man at the wedding. Greater love hath no man." This I find slightly more credible.

A Doubting Thomas

But Thomas, one of the twelve, called Didymus, was not with them when Jesus came. | The other disciples therefore said unto him, We have seen the Lord. But he [Thomas] said unto them, Except I shall see in his hands the print of the nails, and put my finger into the print of the nails, and thrust my hand into his side, I will not believe.

John 20: 24–25

So what does a guy have to do? Jesus has spent chapter upon chapter explaining to his disciples that he's as good as God, that he's going to let himself be crucified, and that he's going to rise from the dead. Then when he does it, some still refuse to believe unless they see it themselves. It's a wonder Matthew (who's supposedly on the scene) doesn't cry, "O ye of little faith!"

The disciple Thomas—famous for doubting—is perhaps singled out unfairly. Mary Magdalene had told the other disciples the same news, but John doesn't say that they believed her. Only when Jesus appears in person and says "Peace be unto you" are we told that they were "glad, when they saw the Lord" (verses 19–20). Nonetheless it is Thomas who openly demands what Othello might call "ocular proof." Eight days later he gets it when Jesus returns, bidding Thomas to stick his finger in the crucifixion wounds, as he had bizarrely requested. Thomas is finally convinced.

Poor Thomas, in addition to being made an example of, has had to suffer by allusion, being labeled over the centuries such things as "wavering Thomas," "unbelieving Thomas," and finally "doubting Thomas" (the last phrase dates to an 1883 issue of *Harper's Magazine*).

Speaking in Tongues

> And when the day of Pentecost was fully come, they [the apostles] were all with one accord in one place. I And suddenly there came a sound from heaven, as of a rushing mighty wind, and it filled all the house where they were sitting. I And there appeared unto them cloven tongues like as of fire, and it sat upon each of them. I And they were all filled with the Holy Ghost, and began to speak with other tongues, as the Spirit gave them utterance.
>
> The Acts of the Apostles 2: 1–4

Today, to "speak in tongues" is to garble together different languages or to speak in some novel lingo no one understands. But this is just the opposite of what the disciples do here, in the passage that inspired the phrase.

The scene is the first Pentecost after Jesus' death. (Pentecost is a Hebrew holy day—the fiftieth day after the first of Passover—now celebrated more by Christians.) The "Holy Ghost"—or inspiring power of God—picks this feast day to fulfill the risen Jesus' last words to his disciples: "Ye shall receive power, after that the Holy Ghost is come upon you: and ye shall be witnesses unto me both in Jerusalem, and in all Judæa, and in Samaria, and unto the uttermost part of the earth" (Acts 1: 8).

If the disciples are going to spread the Gospel to the ends of the earth, they're going to need something better than Berlitz. This is where the Holy Ghost comes in: it descends upon the apostles in the form of "tongues of fire" (also a biblical coinage), not only to inspire them to their task but to retrain their own tongues. The result isn't babble; the disciples speak, not new languages, but some all-purpose tongue that everyone hears as his own (2: 6). ("Tongue" in the sense "knowledge or use of a language" derives from William Tyndale's rendition of this passage in 1526.)

The modern use of "speaking in tongues" was apparently influenced by another New Testament passage, from St. Paul's first letter to the Corinthians: "Now brethren, if I come unto you speaking with tongues, what shall I profit you, except I shall speak to you either by revelation, or by knowledge, or by prophesying, or by doctrine?" (14: 6). Paul uses "speaking with tongues" to refer to the incomprehensible chatter of self-styled prophets, which is really no language at all: lacking "distinction in the sounds," it conveys no meaning, at least if you're not already on the prophet's wavelength. It's like a lot of academic discourse: inspired, certainly, and even enlightening, but gibberish to the uninitiated.

The Road to Damascus AND
To Kick against the Pricks

And as he [Saul] journeyed, he came near Damascus: and
suddenly there shined around about him a light from heaven: |
And he fell to the earth, and heard a voice saying unto him, Saul,
Saul, why persecutest thou me? | And he said, Who art thou,
Lord? And the Lord said, I am Jesus whom thou persecutest: it is
hard for thee to kick against the pricks.

The Acts of the Apostles 9: 3–5

Early Christians (like members of other Mediterranean sects)
placed great emphasis on the conversion experience. And the
most famous convert, and best model, after the crucifixion was
Saul of Tarsus.

Saul, a Hellenistic Jew and a Pharisee, had participated with
the high priests in persecuting and imprisoning early Christians. He played some role in the death of St. Stephen, a great
leader of the Jerusalem congregation, and otherwise "made
havock of the church" (Acts 8: 3).

As chapter 9 begins, Saul, "breathing out threatenings and
slaughter against the disciples of the Lord," is on his way to
Damascus, where the Jerusalem priests have sent him to haul
back Christian sectarians for punishment. But a funny thing
happens on the way: Saul is stricken to the ground and blinded
by a light from heaven, which heralds the voice of Jesus, "the
Lord." Jesus upbraids Saul for persecuting him by persecuting
the faithful and orders him to continue to Damascus for further
instruction. Once there, the "scales fell from his eyes" [*see* p.
270].

Since then, "the road to Damascus" has become a metaphor for a journey of enlightenment or an experience of radical conversion. Christians look to Saul—now better known as "Paul," the Roman form of his name—as the exemplar of the born-again Christian, though they don't require actually hearing a voice from heaven—just the inner experience of calling.

The real voice in Acts also coins another phrase, "to kick against the pricks," by which Jesus means "to vainly resist my inevitable triumph." His literal meaning is "to deliberately strike your foot against sharp objects," an oddly self-defeating form of behavior (like punching a wall in anger) that Jesus likens to Paul's persecution of Christians, which in the end will hurt him more than it hurts them.

The phrase is now used mostly in the sense of "to fight the inevitable" or "to complain about ills one has brought on oneself." D. H. Lawrence uses it both ways at once in *Sons and Lovers* (1913): "Paul [aptly named] was laid up with an attack of bronchitis. He did not mind much. What happened happened, and it was no good kicking against the pricks" (chapter 4).

The Scales Fell from One's Eyes

> And Ananias went his way, and entered into the house; and
> putting his hands on him [Saul] said, Brother Saul, the Lord,
> even Jesus, that appeared unto thee in the way thou camest, hath
> sent me, that thou mightest receive thy sight, and be filled with
> the Holy Ghost. | And immediately there fell from his eyes as it
> had been scales: and he received sight forthwith, and arose, and
> was baptized.

> The Acts of the Apostles 9: 17–18

After encountering Jesus on the road to Damascus, Paul—still
called "Saul" in the text—is literally blind. And he stays that
way for three days, until a disciple named Ananias, inspired by a
vision, lays hands on him. Ananias heals Paul, and, as in the
Gospels, physical healing brings about spiritual illumination—
Paul is "filled with the Holy Ghost." To paraphrase, "the scales
fell from his eyes": he was blind, but now he sees.

The "scales" Acts refers to are not fishy epidermi, but probably cataracts. We don't really know, however, since the English
term "scales" in this sense has only been used in reference (if in-
direct) to Paul's healing—it first appears in the religious poem
Cursor Mundi (ca. 1300), and it was employed again by Wyclif
when he translated Acts in 1382. (The Greek original—*lepides*—
can mean "fish scales" but also "husks" and "shells.")

Whatever it really means, today the phrase is used in the sense
"to realize you were deluded" or "to be suddenly enlightened."
William Ellis, in 1732, was among the first to employ it this way,
writing, in *The Pracitical Farmer,* that "I hope in time the Scales
will be taken off the Eyes of the Landlord's Mind." Though Ellis
isn't entirely clear on the concept, all renters will sympathize.

It Is Better to Give than to Receive

Yea, ye yourselves know, that these hands have ministered unto my necessities, and to them that were with me. | I [Paul] have shewed you all things, how that so labouring ye ought to support the weak, and to remember the words of the Lord Jesus, how he said, It is more blessed to give than to receive.

The Acts of the Apostles 20: 34–35

Paul has taken on the role of chief Christian missionary to the Gentiles. And he's a smashing success, cultivating communities in Rome, Corinth, Ephesus, and elsewhere.

But on his last trip to Ephesus he caused a riot, so this time he calls the church elders of that city to Miletus for consultation. (Besides, he's in a hurry to get back to Jerusalem for Passover.) Paul is nearing the end of his career, and he seems to know it: the tenor of this speech to the Ephesians is valedictory, and he packs in all his best advice on preserving the church from enemies within and without. At the end, he quotes a line (found in none of the Gospels) that he considers Jesus' most essential teaching: "It is more blessed to give than to receive."

Note that Paul doesn't say "better"; we've altered the quote to mean something like "once you're mature you'll see that giving is really much more fun than getting." Neither Paul nor his audience is up to that pretense; what he says Jesus said is that charity will make you blessed—along with being pure at heart, humble, meek, etc. [see p. 170]. And by "give" he doesn't necessarily mean money, though that's often how his words are intepreted today.

Though the phrase (modified or no) is now most commonly addressed to spoiled children, some have seen the virtue of addressing it to society at large. "In conversation, as in other affairs of life," writes Arnold Bennett in his essay "Talking" (*The Savour of Life,* 1928), "it is more blessed to give than to receive. If all taciturn persons would perpend and act upon this deep truth, conversation in Britain would be much more amusing than it in fact is." But only if they avoid such precious terms as "perpend."

A Law unto Themselves

(For not the hearers of the law are just before God, but the doers
of the law shall be justified. | For when the Gentiles, which have
not law, do by nature the things contained in the law, these,
having not the law, are a law unto themselves: | Which shew the
work of the law written in their hearts, their conscience also
bearing witness, and their thoughts the mean while accusing or
else excusing one another). ...

Romans 2: 13–15

In a passage of nearly Shakespearean involution, St. Paul
meditates (for the benefit of the Roman congregation) on the
"law," a word he repeats seven times in these three verses. I won't
blame you if you can't follow the train of thought; certainly
somebody got confused somewhere along the line, because Paul
doesn't mean anything like what we mean by "a law unto themselves."

So what is Paul saying? If you know that he's trying to make
Gentile Christians feel better about not observing Jewish laws
and customs, the passage is easier to decipher. You will not be at
a disadvantage as God judges you, Paul tells them, for lacking
the Mosaic Law or Torah. Righteousness is measured not by
hearing the law, or having it written down for you, but by performing the law—that is, by observing its most important pre-
cepts.

Gentiles may do this without referring to any text save what is
written in their hearts and consciences. If they "do by nature"
what is contained in the law, without "having" the law (learning
the Torah), then they are "a law unto themselves." In short, such
righteous Gentiles have the law *within* themselves.

Perversely, we most often use the phrase "a law unto oneself" not in the positive sense Paul intends, but negatively. We accuse someone of *thinking* he's a law unto himself when he's not—of treating his own whim as a guide while ignoring common judgment and justice. (In this sense it's close to "to take the law into one's own hands," a sixteenth century coinage.) This negative usage had probably been in circulation for a while before it was finally put in writing by Eric Partridge, an expert on proverbs, clichés, and slang, in *Usage and Abusage* (1947). "Certain idiosyncratic, law-unto-themselves writers," he complains, "fall into vagaries when ... they depart from those rules [of usage]." Partridge himself, of course, departs from the Bible.

The Wages of Sin

For when ye were the servants of sin, ye were free from righteousness. | What fruit had ye then in those things whereof ye are now ashamed? for the end of those things is death. | But now being made free from sin, and become servants to God, ye have your fruit unto holiness, and the end everlasting life. | For the wages of sin is death; but the gift of God is eternal life though Jesus Christ our Lord.

Romans 6: 20–23

Congratulations, says Paul to Christ's followers in Rome; while once you were slaves to sin, now you're slaves to righteousness! The King James translation "servants" tones down the Greek, but Paul's slaves *are* paid: the wages of righteousness are "eternal life," while the wages of sin are death. (Paul says wages "is," but that wasn't ungrammatical at the time—"wages" was often treated as a singular noun until the nineteenth century.)

By wages Paul means "ultimate reward," not a weekly com-

pensation. And by "death" he means not physical extinction but spiritual death—the more you sin now, the more you will suffer in the end.

There are, however, many revisions of Paul's assertion. "The wages of sin, mademoiselle, are said to be death," writes Agatha Christie in *There Is a Tide* (1948). "But sometimes the wages of sin seem to be luxury. Is that any more endurable, I wonder?" What a stupid question. In *The Web and the Rock* (1939), Thomas Wolfe gives with one hand and takes back with the other: "The wages of sin were not always and inevitably death, but the wages of seduction were inevitably fatherhood, man's guilty doom, and the utter ruination of another 'pure, sweet girl'" (chapter 11).

Indeed, sin doesn't get the respect any more that it used to. Frederick Lewis Allen in *Only Yesterday: An Informal History of the Nineteen-Twenties* (1931), meditating on the march of progress, notes its cost: "What had departed was the excited sense that taboos were going to smash, that morals were being made over or annihilated, and that the whole code of behaviour was in flux. The wages of sin had become stabilized at a lower level" (chapter 14).

Today, things have finally gone too far. "Wages of Sin Fall," announces a *New York Times* headline from March 1993, "and It's a Problem." The wages in question are no longer paid out to the sinner but collected by the government in the form of so-called "sin taxes" on tobacco, alcohol, and even junk food. The "problem" is that these taxes have worked too well—"people are sinning less." Or, as Ronald Alt, a spokesman for tax collectors, put it early in 1993: "The golden goose of sin taxes is just about cooked"—a bizarre reference, not to the Bible, but to Aesop.

Vengeance Is Mine AND
To Heap Coals of Fire on One's Head

> Recompense to no man evil for evil. Provide things honest in the sight of all men. | If it be possible, as much as lieth in you, live peaceably with all men. | Dearly beloved, avenge not yourselves, but rather give place unto wrath: for it is written, Vengeance is mine; I will repay, saith the Lord.
>
> Romans 12: 17–19

I hate to break the news to all those readers who have ever shouted "Vengeance is mine!" before delivering a payback, but Paul's point is that nobody can say that but God. "I"—not "you"—"will repay, saith the Lord."

Paul says this is written, which is only half true, since he himself puts the phrase in its now familiar form. But he does reach back to Deuteronomy, where, after a jealous Yahweh has chewed out the perverse Israelites [*see* TO HEAP MISCHIEFS, p. 89], he promises destruction for Israel's foolish enemies. "To me belongeth vengeance, and recompense" the LORD avers; the enemies' "day of … calamity is at hand, and the things that shall come upon them make haste" (Deuteronomy 32: 35).

Hardly a letter of love, but Paul manages to twist it to that purpose. Because vengeance is God's, it is not for us to "recompense evil for evil." Rather, we should love our enemies, if not for the sake of Christ-like righteousness, then to make their evil appear worse by contrast. "Therefore if thine enemy hunger, feed him," Paul says generously; "if he thirst, give him drink; for in so doing thou shalt heap coals of fire on his head" (Romans 12: 20). How charitable. This kind of talk just goes to show how brutal biblical life could be.

For this last metaphor—which certainly seems to reserve a sweet form of vengeance to man—Paul reached back once again to Hebrew Scripture, this time quoting directly from Proverbs (25: 21–22), where it is added that "the LORD shall reward thee" for heaping. The English rendition of Romans, though, is actually earlier, tracing to Tyndale's translation of 1526–1534. And it is probably Romans to which William Langland alluded in *Piers Plowman* (the 1377 text) while noting that to "love ... thine enemy in all wise" is to "cast coals on his head."

The Powers That Be

Let every soul be subject unto the higher powers. For there is no power but of God: the powers that be are ordained of God. | Whosoever therefore resisteth the power, resisteth the ordinance of God: and they that resist shall receive to themselves damnation.

Romans 13: 1–2

Some of St. Paul's notions and attitudes haven't dated very well. This passage, for example, which once warmed the hearts of emperors, monarchs, and autocrats, doesn't go down so easily anymore.

Paul himself might have changed his tune had he lived to see the full extent of Rome's persecution of Christians—throwing them to lions and so forth. But that was still in the future as he wrote this letter, in which he insists that Christians bow to the "powers that be"—in other words, the authorities in power. You can serve two masters—God and the emperor—at once, Paul implies, because they're really the same master: the emperor's power was given him by God. Things are the way God wants them to be, so if you resist those in power you're only begging for "damnation."

Paul leaves it to us to figure out what God wants when power is in transition, when two authorities fight, or when revolutions turn former rebels into new powers. One wonders, for example, whether the American colonists incurred damnation for resisting the power of George III, or indeed, to reach further back, whether Pharaoh's power over the Hebrews, too, was ordained by God. I guess the short answer is that God sides with the winners.

A Stumbling Block

> Let us not therefore judge one another any more: but judge this rather, that no man put a stumblingblock or an occasion to fall in his brother's way.

Romans 14: 13

"Stumblingblock" is the invention of translator William Tyndale, and it first appeared in 1526 in this passage from Romans and also in I Corinthians 8: 9. Later translators were so enamored of Tyndale's coinage that they used it to render a number of different Hebrew and Greek terms—it crops up as early as Leviticus 19: 14 and then in ten other passages in both testaments. Tyndale also uses the phrase "stumbling stone" at Romans 9: 13, and this phrase, too, became popular, though it passed out of currency in the late nineteenth century.

Both phrases are rooted in such fifteenth-century formulations as "to stumble at a stone" and "to stumble at a block"—a "block" being the stump of a tree. But where these phrases imply no malice, after Tyndale the phrase "stumbling block" comes to refer to a deliberately placed moral obstacle. Saint Paul instructs the Romans to attend to their own uprightness rather than to judge others' moral failings or, worse, to place occasions for moral failure in others' paths.

Absent in Body, but Present in Spirit

> It is reported commonly that there is fornication among you,
> and such fornication as is not so much as named among the
> Gentiles, that one should have his father's wife. | And ye are
> puffed up, and have not rather mourned, that he that hath done
> this deed might be taken away from among you. | For I verily, as
> absent in body, but present in spirit, have judged already, as
> though I were present, concerning him that hath so done this
> deed.
>
> I Corinthians 5: 1–3

I don't know about you, but I'm more often present in body and
absent in spirit than the other way around. Saint Paul, police-
man to the Gentile churches, didn't have the luxury.

Paul wants to make it clear that just because the Corinthians,
as Greeks, aren't bound by the text of the Torah [*see* p. 273], that
doesn't mean there's no Law in effect. Before he was a Christian
missionary, Paul was a good Jew, and his sensibilites are
offended by various impure acts among his Gentile converts.
For example, he's not pleased to hear that a Corinthian Christian has been caught sleeping with his stepmother—incest, by
the lights of Jewish and Roman law.

What's worse, this man's fellows in the church tolerate such
behavior; rather than mourn over it they are "puffed up" (arrogant). Even if Paul is "absent" from Corinth "in body" (he
writes from Ephesus), he can condemn such evils from afar. For
he is "present" to the community "in spirit"—his judgment and
authority are among them even while he's away.

In case they don't know exactly what he has in mind, Paul issues precise instructions: at the next assembly, as you gather to-

gether in my spirit and "with the power of our Lord Jesus Christ," you are to deliver the culprit "unto Satan for the destruction of the flesh, that the spirit may be saved in the day of the Lord Jesus" (verse 5). In other words, the man is not only to be excommunicated but to be cast out from their society and left to die—all the better for him, so that he doesn't defile himself the more.

Let it be noted that the flesh–spirit dichotomy Paul plays upon here is of Greek origin [see A MERRY HEART, p. 345], and it would be well understood by his Corinthian readers. It's also essential to the early Christian respect for martyrdom, which might have rendered you permanently absent in body but ensured the repose of your spirit in heaven.

It Is Better to Marry than to Burn

For I would that all men were even as I myself. But every man hath his proper gift of God, one after this manner, and another after that. | I say therefore to the unmarried and widows, It is good for them if they abide even as I. | But if they cannot contain, let them marry: for it is better to marry than to burn.

I Corinthians 7: 7–9

This is easily the most infamous of Paul's sayings, and deservedly so. Still, it's been misinterpreted, because many forget that Paul figured the End was near ("the time is short," 7: 29). Thus he thought it best for all to devote themselves to "fasting and prayer" rather than invite Satan's temptations (verse 5). I mean, would *you* want to be caught fornicating when God knocked on the door?

Which is not to say that Paul ever really smiled on the sexual act, or that in fact he wouldn't rather everyone were "as I myself," by which he means totally abstinent. (That would bring about the End if nothing else did.) Luckily, he realizes that "every man hath his proper gift of God," and that celibacy is not within everyone's range. So if you really can't abstain, even if the Last Judgment is tomorrow, you'd better marry now. For marriage, though a distraction from prayer, is better than "burning."

You might think Paul means all fornicators will "burn in hell," a plausible reading of the King James text. Yet all modern translators agree that the Greek for "burn" means "burn with desire"—which is more distracting and dangerous even than marriage. But given Paul's view of sexual sins, I wouldn't put the pun past him.

All Things to All Men

And unto the Jews I became as a Jew, that I might gain the Jews;
to them that are under the law, as under the law, that I might
gain them that are under the law; | To them that are without
law, as without law, (being not without law to God, but under
the law to Christ,) that I might gain them that are without law. |
To the weak became I as weak, that I might gain the weak: I am
made all things to all men, that I might by all means save some.

I Corinthians 9: 20–22

Saint Paul, traveler among the infidels, explains to his Corinthian converts his great achievement. He has spread the faith to all varieties of people—Jews, the law-abiding, the lawless, and the weak. Chameleonlike, he adapted himself to their ways, and in pretending to be like them, gained their trust and ultimately their faith. In effect, the ends, being so noble, justify Paul's means.

Few who quote this line today, though, care about results; the question is usually sincerity. More often than not, we take a negative view of someone trying to be all things to all men—thought a sign of insincerity or weakness. What we often forget, though, is that Paul wasn't "all things to all men" at the same time—he played out his roles in series. In other words, when in Rome, he did as the Romans.

To See through a Glass, Darkly
AND *Faith, Hope, and Charity*

When I was a child, I spake as a child, I thought as a child; but
when I became a man, I put away childish things. | For now we
see through a glass, darkly; but then face to face: now I know in
part; but then shall I know even as also I am known. | And now
abideth fatih, hope, charity, these three; but the greatest of these
is charity.

I Corinthians 13: 11–13

These three verses are among the most influential (and quotable) in the entire Bible, not to mention among Paul's most poetic. Whenever we speak of "putting away childish things," we
quote First Corinthians; whenever we refer to "faith, hope, and
charity," we're using Paul's terms; when we claim to "see
through a glass, darkly," we cite the apostle. But usually we don't
know what we're talking about.

For when it comes to quoting the Bible, we often see through
our glasses darkly. For starters, in Renaissance English "glass"
didn't mean "magnifying glass" or "eyeglass." When Ophelia
calls Hamlet the "glass of fashion" (*Hamlet*, Act 3, scene 1), she
doesn't mean he's just bought a pair of Armanis. She means he's
a "*mirror* of comportment."

Of course, you can't see "through" a mirror; Paul's sense is "by
means of a mirror." Nor is the mirror itself "dark," since by
"darkly" he means "obscurely, with difficulty"—the metal mir-
rors of his day being imperfect reflectors. Paul refers to the limits of mortal vision and understanding, especially when it comes
to divine things. What we can see and know of God here on

earth is only a distorted reflection—like the "shadows on the wall" in Plato's myth of the cave.

But when the End comes, the scales will fall from our eyes, and we shall see God face to face. To put the verse into comprehensible English: "Now we see things dimly, in a mirror, but later we shall see [God] face to face; now I understand things only partly, but then [at the End] I will understand [God] fully and be fully understood [by God]." And when that time comes, we shall put away the things of the world as a man puts away the toys he loved as a child.

What will endure in the afterlife are three things: faith, hope, and (greatest of the three) charity (*agape* in Greek), the three cardinal Christian virtues. The terms "faith" and "hope" are fairly clear, but what Paul means by *agape* is one of those things Catholics and Protestants fight over. Catholics prefer "love," Protestants "charity," which is a little ironic, since it's Protestants who privilege faith over good works.

In truth, *agape* is difficult to translate; it's one of three Greek words for "love," the others being *eros* (sexual love, as in "erotic") and *philos* (brotherly love, as in Philadelphia). What *agape* means depends a lot on context, though "selfless or sacrificing love"—such as Christ's—seems to be the generic meaning. Such love is a divine gift, not something natural to the heart, so it differs from "charity" in the sense of "willing gift and potential tax write-off." Paul himself draws the distinction in verse 3: "Though I bestow all my goods to feed the poor, and though I give my body to be burned, and have not charity, it profiteth me nothing." So don't go offering to be burned at the stake out of selfish motives.

But for the Grace of God ...

For I am the least of the apostles, that am not meet to be called
an apostle, because I persecuted the church of God. | But by the
grace of God I am what I am: and his grace which was bestowed
upon me was not in vain; but I laboured more abundantly than
they all: yet not I, but the grace of God which was with me.

I Corinthians 15: 9–10

"But for the grace of God, there go I," you might pompously
intone as the car behind you gets pulled over. St. Paul—the ultimate source of the line—wasn't so smug; we owe that to John
Bradford, a sixteenth-century Englishman who, while watching
some criminals be hauled off for execution, exclaimed, "But for
the grace of God there goes John Bradford!"

Bradford clearly had this passage from First Corinthians in
mind, though Paul speaks in the affirmative rather than in the
negative. It is "by the grace of God" that Paul is what he is, not
isn't what he isn't, though one implies the other. What he was
was a persecutor of the church; what he is is the hardest-work-
ing missionary in Christendom. But he doesn't want all the
credit.

In fact, Paul implies, left to himself he'd still be an enemy of
Christ. His conversion on the road to Damascus [*see* p. 268] and
subsequent holy career are both gifts of God, given freely, without being earned. This is in fact the very essence of grace: one
cannot work for it—it has nothing to do with merit. Whether
or not Paul means that grace alone makes for salvation is a controversial topic, and perhaps the most important of Luther's arguments with the Church (he said yes, they said no, and then
they called the whole thing off).

In the Twinkling of an Eye AND *O Death, Where Is Thy Sting?*

> Behold, I shew you a mystery; We shall not all sleep, but we shall all be changed, | In a moment, in the twinkling of an eye, at the last trump: for the trumpet shall sound, and the dead shall be raised incorruptible, and we shall be changed. | For this corruptible must put on incorruption, and this mortal must put on immortality. | So when this corruptible shall have put on incorruption, and this mortal shall have put on immortality, then shall be brought to pass the saying that is written, Death is swallowed up in victory. | O death, where is thy sting? O grave, where is thy victory?
>
> I Corinthians 15: 51–55

After explaining to his Greek readers the difference between one's natural body (which is earthly) and one's spiritual body (which is heavenly), Paul goes on to sketch out the basics of resurrection, which Jesus had left rather vague.

According to the Gospels, Jesus himself rose in more or less the same body he died in—which is proved by the episode of "doubting Thomas" [*see* p. 265]. But when the rest of us faithful rise at Christ's Second Coming, it won't be in the "corruptible" natural body we're used to, but in a transformed, "incorruptible" spiritual body no longer subject to decay and death.

This mysterious transformation will happen instantly, or, in Paul's own famous words, "in the twinkling of an eye." The phrase did appear—circa 1300—before Wyclif's 1380 translation, but Paul may well have influenced the earlier usage. What he means is "in the time it takes to blink"—"twinkle" originally meant "wink" or "blink" (but not nod). Eyes still "twinkle," but differently: by sparkling, not winking.

Paul, leaving "twinkle" behind, moves on to what he considers the real payoff: once transformed, we will be immortal. Thus shall the words of the prophet Isaiah be fulfilled: when the LORD returns to Zion, he "will swallow up death in victory" and "wipe away tears from off all faces" (Isaiah 25: 8). "O death," Paul exults, "where [then] is thy sting?" (he means the "sting" or bite of a serpent). "O grave," he gleefully adds, loosely paraphrasing Hosea (13: 14), "where is thy victory?" Paul does not stay for an answer.

One should be grateful that the King James translators took liberties here with Paul's Greek, for what he really wrote was "O death, where is thy victory?"—the substitution "grave" is really much more dramatic. Nonetheless, Paul's poetry is terrific; even better is John Donne's meditational sonnet, "At the Round Earth's Imagined Corners" (1633), which is based on it (with a glance at Revelation—*see* THE FOUR CORNERS OF THE EARTH, p. 314). As a bonus, Donne updates Paul's picture for an age in which the Second Coming is no longer thought to be imminent, at least by most of us.

"Arise, arise / From death," Donne exhorts, "you numberless infinities / Of souls, and to your scattered bodies go" (lines 3–5). Donne imagines that our souls, still in one piece, can find out the particles of our "scattered bodies" and unite them again for the transformation. Of course, one could quibble even with this improvement, since somewhere down the line the particles of our bodies will become particles of other people's bodies, as eventually will the particles of their bodies, etc. So Paul and Donne weren't scientists—I'll take the poetry anyway.

Anathema

The salutation of me Paul with mine own hand. | If any man
love not the Lord Jesus Christ, let him be Anathema Maranatha.
| The grace of the Lord Jesus Christ be with you. | My love be
with you all in Christ Jesus. Amen.

I Corinthians 16: 21–24

At the end of his first letter to the Corinthian church, Paul
bumps aside his secretary to add a salutation in "mine own
hand." Characteristically, he "greets" and "blesses" everyone
while slipping in a little curse on nonbelievers.

The English translators, however, didn't know what to make
of Paul's language, leaving both the Greek *anathema* and the
Aramaic *maranatha* untranslated—and capitalizing them for
good measure. Clearly, if it's targeted at those who "love not the
Lord Jesus Christ," *anathema* can't be anything pleasant, and
William Tyndale (in 1526) and then the good bishops in James's
service (in 1611) must have figured "Anathema Maranatha" was
even worse.

But the two words are not only grammatically separate, they
mean completely opposite things. "Anathema" comes from the
Greek *ana-* (up) *tithenai* (to place), and it originally referred to
something "placed up" as an offering to the gods. In later usage
it came to mean "a thing devoted, not to the gods, but to evil: a
thing accursed" which is how Paul understood it. In other
words, "God's curse be on you, you evil people."

"Maranatha," on the other hand, traces to the Syraic *maran
etha,* "the Lord has come." As such, it's probably a whole new
sentence unto itself, even though in early manuscripts of First
Corinthians the words are connected. On that basis, some (like

the translators) surmised that "*anathema maranatha*" was an intensified version of plain *anathema*: "Curse you, and curse you again, for our Lord has come."

This compounded form shows up in English as late as Harriet Beecher Stowe's *Dred: A Tale of the Great Dismal Swamp* (1856), which does indeed sound dreadful. But since then we've sensibly preferred the simple "anathema," which began circulating on its own in the seventeenth century. It no longer means "a curse," as it did for centuries, or even "a thing accursed," exactly, but more often "someone or something reviled or shunned," as if cursed by the community.

USAGE NOTE: one doesn't say "an anathema," just "anathema." Anthony Holden used the term properly in his article, in the February 1993 issue of *Vanity Fair,* on Princess Diana Spencer. Writing of Diana's stepmother, Raine Dartmouth, Holden asserts that Dartmouth may have brightened the life of Diana's father, but "her pushy, domineering ways were anathema to his children, who took to calling her 'Acid Raine.'"

The Letter Killeth, but the Spirit Giveth Life

> And such trust have we through Christ to God-ward: | Not that
> we are sufficient of ourselves to think any thing as of ourselves;
> but our sufficiency is of God; | Who also hath made us able
> ministers of the new testament; not of the letter, but of the spirit:
> for the letter killeth, but the spirit giveth life.
>
> II Corinthians 3: 4–6

In addition to coining the interesting phrase "to God-ward," Paul pronounces here one of his most memorable dicta: "The letter killeth, but the spirit giveth life."

I know many students who would agree at least with the first part after reading one of Paul's own letters. But of course Paul doesn't mean "epistle"; he means "the letter of the Law," the To-rah. As he sees it, observant Jews are bound by all sorts of rules that the Law itself doesn't give them the strength to fulfill. Worse, the Law condemns them to suffer (or even die) for not observing the very rules that in themselves offer no power of obedience.

What's great about the "new testament" (the new rules of salvation), says Paul, is that God himself, through the Holy Spirit, now offers us grace—the power to do what he wishes us to do. (On grace, *see* BUT FOR THE GRACE OF GOD ..., p. 287.) True righteousness lies in the heart, not in any book of laws. The Spirit, by leading us to act righteously, ensures our salvation and thus gives us "life."

The argument is obviously a little complicated, and few have quoted these lines from Second Corinthians without stumbling on the sense. "Literature, literature, Dick," pronounces one character in Thomas Wolfe's *Look Homeward, Angel* (1929). "It's been the ruin of many a good surgeon. You read too much, Dick. Yon Cassius hath a lean and hungry look. You know too much. The letter killeth the spirit, you know" (chapter 14). Though his citations of Shakespeare's *Julius Caesar* (Act 1, scene 2) are no less misguided, at least he gets the words right.

To Suffer Fools Gladly

> I say again, Let no man think me a fool; if otherwise, yet as a fool
> receive me, that I may boast myself a little. I That which I speak,
> I speak it not after the Lord, but as it were foolishly, in this
> confidence of boasting. I Seeing that many glory after the flesh, I
> will glory also. I For ye suffer fools gladly, seeing ye yourselves are
> wise.
>
> II Corinthians 11: 16–19

Paul is not glad when people find him foolish, but when they do
he makes the best of it.

This is an extension of his "all things to all men" principle [*see*
p. 284]. The Corinthians, in this case, have made it plain that
"fools" (meaning ignorant blowhards) are welcome; in fact, they
"suffer" (put up with) them gladly. These false prophets are
taken more seriously than Paul in some quarters, and his sage
advice is getting lost in the bluster. If that's the way it's going to
be, Paul will play the game in spades.

That is, Paul, never a humble man, will boast the harder—
and thus play the fool—if that's what it takes to get the
Corinthians' attention. And so, to glorify his message by glori-
fying himself, Paul launches into a resumé of his efforts and
sufferings, his lashings and beatings and toil, his cares and anxi-
eties for the churches—all to prove that he must have God on
his side if he can endure so much and gain so little.

Paul's point, then, is that when only fools are favored, then
you have to play the fool. And if there are those among us who
don't suffer fools gladly, they're in the minority, or else there
wouldn't be so many fools about.

To Fall from Grace

Behold, I Paul say unto you, that if ye be circumcised, Christ
shall profit you nothing. | For I testify again to every man that is
circumcised, that he is a debtor to the whole law. | Christ is to
become of no effect unto you, whosoever of you are justified by
the law; ye are fallen from grace. | For we through the Spirit wait
for the hope of righteousness by faith.

Galatians 5: 2–5

Horror of horrors, some new Christians in Galatia (now part of
Turkey) have actually been circumcising themselves! Paul will
not stand for such lapses, apparently spurred on by Jewish
Christians who still cling to the Mosaic Law, and he lays out his
argument here in the harshest possible terms.

Paul's anxiety on such points—a familiar feature of his letters—is a little hard to fathom, but as he saw it the stakes were
high. He was concerned that his Gentile converts not think
Christianity was just a new and improved brand of Judaism.
Rather, it constituted an entirely "new testament" [*see* TO BREAK
BREAD, p. 230] in which righteousness was defined by faith (the
result of grace) and not by adherence to any merely formal rules
and regulations.

To embrace any article of the Torah—such as circumcision—
was to lapse in faith, and in effect to "indebt" yourself to the law
once again (owe your righteousness to it). By accepting the authority of even one regulation, you were denying the absolute
supremacy and efficacy of faith alone—which in Paul's eyes was
the essence of Christianity.

In short, if you seek to justify yourself before God by observing some written law, you are "fallen from grace." Of course, to

"fall" from grace you once had to be "in" it, and Paul doesn't explain how, if grace is a free gift from God that one cannot earn, one could fall from it by his own effort. But it's unkind to fault Paul's logic when he's coined so durable a phrase.

In fact, the phrase is so versatile that it's served all sorts of grammatical functions since Paul's time, from participle ("fallen from grace") to predicate ("to fall from grace") to subject ("her fall from grace"). This last usage is well illustrated in a doubly allusive passage in D. G. van der Vat's review (published in *English Studies,* February 1940) of L. P. Smith's *Unforgotten Years.* Smith, according to van der Vat, "relates, rather amusingly, his father's fall from grace owing to over-indulgence in 'lovingkindness'" [*see* p. 122]. One must admit, though, that there are probably more interesting ways to lapse.

Fear and Trembling

Wherefore, my beloved, as ye have always obeyed, not as in my presence only, but now much more in my absence, work out your own salvation with fear and trembling. | For it is God which worketh in you both to will and to do his good pleasure.

Philippians 2: 12–13

Younger readers may be more familiar with Hunter S. Thompson's trademark—"fear and loathing"—than with the phrase as St. Paul coined it, but nonetheless the original remains in circulation, thanks in part to the English title of one of Søren Kierkegaard's more famous works.

Neither Kierkegaard or Thompson, however, ever had as much cause for fear and trembling as Paul—or in Thompson's case, at least not yet. The apostle is writing to the church at Philippi—one of his favorite places—from the confines of a Roman prison, where he awaits a trial that could spell his death. Yet his tone is relatively tranquil, and indeed, like Socrates before him, he claims actually to welcome death, because it would bring him closer to God.

It is not Paul, then, who fears and trembles now (he did once, at I Corinthians 2: 3). Rather, he enjoins the Philippians to work at their own salvation "with fear and trembling," by which he means "awe and reverence" at God's power rather than "anxiety and fear of punishment." So this phrase is most accurately used in situations where the trembling is more about productive anticipation—or nervous excitement—than existential dread.

To Press toward the Mark

> Not as though I had already attained [salvation], either were
> already perfect: but I follow after, if that I may apprehend that
> for which also I am apprehended of Christ Jesus. | Brethren, I
> count not myself apprehended: but this one thing I do, forget-
> ting those things which are behind, and reaching forth unto
> those things which are before, | I press toward the mark for the
> prize of the high calling of God in Christ Jesus.

Philippians 3: 12–13

St. Paul, warning the Philippians against those "dogs" and "evil
workers" (namely, orthodox Jews) who insist on circumcision
and other rituals, blows his own horn once again. I myself was
circumcised, he tells them; furthermore I am also descended
from Abraham and was once even a Pharisee, a pious zealot, a
persecutor of the church, and a strict adherent of the Mosaic
law. But, he continues, I gave up all the old certainties such
things offered in order to embrace Christ (3: 5–7).

Dwelling on this heroic deed, Paul looks forward to his salvation and fellowship with Jesus Christ. He does not claim to have
already attained these things; but, putting his past behind him,
he continues to reach toward a glorious future, to "press toward
the mark for the prize."

If Paul's phrase seems curious, that's because "mark" is now a
poorer word than in the sixteenth century, when Miles Coverdale used it in translating this passage. When "mark" first appeared in English, circa A.D. 700, it meant "boundary, limit, or
stopping point," later passing through the last of these senses
into "target, object of one's aim." (We preserve this usage in
such phrases as "to hit the mark" and "to miss the mark.")

Coverdale had already used "mark" in Lamentations (3: 12) to mean "target," but here he employs it in a newer sense: "a post or other object placed to indicate the terminal point of a race."

In other words, Paul presents salvation as the finish line of a lifelong, long-distance race. What's important isn't speed but endurance, in which Paul has had few competitors ever since. So don't feel bad if you fall short of his mark.

A Labor of Love

We give thanks to God always for you all, making mention of
you in our prayers; | Remembering without ceasing your work of
faith, and labour of love, and patience of hope in our Lord Jesus
Christ, in the sight of God and our Father; | Knowing, brethren
beloved, your election of God.

I Thessalonians 1: 2–4

Paul, through his scribe Timothy, begins his first letter to his
flock in Thessalonica (Thessaly) with a naked piece of flattery.
He assures the Thessalonians of their "election of God"—in
other words, they are among the new chosen people.

What Paul means by "election"—and whether "election"
properly translates his Greek—is controversial. We don't really
know, for example, whether he believed one's salvation was pre-
destined (some Protestants think so; Catholics deny it). Paul
often insists that salvation comes from faith, which is based in
grace, which one cannot earn through labor. On the other
hand, he sometimes speaks of salvation as something you can
strive for, and here he doesn't stint to praise the Thessalonians
for their faith, hope, and "labour of love."

The Greek for "love" is *agape,* which we've met before [*see* TO
SEE THROUGH A GLASS, DARKLY, p. 285]—it means "selfless be-
neficence." Paul commends the Thessalonians for their charitable works, which is hardly what we mean by "labor of love"
now. The original sense of the phrase survived for a while; the
first allusion to Paul's words (and their repetition at Hebrews
6: 10) is found in the anonymous tract, *The Lady's Calling*
(1673), identified as a sequel to the author's blockbuster, *The
Whole Duty of Man*: "Women ... founded Hospitals, and yet

with a labor of love, as the Apostle styles it, … disdain'd not sometimes to serve in them." In other words, the good ladies not only built hospitals, but also, in the spirit of self-sacrificing love for their fellow man, tended to the sick. Charity today seldom gets its hands so dirty.

Over time, "labor of love" lost its connotations of charity and sacrifice and took on a whole new meaning: "work performed with joy and personal care," which doesn't necessarily involve pain so much as great effort. The only connection to Paul's meaning is that you can expect no material reward—just personal satisfaction—from such labor. (Again, Paul is ambiguous about whether the "work of faith" or "labour of love" will earn you spiritual rewards, like eternal life, later on.)

A Thief in the Night

> But of the times and the seasons, brethren, ye have no need that I write unto you. | For yourselves you know perfectly that the day of the Lord so cometh as a thief in the night. | For when they shall say, Peace and safety; then sudden destruction cometh upon them, as travail upon a woman with child; and they shall not escape.
>
> I Thessalonians 5: 1–3

Times may be tough, Paul tells the Thessalonian congregation, but have no fear: the time is also short. Believe it or not, he presents the imminent end of the world as a comfort—for on that day, "the Lord himself shall descend from heaven with a shout," and "the dead in Christ [that is, Christians] shall rise first" (4: 16).

What may be better, those who persecute Christians are going to rue the day they were born: "sudden destruction" will come upon them. Paul's readers shouldn't inquire too deeply, however, into the exact date of that happy day; only God knows. It is a day one can prepare for (by giving up fornication, for example), but not precisely anticipate. When the Day of the Lord arrives, it will be sudden and unexpected, as "a thief in the night" or as labor comes upon a pregnant woman. (Actually, the former is more unexpected—and harder to prepare for—than the latter, but who's counting?)

Perhaps the "thief in the night" metaphor is a bit ominous, but Paul is looking more to the fate of evildoers than to the reward of the faithful. In any case, those who use the phrase today rarely imply that the thief will be welcome.

The Root of All Evil AND Filthy Lucre

But they that will be rich fall into temptation and a snare, and into many foolish and hurtful lusts, which drown men in destruction and perdition. | For money is the root of all evil: which while some coveted after, they have erred from the faith, and pierced themselves through with many sorrows.

I Timothy 6: 9–10

Timothy is St. Paul's right-hand man in Ephesus, a bustling city in Asia Minor legendary for its flirtations with money and magic. So Paul's counsel to his representative—if indeed Paul wrote the letter, which is doubtful—is appropriate. But beyond this, Paul (or whoever) is just down on money in general: he calls it "filthy lucre" earlier in the epistle (3: 8). (The phrase was coined by William Tyndale in his rendition of 1526–1534; "lucre" comes from the Latin *lucrum,* "profit," which is also the source of "lucrative.")

Money is the "root of all evil" because the desires it fosters tend to start out small, but as they become familiar they become customary and thenceforth sprout like weeds. As Paul sees it, disposable income makes satisfying "foolish and hurtful lusts" too easy and makes keeping the faith a lot less attractive. Some might argue that if poverty is necessary to faith, then faith seems to be a default option rather than a chosen path. But Paul never thought much of the constancy of mortals, and, after all, he was dealing with recent converts who had a hard time shaking off paganism, witchcraft, and filthy lucre.

Fight the Good Fight

Fight the good fight of faith, lay hold on eternal life, whereunto thou art also called, and hast professed a good profession before many witnesses.

I Timothy 6: 12

For I am now ready to be offered, and the time of my departure is at hand. | I have fought a good fight, I have finished my course, I have kept the faith . . . .

II Timothy 4: 6–7

Paul may not have written these two epistles to Timothy, but if not they're pretty good imitations. In the first, the author merely advises Timothy to "fight the good fight of faith," which is the struggle for eternal salvation; in the second, he actually claims to have won.

Paul, the pugilist of God, invokes again the metaphor of righteousness as a kind of race [*see* TO PRESS TOWARD THE MARK, p. 298], which is now finished, at least for him. Those who persecuted and imprisoned him, those who fought against his Christian mission—are now left in the dust, which they will proceed to eat as he basks in the glory of Christ's fellowship.

"To fight the good fight"—now used as a metaphor for "to struggle valiantly against nay-sayers and wrong-thinkers"—has retained its biblical self-righteousness and smugness. Regardless of the outcome, one can always claim to have been on the side of goodness. Former President George Bush, for example, in conceding the 1992 U.S. presidential election on November 3, remarked that he had "fought the good fight, and kept the faith."

Just to prove that the phrase works for winners and losers alike, when Bill Clinton arrived to vote at his polling place in Little Rock, Arkanasas, earlier that same day, he was greeted by this computer-generated banner: "Welcome Home Governor Clinton: You Have Fought a Good Fight and Kept the Faith." Neither Bush nor Clinton's supporters explained what happened to Paul's phrase "I have finished my course," which would in fact be a lot more apt to a presidential "race." This clause is now regularly omitted in citations of Second Timothy—maybe it just doesn't sound as stirring or dignified.

Unto the Pure All Things Are Pure

Unto the pure all things are pure: but unto them that are defiled
and unbelieving is nothing pure; but even their mind and
conscience is defiled. | They profess that they know God; but in
works they deny him, being abominable, and disobedient, and
unto every good work reprobate.

Titus 1: 15–16

Try telling the opponents of naughty pop lyrics that "unto the
pure all things are pure"—one biblical statement with which
they're sure to take issue. Defenders of artistic freedom often
meet the challenge of purity with a statement like this: "Only
those with dirty minds will see anything dirty in it."

In this they seem to have Paul—the alleged but uncertain
author of this letter—on their side. But actually we don't know
what the author thought about the famous Roman spectacles of
his day; his concern here is with that old conflict between the
letter and the spirit, the law and faith [*see* p. 292].

What "Paul" is saying is that all the laws Moses ever con-
cocted aren't going to help you if your "mind and conscience"
are "defiled." To the contrary: evil and impure people will turn
even what is good in the Law to evil and impure purposes. On
the other hand, those who are pure in spirit can live with or
without the Law; everything they do will be righteous and pure,
whether or not orthodox Jews like it.

But the phrase as used today is rarely about laws, but more
often about the dirty business of social estimation. A good example of current usage is to be found in this quotation-happy
passage from the morosely titled *Journal of a Disappointed Man*
(1919) by W. N. P. Barbellion (the many-minded author of

Enjoying Life): "I dissect everyone, even those I love, and my discoveries frequently sting me to the quick. 'To the pure all things are pure,' whence I should conclude I suppose that it is the beam in my own eye. But I would not tolerate being deceived concerning either my own beam or other people's motes" (p. 289). In other words, just because you're impure, that doesn't mean others aren't impure, too, and we're all better off admitting it. Even paranoiacs have enemies.

Faith without Works

Even so faith, if it hath not works, is dead, being alone. | Yea, a man may say, Thou hast faith, and I have works: shew me thy faith without thy works, and I will shew thee my faith by my works. | Thou believest that there is one God; thou doest well: the devils also believe, and tremble. | But wilt thou know, O vain man, that faith without works is dead?

James 2: 17–20

No doubt there are some among you who've never heard this phrase at a cocktail party, but it is familiar to many, and I include it in the interest of equal time.

St. Paul has had his say for epistle after epistle on the merits of faith and the freedom of grace. In contrast, James—the otherwise unknown author of this letter, sometimes presumed to be Jesus' brother—lays more stress on works than on faith. Paul was primarily interested in what a good Christian didn't have to do—namely, obey the letter of the Mosaic law; James is afraid some Christians have gotten the idea that all they have to do to be saved is intellectually assent to the Gospel.

James says that there's no such thing as an armchair Christian. If your beliefs do not move you to act, they are "dead" beliefs, impotent if not unreal. After all, "devils" too believe in God and fear him, and they're not going to be saved any time soon. Even the devil may pose as a Christian (and often has), but the proof of faith is in the pudding. Good works not only show faith, they make it "perfect" (whole and complete). James lays his point right out a few verses later: "By works a man is justified, and not by faith only" (verse 24). Paul would turn in his grave at that one.

The Weaker Vessel

> Likewise, ye husbands, dwell with them [wives] according to
> knowledge, giving honour unto the wife, as unto the weaker
> vessel, and as being heirs together of the grace of life; that your
> prayers be not hindered.

I Peter 3: 7

It's been a while since we last considered the Bible's sexism, but this phrase offers us another good opportunity. The author of First Peter—perhaps the very "rock" on whom Christ built his church [*see* p. 209]—is certainly a little condescending toward women, at least by modern lights. As he instructs husbands on proper conjugal attitudes, he refers to the wife as "the weaker vessel" (in revised versions, "the weaker sex")—where "vessel" is a metaphor for "body" (the "vessel" of the soul).

This isn't the worst Peter says—for example, he's all for wives' "subjection" to their husbands (verses 1 and 5). On the other hand, he calls on wives to be an example in holiness to their mates, who tend to be weaker in that regard. But what we remember is the phrase "weaker vessel," though it has rarely been uttered with a straight face, even in less enlightened times. Oscar Wilde uses it satirically in *The Importance of Being Earnest* (1895), when the governess Miss Prism rebukes Dr. Chasuble for his aversion to matrimony. "You do not seem to realize, dear Doctor," she sniffs, "that by persistently remaining single, a man converts himself into a permanent public temptation. Men should be more careful; this very celibacy leads weaker vessels astray." Her premise is that "No married man is ever attractive except to his wife"—a notion almost as prejudicial, to both parties, as "the weaker vessel."

Alpha and Omega

Behold, he cometh with clouds; and every eye shall see him, and they also which pierced him: and all kindreds of the earth shall wail because of him. Even so, Amen. | I am Alpha and Omega, the beginning and the ending, saith the Lord, which is, and which was, and which is to come, the Almighty. | ... I am Alpha and Omega, the first and the last. ...

Revelation 1: 7–8, 11

The author of Revelation, John (called "the Divine"), begins his apocalyptic epistle by greeting his readers among "the seven churches which are in Asia" (he means "principal churches"; there were others). That taken care of, he then launches into the first of many prophetic visions.

John looks forward to the day when Christ shall return to earth, his presence visible even to those who nailed him to the cross. Clearly, John was writing while at least some of these men were still alive—that is, sometime in the first century—and just as clearly he expected Christ to return mighty soon.

John, reveling in the thought of God's imminent vengeance, presses ahead. Grasping for appropriate titles for the Lord, he echoes his earlier description of "him which is, and which was, and which is to come" (verse 4). Using categories of time to comprehend an eternal God, John alludes to the LORD's explanation of his name at Exodus 3: 14 [see JEHOVAH, p. 57]. Likewise, by having God proclaim himself "the first and the last," John cites Isaiah, where the LORD says, "I am the first, and I am the last; and beside me there is no God" (Isaiah 44: 6).

In case these citations of Hebrew Scripture make his Hellenized audience uncomfortable, John puts the point in terms they're more likely to understand: "I am Alpha and Omega, the beginning and ending, saith the Lord." Alpha and omega are, of course, the first and last letters in the Greek alphabet. As we would say "everything from A to Z," John has God proclaim himself as the One who encompasses the totality of all other things. He preceded them and he will survive them.

But there's more to this than simple ABC's. "Alpha and omega" was also a kind of magical incantation, thought to aid in revelation. The phrase stood for all seven Greek vowels, which together were thought to constitute the name of the most powerful of gods. John's allusion to pagan magic here is ironic, since Revelation is intended to comfort those whose Christian brethren were persecuted for *refusing* to worship pagan gods (such as the Roman emperor). But irony isn't exactly John's forte, as we shall see.

Today we use John's phrase, slightly modified ("*the* Alpha and [*the*] Omega"), in decidedly more secular contexts, where it means "the whole shebang" or "the be-all and end-all." Andre Maurois wrote thus in *Ariel: The Life of Shelley* (1923) of the limits of romantic solitude: "What was the use of all these mountains, of all this blue sky without any friends? Social enjoyment, in some form or other, is the Alpha and Omega of existence." I doubt the Lord would agree, but there you have it. Nor would the Lord approve of all churches, for example Thomas De Quincey's "true church on the subject of opium: of which church," he confesses, "I acknowledge myself to be the only member—the alpha and the omega" (*Confessions of an English Opium Eater,* 1822). De Quincey, by the way, though an associate of Wordsworth and Coleridge, didn't know Shelley.

The Seven Seals AND
The Four Horsemen

And I saw in the right hand of him that sat on the throne [in heaven] a book written within and on the backside, sealed with seven seals. | And I saw a strong angel proclaiming with a loud voice, Who is worthy to open the book, and to loose the seals thereof? | And no man in heaven, nor in earth, neither under the earth, was able to open the book, neither to look thereon. | And I wept much, because no man was found worthy to open and to read the book, neither to look thereon.

Revelation 5: 1–4

I won't keep you on the edge of your seat. The answer to the angel's question is "Jesus Christ," or, to use John's nicknames, "the Lion of the tribe of Juda, the Root of David," who appears as "a Lamb as it had been slain, having seven horns and seven eyes, which are the seven Spirits of God sent forth into all the earth" (verses 5–6).

As you may have noticed, John has a thing for sevens, which is after all the holiest number in Hebrew Scripture [see JUBILEE, p. 79]. There is seven of just about everything in Revelation— seven Asian churches, seven Spirits arranged before God's throne, seven golden candlesticks, seven stars in Christ's right hand, seven proclamations, seven seals, seven trumpets, seven angels, seven "vials" (bowls), seven swans a-swimming, and so on and so forth. Seven, in short, is a very Godly number.

But what, actually, do the seven seals on the heavenly "book" (actually a scroll) represent? From subsequent events, it appears that each seal is one key to the future, each key unlocking part of the scroll, which contains an authoritative report on the

Coming of God's Kingdom. As Christ breaks each of the seals, John is presented with a new vision of what is to be, and some of these visions are rather distressing.

Breaking each of the first four seals, for example, ushers in one of the so-called "Four Horsemen of the Apocalypse." The first, on a white horse, is bent on relentless conquest; the second, on a red horse, represents war; the third, on a black horse, brings famine; and the last, the most fearsome, on his sickly-pale horse, is Death, with Hell tagging behind. The End, in short, will begin with quite a bang.

Opening the fifth seal produces a slightly more tranquil vision of Christ's martyrs crying out for justice, but the sixth seal brings more bad news: earthquakes, eclipses, falling stars, and global cataclysm. Respite arrives with the breaking of the famous seventh seal, which results in "silence in heaven about the space of half an hour" (8: 1). This gives John just enough time to catch his breath before the Last Judgment is unfolded before him, which is when the imagery really starts getting bizarre. More to follow.

The Four Corners of the Earth

> And after these things I saw four angels standing on the four corners of the earth, holding the four winds of the earth, that the wind should not blow on the earth, nor on the sea, nor on any tree.

Revelation 7: 1

We don't know whether or not John imagined the earth was flat; by no means did everyone in his day think so. However, he was stuck with a Scripture that endorsed the flat-earth theory, for Isaiah had already spoken of "the four corners of the earth" (Isaiah 11: 12, first translated by Miles Coverdale).

Englishmen of Coverdale's age, however, knew the earth was round, so the biblical "corner" was taken to mean "an extremity of the earth, a direction or quarter from which the wind blows" (OED). Shakespeare may have had Revelation in mind when he had the braggart Benedick, in *Much Ado about Nothing* (1598) ask, "Sits the wind in that corner?" (Act 2, scene 3)—meaning, "Is that really the size of the situation?" Subsequently, "corner" would lose its winds as well as its angels, though winds' force would often be implied. "We are perfectly safe from that Corner," wrote Jonathan Swift in *The Drapier Letters* (1724), with reference not to angels but to inimical blowhards.

So the phrase has blown strong, even as its original meaning was scattered to the winds. Now we use the phrase to mean "the most remote, far-flung, and exotic locales," often as shorthand for saying "absolutely everywhere." In his essay "Excellent," for example, Robert Lynd lauds those "great colonizing and missionary movements that have carried civilization to the four corners of the earth." How politically incorrect.

Bottomless Pit

And the fifth angel sounded, and I saw a star fall from heaven
unto the earth: and to him was given the key of the bottomless
pit. | And he opened the bottomless pit. … | And there came out
of the smoke locusts upon the earth: and unto them was given
power, as the scorpions of the earth have power. | … And they
had a king over them, which is the angel of the bottomless pit,
whose name in the Hebrew tongue is Abaddon, but in the Greek
tongue hath his name Apollyon.

Revelation 9: 1–3, 11

The seventh seal [*see* p. 312] has been opened and seven angels of
destruction have begun their woeful work. The unenviable task
of the fifth is to loose the swarm of locusts that will torment for
five months "those men which have not the seal of God in their
foreheads," driving them to wish for a death that will not come.
Personally, we'll take a raincheck. (On "the seal of God," *see* the
next entry, p. 316.)

The "bottomless pit" out of which these creatures swarm is,
of course, hell, or *sheol* in Hebrew and *Hades* in the Greek of
Revelation. John Milton also called it "Abaddon" in *Paradise
Regained,* after the name of the king of the locusts. ("*Abaddon*"
in Hebrew means "destruction" or "place of destruction," so the
dark angel easily merges with the place he tends.) The colorful
imagery of this passage is forgotten when we use "bottomless
pit" today to refer to a mere sinkhole.

The Mark of the Beast

And he [the second beast] had power to give life unto the image
of the beast, that the image of the beast should both speak, and
cause that as many as would not worship the image of the beast
should be killed. | And he causeth all, both small and great, rich
and poor, free and bond, to receive a mark in their right hand, or
in their foreheads: | And that no man might buy or sell, save he
that had the mark, or the name of the beast, or the number of
his name. | Here is wisdom. Let him that hath understanding
count the number of the beast: for it is the number of a man;
and his number is Six hundred threescore and six.

Revelation 13: 15–18

Adherents of Revelation have never lacked candidates to fill the
rather large shoes of "the Beast" (a.k.a. "the Antichrist")—from
the pope to the military-industrial complex to Procter &
Gamble. But John never held the latter's old logo up to a mirror—which is how some people claimed to find "the number of
the beast," namely 666.

What John really has in mind is Rome, whose emperor Nero
had made quite a career of persecuting Christians. John depicts
his allegorical "beast" (13: 1) as a servant of the "dragon" (Satan)
with "seven heads and ten horns." The "heads" (according to
17: 9) are the seven hills of Rome and also seven evil emperors,
the sixth of whom (probably Domitian) reigns as John writes.
(John thought the eighth would be Nero returned from a false
suicide—a popular fear of the day.) The ten horns, to continue
deciphering, are "ten kings" from Asia (17: 12) whom John apparently expects to join the hateful Nero when he returns.

Other details of John's account have similar correspondences.
But the identity of a second "beast," who first appears here and

is later called a "false prophet" (16: 13, etc.), is harder to fix. Since the second beast "causeth the earth and them which dwell therein to worship the first beast," he likely represents the priesthood of the imperial cult, which advocated worshiping the emperor as a god.

Which leaves two important questions: how does the priesthood manage to place a "mark" on the hands and foreheads of every man and woman, and what is this "mark"? First off, John doesn't mean a visible mark. Writing in an extremely figurative mode, John darkly condemns the imperial priesthood for ostracizing Christians (among other things, they could not "buy or sell"). Only those who submitted to emperor-worship earned approval—metaphorically, the emperor's "mark"—to join in the literal and figurative marketplace of society. (In contrast, faithful Christian martyrs have upon them the "seal of the living God" [7: 2]. John tells us there will be exactly 144,000 such lucky souls.)

John doesn't care how you choose to envision this "mark"; it could be an icon, or the beast's name, or even "the number of his name." The solution to this puzzle is relatively simple. If you render the Hebrew name for Nero Caesar into Hebrew script, you get *nrwn qsr*; each Hebrew character in turn has a numerical value, which, when summed up, yields the magic number, 666. (Try it yourself: *n* = 50; *r* = 200; *w* = 6; *q* = 100; and *s* = 60. Hebrews, like the Romans, used letters to represent numbers.) The trick works equally well in John's native language, Aramaic.

Armageddon

And the sixth angel poured out his vial upon the great river
Euphrates; and the water thereof was dried up, that the way of
the kings of the east might be prepared. | And I saw three
unclean spirits like frogs come out of the mouth of the dragon,
and out of the mouth of the beast, and out of the mouth of the
false prophet. | For they are the spirits of devils, working
miracles, which go forth unto the kings of the earth and of the
whole world, to gather them to the battle of that great day of
God Almighty. | … And he gathered them together into a place
called in the Hebrew tongue Armageddon. | And the seventh
angel poured out his vial into the air; and there came a great
voice out of the temple of heaven, from the throne, saying, It is
done.

Revelation 16: 12–14, 16–17

We use "Armageddon" as a synonym for "the End of the World"
or "The Ultimate Conflict." But even if you don't know Hebrew, Revelation makes it plain that Armageddon is a "place"
(verse 16), not an event.

But it helps to know Hebrew. "Armageddon" comes from *har
megiddo,* "the mount of Megiddo." Megiddo is an ancient Palestinian city that figures in several passages of Hebrew Scripture
(Joshua 12: 21; Judges 5: 19; I Kings 4: 12; etc.); it is now identified with the Israeli city Tell el-Mutesellim. According to John,
the final conflict between God and the forces of evil will unfold
near Megiddo. He probably picked the place because it was the
site of many legendary ancient battles, stretching back to the
fifteenth century B.C. (Either John's Hebrew or his geography
isn't so good, however; there is no known mountain that fits the
description.)

Before the big showdown, however, there will be more suffering on earth, even beyond the horrors unleashed by the Four Horsemen, the angels of destruction, et al. This time seven plagues—that number again—will be dispensed by seven angels from seven bowls or "vials" full of the wrath of God (thus the phrase, occasionally heard, "to pour out vials of wrath"). Among the plagues will be boils, seas and rivers of blood, sunburn, darkness, the drying of the Euphrates, and, finally, cataclysmic earthquakes.

When the seventh angel finally pours out the seventh vial of wrath, the punishment is complete and God proclaims, "It is done." A great cataclysm destroys all the cities of earth, Rome is split into three, and the forces of evil gathered at Megiddo meet their doom crying out vainly against God, who sends down a plague of hail for good measure. It is time for the Last Judgment.

The Millennium AND Gog and Magog

> And I saw thrones, and they [the martyrs] sat upon them, and
> judgment was given unto them: and I saw the souls of them that
> were beheaded for the witness of Jesus, and for the word of God,
> and which had not worshipped the beast, neither his image,
> neither had received his mark upon their foreheads, or in their
> hands; and they lived and reigned with Christ a thousand years. |
> But the rest of the dead lived not again until the thousand years
> were finished. This is the first resurrection.

> Revelation 20: 4–5

"Millennium," as a common noun derived from Latin, simply
means "a thousand years." But the word also has a particular
religious significance having to do with a purported thousand-
year reign of Christ and his martyrs upon the earth after the
Second Coming. (John tells the story but doesn't use the word
"millennium.")

While all this is going on, "that old serpent"—namely, "the
Devil, and Satan" (20: 2)—will be sitting in chains, which is the
good news. The bad news is that the rest of us are going to remain dead until the millennium ends. The other bad news is
that at the same time Satan shall be set free to go and "deceive
the nations which are in the four quarters of the earth, [while
seeking] Gog and Magog, to gather them together to battle"
(verse 8). More good news, though, is that God is going to burn
them all to a crisp with fire from heaven and then toss the Devil
into the lake of fire and brimstone, "where the beast and the
false prophet are" (verse 10). It should be fine company.

Regarding the "Gog and Magog" business, John harks back
to the Book of Ezekiel, which he seems to misunderstand. In

Ezekiel, Gog is "the chief prince of Meschech and Tubal" (Ezekiel 38: 2), two regions of central Asia Minor. ("I am against thee, O Gog," adds the Lord.) "Gog" is in fact probably a pseudonym for Gyges, king of Lydia in the seventh century B.C., by legend the possessor of a ring of invisibility. Magog in Ezekiel, on the other hand, is a place, not a person—namely, "the land of Gog" (from the Akkadian *mat Gog*). What John was thinking, I don't know, but he treats both Gog and Magog as evil nations who will ally themselves with Satan against God's people.

"Millennium" was first used to name Christ's thousand-year reign about a generation after the King James Version was published. It became a metaphor for a future time of happiness and prosperity, as in Lord Byron's *Marino Faliero* (1820): "But this day, black within the calendar, / Shall be succeeded by a bright millennium."

A New Heaven and a New Earth
AND *The New Jerusalem*

And I saw a new heaven and a new earth: for the first heaven and
the first earth were passed away; and there was no more sea. |
And I John saw the holy city, new Jerusalem, coming down from
God out of heaven, prepared as a bride adorned for her husband.
| And I heard a great voice out of heaven saying, Behold, the
tabernacle of God is with men, and he will dwell with them, and
they shall be his people, and God himself shall be with them,
and be their God. | And God shall wipe away all tears from their
eyes; and there shall be no more death, neither sorrow, nor
crying, neither shall there be any more pain: for the former
things are passed away.

Revelation 21: 1–4

At the end of the Millennium, God will finally render his Last
Judgment, which we've been hearing so much about. Those
whose names and deeds are recorded in the "book of life"
(20: 12) shall be saved; but those who are "not found written in
the book of life" shall be "cast into the lake of fire" (20: 15),
where the Devil frolics with the Beast and the False Prophet.
(This book, unfortunately, isn't available in stores.)

The Last Judgment is God's ultimate spring cleaning, just in
time for the arrival of a very special guest. The old heaven and
old earth are swept away to make room for better versions; from
the "new heaven" descends to the "new earth" a spanking "new
Jerusalem," which is described as "prepared as a bride adorned
for her husband." The happy groom is no other than Jesus
Christ himself, who is apparently delighted with a spouse twelve
thousand stadia (about 1,400 miles) square, and who has twelve
pearly gates rather than eyes, ears, a mouth, etc.

But of course John indulges here in allegory. The "new Jerusalem" stands collectively for the martyrs and the faithful, the holy congregation, who will symbolically "marry" Christ by joining with him in righteousness forever. There shall no longer be death, or sorrow, or pain, or tears, just joyful basking in the glory of God.

The idea of a "new Jerusalem" has roots in Hebrew Scripture; the Psalmist, for example, alludes to "the city of the LORD of hosts, ... the city of our God: God will establish it forever" (Psalm 48: 8). In the book of Isaiah, God promises to "create new heavens and a new earth: and the former shall not be re-membered, nor come into mind" (Isaiah 65: 17). St. Paul, too, had spoken of a "Jerusalem which is above, ... which is the mother of us all" (Galatians 4: 26); and in Hebrews we find mentioned "the city of the living God, the heavenly Jerusalem" (Hebrews 12: 22). John reflects the rabbinic notion that the city of God on earth—the actual Jerusalem—shall be replaced in the life to come with an idealized, eternal version, which shall be a new Paradise.

References to such a city today, however, are less grandiose. Rose Macaulay writes of the kind of "new Jerusalem" most of us are ever likely to see in *Told by an Idiot* (1923): "Gold and purple and crimson. Silver and scarlet and gold. Fluttering pennons on tall Venetian masts. The Mall was a street in fairyland, or the New Jerusalem." Disneyland hadn't been built yet, nor the first shopping mall, though such places currently pass for versions of paradise.

Purgatory

There are suggestions in the books of Second Maccabees and First Corinthians of a place neither heaven nor hell, where sinners who are basically just will suffer temporarily before resurrection. Catholic theologians advanced on this basis the doctrine of "Purgatory," a place of purification serving as a way station between death and salvation for lower-grade sinners. The notion was attacked by early Protestants, one of whom called it "a fond thing vainly invented."

In this section of the book, I (remaining neutral) collect both fond things vainly invented—that is, phrases falsely thought of biblical origin—and entries of less importance or currency than those in the main text, along with a few side notes and curiosities. I deal first with phrases of the former type in "Faux Bible" (which begins immediately below) and those of the second type in "Pages of Refuge" (which begins on p. 333).

Faux Bible

THE APPLE OF ONE'S EYE

This phrase, found at Deuteronomy 32: 10; Psalm 17: 8; and Proverbs 7: 2, is occasionally attributed to the English Bible. But it had already appeared by A.D. 885, at the latest, well before the first translation of any Hebrew Scriptures. For a time— at least into the nineteenth century—the phrase meant not only "someone or something cherished" but also "pupil."

TO BE BESIDE ONESELF

In the sense of "be out of one's mind," the phrase does appear in the King James Version of the Acts of the Apostles (26: 24): "Paul, thou art beside thyself; much learning doth make thee mad." But the phrase isn't biblical; it dates back at least to the late fifteenth century. However, "much learning doth make thee mad" is biblical as well as true.

BETTER NEVER TO HAVE BEEN BORN

In Matthew's Gospel (26: 24) we find the line, "It had been good for that man if he had not been born." But the saying originates in Sophocles' *Oedipus at Colonus,* written nearly five centuries earlier. "Never to have been born is best," chants the chorus of elderly gentlemen, who've had plenty of time to come to that conclusion.

CLEAR AS CRYSTAL

Though this phrase appears at Revelation 22: 1 ("And he [the angel] shewed me a pure river of water of life, clear as crystal, proceeding out of the throne of God and of the Lamb"), it was already in circulation before any translation of that book. The earliest citation in the OED, however, is from the *Cursor Mundi* (ca. 1300), a religious poem full of allusions to the Bible. The phrase "crystal clear" appeared by the early sixteenth century.

A CONTRITE HEART

It is sometimes said that "a contrite heart" derives from Psalm 51: 7, but "contrite of heart" appeared in the fourteenth century, "contrite in heart" in the fifteenth, and "contrite hearts" in the sixteenth.

Don't know him from Adam

In other words, "I wouldn't be able to tell him apart from Adam" (someone we've all heard of but never seen). No one in the Bible ever says this, of course, but Englishmen have used "Adam" in any number of expressions that would have puzzled the original. This phrase dates to 1784, when an anonymous hand wrote in the serial *London Sessions* that "Some man stopped me, I do not know him from Adam." Another familiar saying, "as old as Adam," came later, tracing to 1867, when the pseudonymous "Colonist" wrote, "Though as old as Adam, love is still the theme that interests all hearts in all countries." Since both persons are so coy about their identity, I wouldn't know them from Adam (or Eve).

to Give up the ghost

John Wyclif, in translating Matthew 27: 50 in 1388, was indeed the first to use "up" in the phrase "to give up the ghost." But "give the ghost" was in use by the early fourteenth century, and it may trace back to 900. The now familiar version also appears at Job 14: 10; Jeremiah 15: 9; Luke 23: 46; and John 19: 30.

God forbid!

"God forbid!" gasps the audience of priests, lawyers, and elders as Jesus wraps up a parable aimed right in their direction (Luke 20: 16). Jesus hints that all the jealous hypocrites who seek his death will ultimately be crushed under God's mighty fist. This is a conclusion God will in fact *not* forbid; on top of that the phrase doesn't originate here, but rather in the thirteenth century poem *Cursor Mundi.* If it's any consolation, that poem does draw heavily on the Bible, but in this case no particular passage is cited.

the Golden Rule

"Therefore all things whatsoever ye would that men should do to you, do ye even so to them," says Jesus (Matthew 7: 12): "for this is the law of the prophets." What Jesus doesn't say is that it was also a common saying among both the Greeks and the Romans, who bequeathed it to the Jews. Furthermore, it's unclear where this "law" may be found among the "prophets," though Jesus may refer to Leviticus 19: 18: "Thou shalt love thy neighbour as thyself" [*see* p. 77]. In any case, it is his version rather than Leviticus's that became known as the "Golden Rule," first referred to by Robert Godfrey in 1674 as the "Golden Law." "Golden Rule," which actually predates Godfrey, was originally a mathematical term; only in the nineteenth century, it seems, was the name given over to "do unto others as you would have them do unto you," which is a paraphrase of Jesus rather than a quotation.

an Ivory tower

Addressing himself to a "prince's daughter," the singer of The Song of Solomon 7 (verses 3–4) gets carried away with his romantic similes: "Thy two breasts are like two young roes that are twins. | Thy neck is as a tower of ivory"; even better, "thine eyes [are] like fishpools in Heshbon, by the gate of Bathrabbim: thy nose is as the tower of Lebanon which looketh toward Damascus" (as opposed, say, to the tower that looketh toward Tyre). Obviously, the singer doesn't have Oxford or Columbia in mind when he compares the princess's neck to "a tower of ivory," and anyway Chaucer had beaten Wyclif to the punch by about twenty years. "Her throat," he writes in *The Dethe of Blaunche* (ca. 1369), "Seemed a round tower of ivory." I guess that in the fourteenth century that was considered high praise.

Jumpin' Jehoshaphat!

Several persons in the Hebrew Bible are named "Jehoshaphat," and no one knows which of them—none is singled out as a leaper—came to be honored when, in nineteenth-century America, the name was turned into a euphemistic substitution for "Jesus!" (At some point thereafter, the second *h* was removed.) "Jumping Jehoshaphat!" (actually, "Great jumping Jehoshaphat!") first appeared in 1935, in Georgette Heyer's *Death in the Stocks,* which I haven't read but which sure sounds gripping. The name "Jehoshaphat," which means "Yahweh judges," is also that of a valley mentioned in the Book of Joel as the place where God shall judge the enemies of Israel. It is perhaps better known today by Joel's other term, "the valley of decision" (Joel 3: 14).

the Last gasp

"At the last gasp" appears in the Authorized Version in the Apocryphal Second Book of the Maccabees (7: 9), and some believe this is the original source of the phrase. But it had already been written down by 1577, in the form "unto the last gasp."

"a Mess of pottage"

This is what Jacob's brother Esau (infamously) traded his birthright for, but the phrase appears nowhere in the original text. It appears, rather, in the chapter heading to Genesis 25 in various sixteenth-century Bibles. The King James Version refers (at verse 34) only to the "bread and pottage [stew] and lentiles [*sic*]" Jacob serves Esau in return for the rights due Isaac's eldest son. Nonetheless, "mess" (meaning "a serving of food") would be remembered and "to sell one's birthright for a mess of potage" quoted in reference to bad bargains where one gives up something permanent or priceless for something temporarily gratifying.

ORIGINAL SIN

If you thought mankind's "original sin" was eating the forbidden fruit, you may be surpised to learn that the word "sin" never occurs in J's account of that episode; in fact, it first occurs in the story of Cain and Abel [*see* p. 24]. "Original sin" is not a biblical term or, in the sense of "inborn sin," a biblical concept; the notion was developed by Catholic theologians and formalized only in the sixteenth century. Some support for it is found in St. Paul's Epistle to the Romans: "Wherefore, as by one man sin entered into the world, and death by sin; and so death passed upon all men, for that all have sinned" (5: 12). The wording is ambiguous, and Paul may simply be reprising Genesis 3, in which mankind is condemned to mortality on account of Adam and Eve's transgression.

"PHYSICIAN, HEAL THYSELF"

Though the phrasing, from Luke 4: 23, may originate in the Bible, Jesus himself identifies the line as a "proverb." In fact, the saying was common both in Greek and Latin long before the composition of the Gospels.

TO PLAY THE FOOL

"Behold," says Saul in a moment of repentance for his treatment of David, "I have played the fool, and erred exceedingly" (I Samuel 26: 21). But "to play the fool" is not a biblical phrase; it was already in circulation by 1426.

THE PROMISED LAND

This phrase does not appear in the King James Bible [*see* JACOB'S LADDER, p. 41], though we do find "land of promise" in the Epistle to the Hebrews, whose author speaks of Abraham sojourning "in the land of promise, as in a strange country" (11: 9). The form "promised land" first appeared in John Milton's *Paradise Lost* (1667).

TO RAISE CAIN

This phrase began life in early nineteenth-century America as a more polite way of saying "to raise the devil." (Cain, as the first criminal, was as good a candidate as any, I suppose.) In this context, "raise" means "stir up," not "rear," but the first person to use the phrase in writing availed himself of the pun: "Why have we every reason to believe that Adam and Eve were both rowdies?" quizzed an anonymous hand in one 1940 edition of the St. Louis *Daily Pennant.* "Because ... they both raised Cain."

TO REAP WHAT YOU SOW

"Be not deceived," thunders Paul in his epistle to the Galatians; "God is not mocked: for whatsoever a man soweth, that shall he also reap" (6: 7). While one may be grateful to Paul for his kinder, gentler version of "to reap the whirlwind" [*see* p. 156], one cannot thank him for the phrase itself, at least not its English rendition, which was in circulation (in an early form) by the thirteenth century. The poet John Lydgate, in *The Assembly of Gods* (ca. 1420), first put it into modern English before Galatians was translated: "Such as ye have sowe [*sic*] / Must ye needs reap."

THIS VALE OF TEARS

This phrase, referring to our miserable earthly existence, is sometimes said to derive from Psalm 84, where the King James Version mentions a certain "Vale [Valley] of Baca," earlier translated by Miles Coverdale as "vale of misery." While it's true that *baca* does mean "weeping" in Hebrew, in this context it refers rather to "baca trees," a sort of balsam that "weeps" its gum. Such trees were found in the Valley of Baca, a dry plain crossed by pilgrims on their way to Jerusalem. And indeed while "vale of misery," "vale of adversity," "vale of trouble, of woe, and of heaviness," "vale of trouble and distrees," and "vale of weeping" were all in circulation as Coverdale tranlsated Psalms, the phrase "vale of tears" was committed to writing only in 1618, by Sir Walter Raleigh.

AT WIT'S END

Enumerating all the ways God exerts his power over men, the Psalmist tells how sailors "see the works of the LORD, and his wonders in the deep" (Psalm 107: 24)—by getting tossed up and down in storms. "They reel to an fro," chuckles the author, "and stagger like a drunken man, and are at their wits' end" (verse 27). A humorous verse, so it's a pity "at wit's end" isn't really the Psalmist's coinage. The phrase first appeared in John Langland's *Piers Plowman* (1377).

ET AL.

Other phrases that never appear in the English Bible are discussed in the text. These include "forbidden fruit" (*see* p. 15); "Adam's apple" (p. 16); "ashes to ashes, dust to dust" (p. 20); "Heaven's gate" (p. 42); Jonah and "the whale" (p. 158); the "straight and narrow path" (p. 186); the "three kings of Orient" (p. 166); "old wine in new bottles" (p. 192); "it's better to give than to receive" (p. 271); and "millennium" (p. 320).

Pages of Refuge

AN ABOMINATION OF DESOLATION

In an apocalyptic passage of Matthew (24: 15), Jesus foretells the End of all things, when his disciples "shall see the abomination of desolation, spoken of by Daniel the prophet"—namely, at Daniel 9: 27; 11: 31; and 12: 11. What Daniel referred to, apparently, was the placing of a statue of Zeus (this is the "abomination") in the Jerusalem Temple in 168 B.C., which was to foretell the coming of "desolation" upon Israel. What Jesus seems to mean is that, at the beginning of the End, Israel shall be overrun by hostile forces and there shall be a "great tribulation, such as was not since the beginning of the world to this time, no, nor ever shall be" (Matthew 24: 21).

ABRAHAM'S BOSOM

"Into Abraham's bosom" is where angels carry the late beggar Lazarus in the Gospel according to Luke (16: 22–23). Luke relies on the old Jewish idea that Abraham, first and greatest of Hebrew patriarchs, presides over some sort of resting place for the spirits of good men. (Genesis, though, says nothing of the sort.) Exactly where Abraham and his "bosom" are supposed to be is unclear. Jewish beliefs at the time on heaven and hell (*sheol* in Hebrew, or *Hades* in Greek) were diverse; perhaps Lazarus is carried straight into heaven, but more likely he finds himself resting on Abraham's chest in some paradisiacal waiting room, which might not even be all that far from hell. In fact, the rich man who in life refused to feed Lazarus crumbs from his table, who now roasts in hellfire, can easily spy on Lazarus and Abraham. Maybe Abraham's bosom is Purgatory, but who knows? All one can say for sure is that "to sleep in Abraham's bosom" was proverbial by the mid-1500s. The allusion was familiar enough by the end of the century that Shakespeare could make a joke of it, having Hostess Quickly proclaim, "Nay, sure, [Falstaff's] not in hell: he's in Arthur's bosom, if ever a man went to Arthur's bosom" (*King Henry the Fifth*, 1599).

"ALMOST THOU PERSUADEST ME TO BE A CHRISTIAN"

This, according to the Acts of the Apostles (chapter 26) is what King Herod Agrippa II of Judea and Samaria, a Jew, says to an imprisoned St. Paul when the latter argues for his belief in Christ. But almost isn't good enough; Agrippa seems to be having a little fun at Paul's expense. At the time, "Christian" was a relatively new term for followers of Jesus; according to an earlier passage of Acts (11: 26), "the disciples were called Christians first in Antioch," circa A.D. 45–46.

"BABYLON IS FALLEN, IS FALLEN, THAT GREAT CITY"

In the first part of the book of Isaiah, the prophet has a vision of the future destruction of one of Judah's nemeses: "Babylon is fallen, is fallen; and all the graven images of her gods he [the LORD] hath broken unto the ground" (Isaiah 21: 9). Babylon did fall, but centuries later it was resurrected by the author of Revelation. As Jesus stands triumphant on Mount Zion, an angel appears to say, "Babylon is fallen, is fallen, that great city, because she made all nations drink of the wine of the wrath of her fornication" (Revelation 14: 8). The reference here isn't to the erstwhile city, but rather to that latter-day evil empire, Rome. Rome, of course, fell, too, when the Visigoths sacked it in the fifth century. But, as of this writing, Jesus has not yet reappeared on Mount Zion.

IT BITETH LIKE A SERPENT, AND STINGETH LIKE AN ADDER

This is what the author of Proverbs (23: 32) has to say for wine, which will also make "Thine eyes ... behold strange women, and thine heart ... utter perverse things" (verse 33). The author of Ecclesiasticus, however, takes a different position: "What life is then to a man that is without wine? for it was made to make men glad" (31: 27).

"BLESSED ART THOU AMONG WOMEN"

The beginning of the "Hail Mary"—a Christian prayer second only to the Lord's Prayer in fame and familiarity—is a reformulation of one verse from Luke's Gospel: "And the angel came in unto her [Mary], and said, Hail, thou that art highly favoured, the Lord is with thee: blessed art thou among women" (1: 28). The rest—"blessed is the fruit of thy womb, Jesus," etc.—was devised centuries later.

"BREAD" PHRASES

Besides "man does not live by bread alone," "to cast bread upon the waters," "daily bread," "loaves and fishes," "to break bread," and (if you count it) "manna from heaven," a few other biblical "bread" phrases have achieved modest fame. "The bread of affliction," from Deuteronomy 16: 3, refers to unleavened cakes eaten during Passover to commemmorate the times of "affliction" in Egypt. The book of Proverbs speaks, in its typically sexist way, of the virtuous wife who "looketh well to the ways of her household, and eateth not the bread of idleness" (31: 27). Isaiah speaks more famously of "the bread of adversity, and the water of affliction" (Isaiah 30: 20), which is a metaphorical reference to the hardships of exile in Babylon. Finally, in the Gospel according to John, Jesus refers to himself as "the bread of life": "he that cometh to me shall never hunger; and he that believeth on me shall never thirst" (John 6: 35). In each case, except in the more literal Deuteronomy, "bread" means "the basic stuff."

A CHARIOT OF FIRE

As the prophet Elijah chats one day with his disciple Elisha, "Behold, there appeared a chariot of fire, and horses of fire, and parted them both [Elijah and Elisha] asunder; and Elijah went up by a whirlwind into heaven" (II Kings 2: 11). So much for Elijah's mission on earth. The chariot of fire is obviously a divine vehicle, a public transit system to heaven, if you will; it would later be immortalized as the title of the Hollywood film *Chariots of Fire: The Movie* (as opposed, for example, to *Chariots of Fire: The Soundtrack*).

"CHARITY SUFFERETH LONG, AND IS KIND"

This is one of St. Paul's better known arguments (from I Corinthians 13: 4) in favor of *agape* ("charity" or "love"), which he considers the greatest Christian virtue [*see* FAITH, HOPE, AND CHARITY, p. 285].

THE CHILDREN OF LIGHT

This phrase appears several times in the New Testament—for example, at Luke 16: 8 ("For the children of this world are in their generation wiser than the children of light") and John 12: 36 ("While ye have the light, believe in the light, that ye may be the children of light"). In Greek literally "the sons of light," the expression seems to refer to the community of the righteous; it was also the term used by the authors of the Dead Sea Scrolls to refer to themselves as a body of the "elect" (those chosen for salvation). The doctrines of the Dead Sea sect—probably Essenes—are now believed to have influenced John's Gospel, if not Jesus himself.

CITIES OF REFUGE

The LORD uses this term at Joshua 20: 2, referring back to Deuteronomy 4: 41–43, where Moses sets apart three cities in Transjordan as places of safety for those who "kill [their] neighbour unawares" (commit manslaughter). In Joshua, such "cities of refuge" are intended for accused murderers, who would be safe from revenge until their cases were judged. The phrase was coined by Wyclif in his 1388 revision of Joshua 21: 13.

CONSIDER THE LILIES OF THE FIELD

"Consider the lilies of the field, how they grow; they toil not, neither do they spin," says Jesus (rather poetically) to the multitude at Matthew 6: 28. In other words, lilies do nothing to "earn" God's making them grow and flower; all the better, then, will he care for mankind—"Shall he not much more clothe you, O ye of little faith?" (verse 30).

THE CROWN OF LIFE

In the General Epistle of James, the author claims that "The Lord hath promised" the "crown of life" to those that love him (1: 12). In biblical literature, crowns are both festive and signs of triumph and privilege; here the "crown of life" is a symbol of the eternal life that the faithful will enjoy, as a special reward. The image reappears in Revelation (2: 10), where we also find references to "the book of life," a record of those who are to be saved [see A NEW HEAVEN AND A NEW EARTH, p. 322].

DANIEL IN THE LION'S DEN

The hero Daniel [see FEET OF CLAY, p. 152, etc.] is put on the spot when his enemies convince the Persian king Darius to forbid prayer to any god save himself. When Daniel continues praying to Yahweh, Darius (reluctantly) condemns him to be tossed "into the den of lions" to meet his doom (Daniel 6: 16). Of course, with the LORD's help, Daniel escapes unscathed; Daniel's enemies, however, don't fare so well when Darius orders *them* to be thrown to the lions, who "brake [*sic*] all their bones in pieces" (verse 24). This famous story did influence usage of the phrase "in the lion's den" (meaning "up against real trouble"), but it isn't the source. "Den" was used as the name of the feline's habitation as early as the thirteenth century, and we may safely assume that even then no one was eager to venture too far into one. The related phrase "to beard the lion in his den" (which Daniel doesn't do) is a nineteenth-century coinage.

TO DIE THE DEATH

Once again rebuking the Pharisees, Jesus points out that "God commanded, saying, Honour thy father and mother: and, He that curseth father or mother, let him die the death" (Matthew 15: 4, a reference to Exodus 21: 12–17; compare Mark 7: 10). One wonders what else one could die except "the death"—die the head cold? Die the toothache? Die the life? In any case, the Pharisees have been questioning the disciples' neglect of tradition (in this case, washing your hands before dinner). Rather than apologize for such hygienic lapses, Jesus launches a countercharge: you Pharisees should talk, when you don't even honor your parents, which is explicitly demanded by the Law! Score another one for the Messiah.

"THE END OF ALL THINGS IS AT HAND"

At least, so thought the apostle Peter (I Peter 4: 7), as did St. Paul, and possibly Jesus, too. Christianity began as an apocalyptic religion, based partly on the belief that God's kingdom was about to come. When it didn't, certain adjustments had to be made.

"ALL FLESH IS AS GRASS"

This is a simile the apostle Peter picks up (I Peter 1: 24) from the book of Isaiah: "All flesh is as grass, and all the goodliness thereof is as the flower of the field: | The grass withereth, the flower fadeth: because the spirit of the LORD bloweth upon it: surely the people is grass" (Isaiah 40: 6–7). Peter leaves the main point intact (that is, we all die), but he drops the reference to God's mowing the people down. Instead, he adds: "But the word of the Lord endureth forever" (I Peter 1: 25).

THE FURNACE OF AFFLICTION

Along with the "lake of fire burning with brimstone" and the "bottomless pit" this is a place one might happily avoid. But where the lake and the pit are reserved for especially nasty characters (such as the Beast), the LORD has sent all Israel through the "furnace of affliction," a series of bitter trials meant to prove his chosen people's mettle (Isaiah 48: 10).

"GOD IS NO RESPECTER OF PERSONS"

"The Lord is judge," writes Ecclesiasticus, "and with him is no respect of persons" (35: 12). In the Protestant Bible the line is first found, in more familiar form, in the book of Acts: "Then Peter opened his mouth, and said, Of a truth I perceive that God is no respecter of persons" (Acts 10: 34). To translate: God doesn't play favorites; he doesn't care who you are—whether king or clown, Jew or Gentile; what counts is your righteousness. I'm glad Peter didn't say this *without* opening his mouth.

THE GOLDEN BOWL

Toward the end of his lecture, Ecclesiastes waxes poetic on death: "Or ever the silver cord be loosed, or the golden bowl be broken, or the pitcher be broken at the fountain, or the wheel broken at the cistern. | Then shall the dust return to the earth as it was: and the spirit shall return unto God who gave it" (12: 6–7). Man's life is like a golden "bowl" (lamp) strung from a silver cord, and like a fragile pitcher cast down by a wheel (pulley) into a vital well. As the cord snaps, the lamp breaks, the pitcher splits, and the well goes dark and dry, we return to dust. If Ecclesiastes lived in the second century B.C., he may have been familiar with another "golden bowl," found in Greek myth. That one is really just a bowl, the vessel Heracles borrows from Helios (the Sun) to skim over the seas and slay another hideous monster. But where Ecclesiastes' bowl is a figure of death, Hercules' bowl carries him to the Garden of the Hesperides, where he finds the golden apples of immortality.

A GRAIN OF MUSTARD SEED

Following up on one seed parable [*see* TO FALL BY THE WAYSIDE, p. 201], Jesus proposes another, comparing the kingdom of heaven to "a grain of mustard seed" (Matthew 13: 31)—the "least [tiniest] of all seeds." (Unfortunately, he's wrong.) But while the mustard seed is humble, if well sown it will grow bigger and bigger, to become "the greatest among herbs" (verse 32). In case you were about to jump in to defend coriander, by "greatest" Jesus means "biggest"; once again, he exaggerates, but who's counting. What he's getting at is no mystery: he and his tiny band of disciples are the mustard seed from which will grow a glorious congregation, the "tree" of God's kingdom.

INFAMOUS BIBLES

"He that hath ears to hear, let him hear," says Jesus in the Gospel according to Mark (4: 9). But an edition of the Bible printed in 1810 renders the verse thus: "Who hath ears to ear, let him hear." This bit of absurdity earned the edition infamy and the nickname "The Ears to Ear Bible." Other notable editions are the "Wicked Bible" (1631), which altered the seventh commandment (Exodus 20: 14) to read, "Thou shalt commit adultery"; the "Treacle Bible" (or "Bishops' Bible," 1568), in which Jeremiah 8: 22 reads, "is there no treacle in Gilead" (the King James Version gives "balm in Gilead"); the "Lions Bible" (1804), which refers at I Kings 8: 19 to the "son that shall come forth out of thy lions"; the "Placemaker's Bible" (1562), in which Jesus invents a new beatitude: "Blessed are the placemakers" (Matthew 5: 9); the "Unrighteous Bible" (1653), where St. Paul tells us in no uncertain terms that "the unrighteous shall inherit the Kingdom of God" (I Corinthians 6: 9); the "Sin On Bible" (1716), which has Jesus tell a man he's healed to "sin on more" (John 5: 14); the "Breeches Bible" (1560, better known as the Geneva Bible), which informs us that Adam and Eve "sewed fig-tree leaves together, and made themselves breeches" (Genesis 3: 7); the "Bug Bible" (Coverdale's version of 1535), which instead of the King James's "Thou shalt not be afraid for the terror by night" (Psalm 91: 5) gives, "Thou shalt not need to be afraid for any bugs at night"; the "Printers Bible" (1702), in which the Psalmist rails against "printers" who have "persecuted me with-out a cause" (Psalm 119: 161; he really means "princes"); and the "Large Family Bible" (1820), in which, at Isaiah 66: 9, the LORD asks rhetorically, "Shall I bring to the birth and not cease to bring forth?" (it should read, "cause to bring forth"). These and other editions are discussed under "Bible" in *Brewer's Dictionary of Phrase and Fable* (HarperCollins).

JESUS' LAST WORDS

In the Gospels of Matthew and Mark, Jesus uttered no words as he died—he only "cried with a loud voice, and gave up the ghost" (Mark 15: 37; see Matthew 27: 50). His last statement in these two Gospels, delivered a few verses earlier, is "Eloi, Eloi, lama sabachthani?," that is, "My God, my God, why hast thou forsaken me?" (Mark 15: 34; see Matthew 27: 46). According to Luke, however, "When Jesus had cried with a loud voice, he said, Father, into thy hands I commend my spirit: and having said thus, he gave up the ghost" (Luke 23: 46). In John, on the other hand, "He said, It is finished: and he bowed his head, and gave up the ghost" (John 19: 30). In short, the only thing the Gospels agree on is that Jesus gave up the ghost.

to Keep house

This phrase was first used by Miles Coverdale as he translated Psalm 113: 9 in 1535. The LORD, according to Coverdale's version, "maketh the barren woman to keep house." But he didn't mean "maintain the household," as we do; he meant "have a place to live." The Revised Standard Version makes the sense clear: "He gives the barren woman a home."

the Key of knowledge

This "key" is different from the "keys of the kingdom" that Jesus grants to Peter. "Woe unto you, lawyers!" he cries at Luke 11: 52, "for ye have taken away the key of knowledge." Keys may have been at the time symbols of professional learning (the emblems, for example, of doctors and lawyers); if so, Jesus begs to be contrary. Rather than promoting knowledge, lawyers, with their slavish devotion to the letter of the law and their vain trust in mortal judgment, actually impede true knowledge (that is, of God), which resides in the heart, not in the law.

"the Kingdom of God is within you"

This is Jesus' reply (at Luke 17: 21) to another of the Pharisees' queries. They want to know exactly when the kingdom of God is going to come, since Jesus spends so much time promising it. Jesus doesn't really answer them; he refuses to specify any date for the End, pointing out instead that in some sense the kingdom of God is already here "within you" (or, depending on how you translate the Greek, "among you" or "within your grasp"). That is, the Spirit is among believers here and now, though of course the Pharisees aren't believers.

LATINISMS

Some biblical expressions are fairly well known in Latin translation, even beyond Catholics of a certain age: *fiat lux,* for example, which means "Let there be light" (Genesis 1: 3). Others include: *in principio* ("In the beginning," Genesis 1: 1); *sanctum sanctorum* ("Holy of holies," the "inner sanctum" of the Israelite tabernacle, Exodus 26: 34); *de profundis* ("Up from the depths," Psalm 129: 1); *vanitas vanitatum* ("Vanity of vanities," Ecclesiastes 1: 2); *pax vobis* ("Peace be unto you," Luke 24: 36); *quo vadis?* ("Where are you going?" John 16: 5); *ecce homo* ("Behold the man," John 19: 5); and *noli me tangere* ("Don't touch me," John 20: 17). Finally, the prayer known as the "Magnificat" is named after its first word, pronounced by Jesus' mother Mary at Luke 1: 46: *Magnificat anima mea Dominum* ("My soul doth magnify the Lord").

"LET NOT THE SUN GO DOWN UPON YOUR WRATH"

If you are angry, St. Paul writes to the church at Ephesus, "Sin not; let not the sun go down upon your wrath: | Neither give place to the devil" (Ephesians 4: 26–27). In other words, don't go to bed mad—sound advice whether or not you're a Christian.

THE LORD'S ANOINTED

This is William Tyndale's translation of a phrase first found at I Samuel 16: 6, where the prophet Samuel applies it (mistakenly) to Eliab, David's eldest brother. It is David, of course, who is truly the LORD's anointed, that is, the man chosen by God to lead the Israelites. "Anointed" in the sense "divinely chosen" is a figurative use of the term, based on the literal sense "to smear with oil as a symbol of blessing." The LORD doesn't need to use oil or anything else.

THE MAN

In the sense "the man for the job" or "the man I had in mind," Miles Coverdale coined this expression in translating II Samuel 12: 7, where the prophet Nathan informs David, "Thou art even the man" to be king. (In the King James Version, the verse reads: "Thou art the man. Thus saith the LORD God of Israel, I annointed thee king over Israel, and I delivered thee out of the hand of Saul.") The variant form, "the very man," was coined by Shakespeare in *Much Ado about Nothing* (1598).

A MERRY HEART

"A merry heart maketh a cheerful countenance," Proverbs insightfully notes, "but by sorrow of the heart is the spirit broken" (15: 13). Not a verse that by itself proves the wisdom of Solomon, the book's reputed author. It is worth noting, however, that the Hebrews regarded the individual as an organic whole, in which heart, mind, and spirit were at one, which is the point of the proverb. In this regard they would differ from the dualistic Greeks of classical times, who thought happiness rested in part on reason's controlling irrational emotions (the "heart"). If our adoption of "merry heart" and "merry-hearted" (Isaiah 24: 7) from the King James Bible is any indication, it seems we're more Jewish than Greek at heart.

"MY TIME IS AT HAND"

The use of "time" to mean "time of death" traces back to an early translation (ca. A.D. 1000) of Matthew 26: 18, where Jesus tells his disciples to "Go into the city [Jerusalem] to such a man, and say to him, The Master saith, My time is at hand; I will keep the passover at thy house with my disciples." The disciples, if not the host, must know what he means, which will make this Passover a somber occasion.

THE PATIENCE OF JOB

"Behold," writes James in his epistle, "we count them happy which endure [suffering]. Ye have heard of the patience of Job, and have seen the end of the Lord [that is, how the Lord dealt with him]; that the Lord is very pitiful, and of tender mercy" (James 5: 11). Without judging God's pity and mercy from the record, reasonable people might disagree about Job's patience.

PISGAH

At Deuteronomy 3: 27, Yahweh tells Moses to "Get thee up into the top of Pisgah, and lift up thine eyes westward, and northward, and southward, and eastward, and behold it with thine eyes: for thou shalt not go over this Jordan." "It" is the promised land of Canaan, and it will be up to Moses' protegé Joshua to lead his people there. What God doesn't mention, however, is that Moses will drop dead after taking in the view (34: 5). The Hebrew common noun *pisgah* refers here to the uppermost ridge of a mountain, though the translators thought it was a proper name for Mount Nebo, which lies east of the River Jordan. Later, "Pisgah" came to refer in English to a magisterial, if detached, prospect, a high point from which we peer into a hopeful future. Most people forget about Moses' death, but it adds another layer of tragedy to the speech the Reverend Martin Luther King, Jr. delivered the day before he was assassinated: "I've been to the mountaintop," King said. "And I've seen the promised land. I may not get there with you."

President Bill Clinton

In his Inaugural Address on January 20, 1993, Mr. Clinton quoted a line from St. Paul's Epistle to the Galatians, in the King James rendition: "Let us not be weary in well doing: for in due season we shall reap, if we faint not" (6: 9). In other words, hard work pays off. I must confess that I haven't heard the line quoted more often on the street since.

THE PRINCE OF PEACE

This is an epithet found, along with "Wonderful, Counsellor, The mighty of God, The everlasting father," at Isaiah 9: 6. The author was probably referring to Cyrus II, the Persian emperor who freed the Jews from their Babylonian captivity and helped restore the Jerusalem Temple. But Jews and Christians alike would later interpret this passage as a reference to the Messiah.

THE QUEEN OF SHEBA

The queen, who makes her appearance in chapter 10 of First Kings, ruled over Sheba (or Saba, or Seba), a wealthy land roughly equivalent to modern-day Yemen. She is best remembered for her riches, a small portion of which she bestows on Solomon once he has passed her test of "hard questions." Solomon, in fact, far exceeds the reports of his wisdom; "Behold," the queen says in amazement, "the half was not told me" (verse 7). She even goes so far as to praise Yahweh. The queen makes a mysterious reappearance in the Gospels, where Jesus refers to her obscurely (Matthew 12: 42 and Luke 11: 31).

THE QUICK AND THE DEAD

"The quick and the dead"—first used at Acts 10: 42—means simply "the living and the dead," and this more modern way of putting it is common to all revisions of the Authorized Version. Surely this is a rueful injustice to the elegant and quotable Renaissance phrasing, wherein "quick" derives from the Old English "cwic" ("alive"). The sense "rapid, swift" dates only from about the thirteenth century, although it follows naturally from the word's original meaning. Being quick, a thing was animate, and therefore lively and in motion. (Notice that "lively" itself derives from the same idea.)

RACHEL WEEPING FOR HER CHILDREN

It is Jeremiah who makes this reference to the biblical matriarch (Jeremiah 31: 15), though in his text the name is spelled "Rahel." She is figuratively God's bride, mother of Israel (though married to Israel, or Jacob, in Genesis); and here she weeps for the exile of her "sons." The Scripture-quoting Matthew repeats the line in describing Herod's massacre of the innocents (Matthew 2: 18; *see* p. 167).

THE SEVEN PILLARS OF WISDOM

"Wisdom," writes the author of Proverbs anthropomorphically, "hath builded her house, she hath hewn out her seven pillars" (9: 1). Wisdom, it seems, was the first of God's creations and is still easily found by those who seek her. But exactly where her house is and what its seven pillars represent is never specified. Ancient scientists, however, as fond of the number seven as the Hebrews were, speculated that the world itself was held up by seven pillars (and we find "pillars of the earth" elsewhere in the

Brush Up Your Bible

Bible, as at I Samuel 2: 8). Yet no one would confuse the entire world with Wisdom's house.

A SHINING LIGHT

John coined this phrase, in the sense of "a person of conspicuous excellence," in his Gospel, where Jesus refers to John the Baptist as "a burning and a shining light" in which the Jews who now oppose Jesus (who is far greater) were "willing for a season to rejoice" (John 5: 35). The phrase had already appeared in Proverbs (4: 18), but there it is used more literally, and it is John's Gospel (via Tyndale's translation of 1526) that established the modern usage.

TO SIT AT SOMEONE'S FEET

Miles Coverdale coined this phrase in 1535 while translating Luke's Gospel: "Mary ... sat her down at Jesus feet, and harkened unto his word" (10: 39). It always implies an attentive and reverential attitude, though such an attitude may of course be viewed ironically. The journal *Nature,* for example, reported in 1971 that "there are far more universities per square mile in Britain than are necessary to enable students to sit at the feet of some teacher or other." The "Mary" Luke mentions, by the way, is the one sometimes identified with Mary Magdalene [*see* MAUDLIN, p. 245].

SUFFER THE LITTLE CHILDREN

Jesus, as we have seen, is a great friend to the little ones [*see* A MILLSTONE AROUND YOUR NECK, p. 213], which he proves again with this phrase. The disciples, protective as always of their master as he preaches the Gospel, yell at some people who have brought young children before Jesus. But this in fact angers him. "Suffer [permit] the little children to come unto me," he orders them, "and forbid them not: for of such is the kingdom of God" (Mark 10: 14; also Matthew 19: 14 and Luke 18: 16).

SUFFICIENT UNTO THE DAY IS THE EVIL THEREOF

What this means, in a nutshell, is that things are bad enough on any given day that it isn't necessary for you to make them worse. The phrasing is from Coverdale's rendition, in the Great Bible of 1640, of Matthew 6: 34, where during the Sermon on the Mount Jesus advises the crowd to take care of one day at a time, and forget about tomorrow—worrying doesn't solve anything and is an "evil" unto itself.

A TINKLING CYMBAL

A tiny, empty sound, paralleled by St. Paul (I Corinthians 13: 1) with the blustery noise of "sounding brass." These are what Paul says he will be reduced to, even if he speaks with "the tongues of men and angels," without charity, greatest of Christian virtues [*see* FAITH, HOPE, AND CHARITY, p. 285].

"TOUCH NOT; TASTE NOT; HANDLE NOT"

This is Paul's summary (Colossians 2: 21) of the "commandments and doctrines of men," a series of rigid and meaningless prohibitions that have nothing to do with the things that really matter and will endure—namely (all join in), faith, hope, and charity.

TOUCH PITCH AND BE DEFILED

"He that toucheth pitch," sermonizes Joshua ben-Sira, author of Ecclesiasticus, "shall be defiled therewith; and he that hath fellowship with a proud man shall be like unto him" (13: 1). Pitch is a particularly sticky residue of tar, both filthy and tenacious. To translate: contact with filth will make you filthy, or, as Saint Paul will put it (borrowing from the Greek dramatist Menander), "Evil communications corrupt good manners" (I Corinthians 15: 33). The company of the vain will corrupt you, no matter how modest, humble, or pure you may be. I've heard William F. Buckley, Jr. use this line, but it's relatively unfamiliar in less lofty circles. Perhaps that's because the book of Ecclesiasticus has for centuries been banished from Jewish and Protestant Bibles, though it remains a part of the Catholic canon.

THE VALLEY OF THE SHADOW OF DEATH

Yet another biblical valley, this is mentioned in the famous Psalm 23, the one that begins, "The Lord is my shepherd." The author, knowing God is ever with him, fears nothing, not even the "valley of the shadow of death" (verse 4). Though poetic and suggestive, the phrasing—based on Coverdale's translation—isn't precise; better is the New English Bible's rendition: "a valley dark as death." Imprecise or not, Isaiah adopts the phrase in referring to certain "people that walked in darkness"; they "dwell in the land of the shadow of death" (Isaiah 9: 2).

WHAT IS TRUTH?

"*What is truth?* said jesting Pilate, and would not stay for an answer." This formerly famous first line opens "Of Truth," the first piece in Francis Bacon's *Essays* (1597), the first book of essays in English. Bacon is citing the Gospel according to John (chapter 18), where Jesus defiantly informs Pilate that he came into the world to "bear witness unto the truth. Every one that is of the truth heareth my voice" (verse 37). In reply, "Pilate saith unto him, What is truth? And when he had said this, he went out again unto the Jews, and saith unto them, I find in him no fault at all" (verse 38). Obviously enough, Pilate's question is rhetorical—he's "jesting," to quote Bacon; the Roman seems to have been among the school of skeptics.

THE WHORE OF BABYLON

Among the bizarre characters John the Divine encounters in Revelation is the infamous "Whore of Babylon," whom he describes thus: "I saw a woman sit upon a scarlet coloured beast, full of names of blasphemy, having seven heads and ten horns. | And the woman was arrayed in purple and scarlet colour, and decked with gold and precious stones and pearls, having a golden cup in her hand full of abominations and filthiness of her fornication: | And upon her forehead was a name written, MYSTERY, BABYLON THE GREAT, THE MOTHER OF HARLOTS AND ABOMINATIONS OF THE EARTH" (Revelation 17: 3–5). What all these details add up to is that the "Whore" is Rome (the city, as opposed to the "Beast" of the extended empire). Early Protestants were particularly fond of this allegory (with which they tarred the Church of Rome), but one rarely hears this sort of talk anymore.

THE WISDOM OF SOLOMON

As Solomon succeeds his father David to the crown of Israel and Judah, he prays to the LORD for "an understanding heart to judge thy people, that I may discern between good and bad: for who is able to judge this thy so great a people?" (I Kings 3: 9).

God, pleased and surprised the Solomon didn't ask for a long life or lots of money, readily grants the request. Solomon proves his wisdom, which was to become legendary, right away, by resolving a dispute between two harlots over a baby. (You know the tale: he proposes to cut the child in half—I Kings 3: 16–28). Solomon's sagacity would go on to inspire a few English proverbs (now out of circulation), such as: "Solomon was a wise man, and Samson was a strong man, yet neither of them could pay money before they had it." By the way, though the king refrained from any greedy petitions, he did become very wealthy.

Index of Words and Phrases

Lucifer, 113

magi, 166, 235, 241
magnificat anima mea Dominum, 344
magnum, 104
mammon, 180
man, 345
man after his own heart, 96
man does not live by bread alone, 87–88
manger, 241–242
manna from heaven, 63, 87
many are called, but few are chosen, 218–219
mark of Cain, 26
mark of the Beast, 316–317
Massacre of the Innocents, 167
maudlin, 245
measure for measure, 182
mene, mene, tekel, upharsin, 155
merry heart, 345
mess of pottage, 329
Methuselah, 28, 29, 31
methuselah, 104
Millennium, 320–321, 322
millstone around your neck, 213–214
money changers, 220
mote in the eye, 183, 307
my God, my God, why hast thou
    forsaken me?, 239, 342
my name is legion, 240
my son was dead, and is alive again, 249
my soul doth magnify the Lord, 344
my time is at hand, 345

nebuchadnezzar, 104
new heaven and a new earth, 322–323
new Jerusalem, 322–323
new testament, 230, 292, 295
new wine in old bottles, 192
Ninevah, that great city, 158
Noah's ark, 31–32, 33
Nod, 26–27
noli me tangere, 344
nothing new under the sun, 129

O death, where is thy sting?, 288–289
O ye of little faith, 190–191, 337
old as Adam, 327
old as Methuselah, 28
old wine in new bottles, 192
onanism, 44–45
one of these days, 99–100
original sin, 330
Our Father, 178
our vines have grown tender grapes, 135
out of the mouths of babes, 121

painted Jezebel, 106
parting of the waters, 60–61
Passover, 56
patience of Job, 346
pax vobis, 344
peace be unto you, 265, 344
peace dividend, 138
pearls before swine, 184
pearly gates, 322
Pentecost, 266
Pharisees, 169
Philistine, 93–94
physician, heal thyself, 330
pillar of salt, 39–40
Pisgah, 83, 346
place whereon thou standest is
    holy ground, 50
play the fool, to, 330
plowshare, 137
pour out vials of wrath, 319
powers that be, 279
press toward the mark, to, 298–299
pride goes before a fall, 127
pride goeth before destruction, 127
Prince of Peace, 347
prodigal, 250
prodigal son, 248–250
promised land, 42, 85, 331, 346
Purgatory, 325
put away childish things, to, 285
put words in one's mouth, to, 102

thorn in the flesh, 86
thorn in your side, 85–86
thou are weighed in the balance, and art
  found wanting, 155
thou shalt have no other gods before me, 64
thou shalt not bear false witness against
  thy neighbor, 65
thou shalt not commit adultery, 65
thou shalt not covet thy neighbor's house, 65
thou shalt not covet thy neighbor's wife, 65
thou shalt not kill, 65
thou shalt not steal, 65
thou shalt not take the name of the
  LORD thy God in vain, 65
Three Wise Men, 166–167
tidings of great joy, 241–242
tinkling cymbal, 350
tongues of fire, 266
touch not, 350
touch pitch and be defiled, 350
Tower of Babel, 35–36
Tree of Knowledge, 15–16, 20
Tree of Life, 15, 22
truth shall make [set] you free, 259
turn the other cheek, to, 176, 181, 234
turn, turn, turn, 130
two are better than one, 131
two heads are better than one, 131
two-edged sword, 123–124

unto the pure all things are pure, 306–307
up from the depths, 344

vale of tears, 332
valley of the shadow of death, 351
vanitas vanitatum, 344

vanity of vanities, 128, 344
vengeance is mine, 277–278
very man, 345
voice crying in the wilderness, 139–140
voice of the turtle, 135

wages of sin, 275
walk on water, to, 205–206
wash your hands, to, 235–237
water into wine, 255
way of all flesh, 90
way of all the earth, 90
weaker vessel, 309
weighed in the balance, 154–155
what God hath joined together ..., 215
what hath God wrought!, 83–84
what is truth?, 351
wheels within wheels, 150–151
where are you going?, 344
white as snow, 136
whited sepulchres, 224–225
who lives by the sword shall die by
  the sword, 233–234
Whore of Babylon, 352
whosoever will save his life shall
  lose it, 212
wide is the gate, and broad is the way,
  that leadeth to destruction, 186
wisdom of Solomon, 352
wolves in sheep's clothing, 187–188
woman, 19
word made flesh, 253–254
writing on the wall, 154–155

Yahweh, 57–59
ye cannot serve God and mammon, 180

General Index

This is a selective index of proper names, biblical books, and miscellaneous religious feasts, rituals, and concepts. For common words and phrases, please see the preceding "Index of Words and Phrases." Books of the Bible are given in *italics,* according to their titles in the Authorized Version.

Aaron, 55, 62, 71, 75, 81–82
Abaddon, 315
Abel, 24–25, 26, 330
Abraham, 5, 37, 39, 41–42, 51, 57, 72, 259, 298, 331, 333–334
Absalom, 102
Acts of the Apostles, 72, 143, 162, 266–272, 326, 334, 340, 348
Adam, 14–20, 22, 24, 36, 57, 216, 327, 330, 331, 342; *see also* EVE
Ælfric, x, 51, 52
Aesop, 187, 276
Ahab, 105–107
Ahitophel [Achitophel], 111
Alexander the Great, 153
Amos, 2, 94
Ananias, 270
Antichrist, 316
Apocrypha, xiii
ark, 31–32, 33
Ark of the Covenant, 32
Armageddon, 318–319
Authorized Version, *see* BIBLES: AUTHO-RIZED VERSION *and* BIBLES: KING JAMES BIBLE
Azazel, 75–76, 112, 180

Baal, 84, 105, 109, 120, 221
Babel, 35–36
Balaam, 83–84
Balak, 83
baptism, 168
Barabbas, 236
Beast, 316–317, 322, 340, 352

beatitudes, 170
Bede, the Venerable, x
Beelzebub, 197
Behemoth, 119–120
Belshazzar, 154–155
ben-Sira, Joshua, 350; *see also* ECCLESIAS-TICUS, WISDOM OF JESUS THE SON OF SIRACH, OR
Bibles: Authorized Version, ix, xii–xiii; Bishops' Bible, xii, 341; Breeches Bible, 342; Bug Bible, 342; Coverdale Bible, xi; Ears to Ear Bible, 341; Geneva Bible, xii, 116, 128, 257, 342; Great Bible, xi; Gutenberg Bible, x; King James Bible, ix, xii–xiii; Large Family Bible, 342; Lions Bible, 341; Masoretic Text, 3; Matthew Bible, xi; New Revised Standard Version, xii; Placemaker's Bible, 341; Printers Bible, 342; Revised Standard Version, xii; Revised Version, xii; Septuagint, 3, 9, 139; Sin On Bible, 342; Treacle Bible, 341; Unrighteous Bible, 341; Vulgate, x, 75, 79, 139, 148, 179; Wicked Bible, 341
Book of the Covenant, 70
born-again Christians, 256–257
Bradford, John, 287
brimstone, 39–40
Buckley, William F., Jr., 351
Bush, George, 50, 146, 304–305

Cain, 24–27, 330, 331
Calvary, 251
Canaan, 37, 46, 83, 85, 140, 346